A DREAM PLAY

AND FOUR CHAMBER PLAYS

A DREAM PLAY
AND FOUR CHAMBER PLAYS

By August Strindberg

Translations and Introductions
by Walter Johnson

The Norton Library
W·W·NORTON & COMPANY·INC·
NEW YORK

First published in the Norton Library 1975
by arrangement with the University of Washington Press

Books That Live
The Norton imprint on a book means that in the publisher's
estimation it is a book not for a single season but for the years.
W. W. Norton & Company, Inc.

Library of Congress Cataloging in Publication Data
Strindberg, August, 1849-1912.
   A dream play, and four chamber plays.
   (The Norton library)
   Reprint of the ed. published by the University of
Washington Press, Seattle.
   CONTENTS: A dream play.—The ghost sonata.—Stormy
weather. [etc.]
   I. Johnson, Walter Gilbert, 1905-   II. Title.
PT9811.A3J58 1975   839.7'2'6   75-25573
ISBN 0-393-00791-X

Printed in the United States of America
1 2 3 4 5 6 7 8 9

Preface

IN THIS VOLUME are new translations of *A Dream Play* (1901) and four of Strindberg's chamber plays: *Stormy Weather* (1907), *The House that Burned* (1907), *The Ghost Sonata* (1907), and *The Pelican* (1907).

Two of these plays have been generally admired and frequently produced both in Sweden and abroad. *A Dream Play* and *The Ghost Sonata* are not only great and highly influential theater, but excellent literature as well. The other three deserve far more attention and serious consideration both as works of literary art and as theater pieces than they have yet received. Careful study will reveal insights and dramatic potentials that even in Sweden have been rarely perceived except, in a way, for *The Pelican*. Swedish performances of that play have been appreciated too often, however, for autobiographical elements fixed upon by Strindberg relatives, friends, acquaintances, enemies, and sensationalists.

All of these plays are closely related in substance and, far more than a cursory reading would suggest, in form. All of them deal with the human condition or, shall we say, the nature of the world about man and the experience—individual, yet universal—he must endure on his journey through life to death. *A Dream Play* reveals clearly how Strindberg believed human beings live on earth, the home of all of us; the chamber plays reveal what lies behind the façades of houses that may look very much like homes. And in all five plays, Strindberg suggests that the real home of man is not in this world of appearances, but in an original world of reality beyond the grave.

In these translations I have tried as in my earlier translations of Strindberg plays to be faithful to the Strindberg idiom and to his intention. I have made no effort to rewrite or to adapt, for Strindberg knew very well what he was doing, and he rarely nodded.

I am particularly grateful to Dr. Gustaf Hilleström of Stockholm for helping me secure illustrations for this volume and for giving me the opportunity to witness his production of *A Dream Play* in my translation while he was a Walker-Ames Professor at the University of Washington in 1970.

WALTER JOHNSON

Contents

A DREAM PLAY

AND FOUR CHAMBER PLAYS

Introduction to

'A Dream Play'

EMIL SCHERING, Strindberg's German translator, was more than a little puzzled by *A Dream Play* when he read it for the first time, and he told Strindberg so. In reply he received a letter, part of which is an excellent supplement to Strindberg's prefatory note as an explanation of what the author intended:

> How to understand *A Dream Play?*
> Indra's daughter has descended to Earth to find out how human beings have it. And there she learns how difficult life is. And the worst is: having to injure or do harm to others if one wants to live. The form is motivated in a preface: the conglomeration out of a dream in which, however, there is a definite logic. Everything *irrational* becomes believable. Human beings appear at several points and are sketched, the sketches flow together; the same person splits into several persons only to form into one again.
> Time and place do not exist, a minute is equal to many years, etc.

If one examines the foregoing and the prefatory note immediately preceding the play, one has the key to both its substance and its form.

The age-old notion that the core experiences of his lifetime flash in review through the mind of a dying human being may conceivably have been Strindberg's point of departure in planning a play that would deal with the nature and quality of the human experience, not as they concerned him alone but as they apply to people generally. The notes preserved in the Strindberg collection in the Royal Library in Stockholm demonstrate, moreover, that—as he had promised in *To Damascus* III—he did not intend to present another account of his personal suffering.

The notes clearly indicate careful planning in both selection and arrangement of material about the human experience. A few of these notes will suggest the evolution of his planning:

1. *The Seasons*
   A: *Spring*
   B: *Late summer*
   C: *Winter*
   D: *Spring again*

2. *Indra's Daughter*
       The Idea
   Alles Beides. Both-And.
       For good and evil.
   The four seasons: Spring, Summer, Autumn, Winter
                     childhood youth   aging   old age
                   Night and day.
   Act I = Spring
       The dolls (puppets)
       The school
   Act II = Summer
       The fiancée
       The wife
   Act III = Autumn
       The children
       The son-in-law   moving—the birds of passage
   Act IV = Winter
       The widow—Aloneness [solitude]
       The grave—spring—rebirth

3. *The Growing Castle*
   Act I: (a) Outside the castle
            (b) In the castle
            (c) At the mother's
                home

4. *The Dream Play*
   I.   1. The castle in the
            hollyhock forest
         2. The officer's room in
            the castle

(d) In the corridor
(e) At the lawyer's
(f) In the church by the organ
(g) In Fingal's Cave
Act II: (a) The lawyer's living room
(b) Foulstrand
(c) Fairhaven
Act III: (a) Fingal's Cave
(b) The corridor
(c) Outside the castle

II.

III.

3. The mother's room
4. The theater corridor
5. The lawyer's office
6. The church with the organ
7. Fingal's Cave
8. The lawyer's office
9. Foulstrand
10. Fairhaven
11. The school
12. By the Mediterranean
13. Fingal's Cave
14. The theater corridor
15. The castle in the hollyhock forest with a backdrop of human faces.

In another note Strindberg indicates that he had planned to have Agnes go through a full lifetime:

School; the Girl and her suitors; marriage and the kitchen; the children and the nursery; the widow and solitude; the end in death. What she has then learned is the following: life is difficult, human beings are about what they can be, everything is fragile and therefore seems treacherous, everything is very contradictory and therefore seems very evil; life is something transitory materially and therefore seems very cynical. Life is the pilgrimage of a soul in a human body (= animal body) and therefore it contracts and contracts, is painful and flawed.

Not only do these outlines and notes suggest a great deal about the evolution of the planning of the play but they introduce the basic facts about its substance and form.

Strindberg's purpose was, then, to interpret human life on a new basis: not through what the five senses and reasoning power alone have to say about it when the censor is functioning, but primarily through what memory, imagination, the dream experience in its various forms, and the unconscious have to say about it when they are not controlled by consciousness or, if you will, by a censor that insists on controls represented by reasoning and logic. What Strindberg was doing, in other words, was using sources of insight into man and his world previously tapped to some degree in all forms of literature and especially in lyric poetry, but never exploited, deliberately and fully, by Strindberg's predecessors in drama and theater. Earlier dramatists had certainly used their powers of imagination and their memories and had touched on the unconscious, but none of them had written a play designed to tell the truth about God, man, and the universe in a form deliberately imitative of a dream.

The flow from memory and the unconscious touches on almost every phase of Strindberg's own life and of every human being's life experience. A look at the content of the play, scene by shifting scene, is useful:

Personal	*Universal*
1. *The Officer:* there had been some talk when Strindberg was young about his becoming an officer (the military academy Karlberg; the military drill fields nearby; Hästkasernen, the cavalry barracks on Sturevägen).	Military life, yes, but much more than that. The age-old question: What are you going to be when you grow up? Unfulfilled childhood dream. Even if fulfilled, fulfillment a prison.
2. *Parental home:* early death of mother. Conflicts. Wife vs. husband. Servant. Parent-child: extracted promises.	Family relationships: the inevitability of conflicts when people are brought together in "home."
3. *Doorkeeper at the theater-opera:* Actors, singers, employees. Strindberg and two actress wives: the never-ending pursuit of Victoria. The fishing box	Theater (or any professional) world and its conflicts. Labor conditions. The eternal dream: gaining the perfect mate. Police regulations and police interfer-

Personal (cont.)

and the net: fishermen active in Stockholm Stream in plain view of the theater-opera.

4. *The Lawyer's Office:* Strindberg's consultation with lawyers (three divorces).

5. *Commencement:* Strindberg's unhappy experiences at the University of Uppsala; the rejection of his thesis and his failure in chemistry.

6. *Fingal's Cave:* endless reasons for complaining about himself, others, his environment, and the Creator; perfection vs. actuality.

7. *Marriage:* before and after. Dream and reality: fulfillment vs. the facts of marital life— human needs, individual preferences and peculiarities. The short hard accents.

8. *Foulstrand-Fairhaven:* a trip to Italy and renewed awareness of injustice at home and abroad. Physical afflictions; human handicaps and limitations.

9. *School teaching:* classroom experience as a young man; in effect a teacher throughout his lifetime.

10. *The Coalheavers:* the trip to Italy and renewed awareness of social injustice everywhere.

Universal (cont.)

ence. "Not quite what I had hoped for."

Human sins and crimes. Legal controversies. What man does to his fellow man.

The lot of man: some are taken up, others left behind. And the lot of those who receive the rewards?

Universal concentration on the ego. Universal complaining. The finite human being: imperfections and frustrations. Whom and what to blame?

Human marital unions: food, shelter, and clothing; adjustments. Cabbage, beauty, hairpins—representative of universal marital problems.

The privileged vs. the underprivileged; appearance vs. reality; theory vs. practice. The big question: Is anyone spared? Can anyone's good fortune bear scrutiny?

Who isn't a teacher—in one way or many? The eternal repetition; discipline; having to mature; doing one's lessons over.

Political, economic, and social distinctions; labor conditions; regulations; police. Govern-

Personal (cont.)

Universal (cont.)

ment. The right-thinking people's role—to preserve the status quo.

11. *Fingal's Cave:* Strindberg's conviction that he had poetic insight into the truth about God, man, and the universe.

The lot of man: "Man is to be pitied."

12. *The corridor at the theater:* his first and third wives were actresses; waiting and observing. The cloverleaf opening in one of the doors in the corridor at the theater-opera house. The inadequacy of intellectual and moral leaders.

Universal interest in the meaning of life. Can even the most highly educated supply the answers to the basic questions?

13. *The riddle of life:* poet's insight: man the union of divinity and dust (spirit and body); life = dream, phantom.

General sensing of the limitations of human beings, not least their ability to communicate in words.

14. *The procession-review of "characters":* himself and others (as he "saw" them).

The parade of fellow human beings, rarely if ever well known, in one's life.

15. *The burning of the castle:* the coming release of his soul or spirit and those of others from the prison of earthly life.

The release from the prison of living, from the anguish of life.

Even this brief outline and its suggestions of universal parallels are nothing but extensions of the plans Strindberg himself drew up before he wrote *A Dream Play,* but they should help to make clear Strindberg's intention and indicate his conclusions.

The play illustrates in one area of life after the other the conflicts that result from man's egotistic desire and even demand for perfection here and now and the very finite nature of life itself. Strindberg's testimony is summarized in the memorable recurring statement of the central theme: "Man is to be pitied" (*Det är synd om människorna*). The conviction that earthly life is essentially but not entirely suffering is based on Strindberg's concept of human nature: "These are my children! Each one by himself is good, but all you have to do to turn them into demons is to bring them together." Among the innumerable causes of consequent human suffering synthetically presented are man's egotistic desires—for love, knowledge, fame, power and place, wealth, and possessions.

A Dream Play presents a remarkably rich and impressively complete treatment of the human condition poetically perceived and poetically presented. It gives us Strindberg's fullest post-Inferno statement of personal belief about the forces controlling this world in which we live, the very texture of that world, and the misery and the glory of human life. It is a statement that is both negative and positive. Strindberg neglects neither the beauty nor the ugliness in the world or in man; he is as aware of the moments of intense joy as he is of the periods of despair and suffering and the boredom of monotonous repetition.

The substance of *A Dream Play* may well be said, however, to be an expression of modern pessimism, emphasizing as it does the extreme limitations placed on every human being by his senses and all of his other powers, the extreme difficulty of controlling everyman's key problem—his ego, and the slight possibilities for improvement in a human community made up of individuals, all of whom are struggling not only for survival but for personal advantage and advancement. It is in such matters that Strindberg's significance for the Age of Anguish, our time, primarily lies, and it is interesting to note that what Strindberg says in *A Dream Play* (and elsewhere, particularly in other post-Inferno works) has interesting parallels with Freud's Adjustment, Adler's Compensation, and Jung's Persona.

If any character may be said to outrank all others in the play, it must be Agnes, Indra's daughter, who has descended to earth to find out "how human beings really have it." Agnes is a Christ figure with differences: she has come to earth not to serve as a guide for human beings and a scapegoat for them, but to learn about them through observation and full participation in living and to report on her findings later on. It is highly appropriate that she is a female being. Although Strindberg was so frequently and firmly labeled a woman hater that he himself believed the charge on occasion, he adored women even when he objected violently to certain manifestations of the emancipated woman and saw in woman (the individual's Victoria) the one possibility for the individual man's fulfillment and completion. Woman as the complement is one theme that runs through almost all of his major creative works; nowhere else is the theme so fully and clearly treated, however, as in *A Dream Play*.

Agnes becomes a human being in order to discover through personal experience the truth about man and his lot. She not only observes the human animal in his social and gregarious activities; she marries, becomes a mother, and faces the problems implicit in the marital and parental state, only to be brought into the conflict between family duties and obligations to herself as an individual and as a member of the larger community. To be sure, Agnes does take on the burdens of her fellow beings by putting on the Doorkeeper's shawl, she does take on the burden of others' suffering, and through her insight she understands their unhappiness and suffers for them sympathetically. But the one who has to bear the crown of thorns is the Lawyer, a human being who does not have Agnes' means of escape from the facts of a harsh and brutal earthly reality. While Agnes is a Christ figure in that she takes on the burden of being imprisoned in human flesh, and that she observes and experiences human living in order to report to and mediate for man with higher beings, the Lawyer serves as a Christ-like scapegoat here and now without visible reward or means of escape.

For the presentation of his major statement about man and his world, Strindberg selected a fascinating combination of "an insignificant basis of reality" and the dream experiences in various forms.

He did not place major emphasis on the self-control and logical thinking that, hopefully, assert themselves when the adult is conscious and awake. The play does not present the results of any searching analysis that is the method of adult human thought. Instead Strindberg exploited a region of human experience out of reach of either direct observation or direct introspection. That region is, of course, the unconscious with its world of distorted and seemingly disconnected but remembered activities. It has much to do with the dream in any of its forms such as the dream proper, hallucination, and daydreaming. It has to do with the memory, that storeroom of transformed, suppressed, and frequently tidied up recollections. It has to do with the imagination and with fantasy.

What needs to be emphasized in Strindberg's own explanatory note—the finest possible introduction to *A Dream Play*—is "the disconnected but apparently logical form." It is a form that permits the human being represented by the poet-author to get at truth about man and his world, and there is, Strindberg believed, justification for believing that the truth arrived at synthetically, by insight, through the logic of the dream, is probably more reliable than the result of analysis of the material observed and reported by the senses and scrutinized and studied by the reasoning power.

In such a play there will be no characterless characters as Strindberg defined them in the Preface to *Lady Julie*. Agnes, for example, for all the attention given her, is not analyzed; her complexity and dynamic quality are sensed, not demonstrated or illustrated in the laboratory manner. What is true about Agnes is even more strikingly true of the other "characters" or, better still, types. Note the "cast":

1. The Glazier, the Father, the Doorkeeper, the Billposter, the Singer, the Ballet Girl, the Chorus Girl, the Prompter, Chorus Members, Supers, the Policeman, the Lawyer, Audience, the Three Candidates, Voices, the Old Fop, the Old Coquette, Her "Friend," the Poet, He, She, the Pensioner, Ugly Edith's Mother,

the Children, the Maids, the Naval Officer, the Schoolboys, the Dancers, the Schoolmaster, the Newlyweds, the Blindman, the Coalheavers.

2. The Officer (Alfred), the Mother (Kristina), the Quarantine Master (Ordström).

3. Lina (I), Victoria, Kristin, Ugly Edith, Lina (II), Alice.

The fact that most of them have no identifying names at all is significant. The fact that the Officer, the Mother, and the Quarantine Master receive the names Alfred, Kristina, and Ordström ("stream of words") is incidental. The fact that the two Linas, Victoria, Kristin, Ugly Edith, and Alice are identified by names does not individualize them; they are merely the servant, the virtuous but unrewarded daughter (wife and mother), the ideal woman (usually heard but not seen), the maid who pastes and pastes, the girl handicapped by physical ugliness, and the apparently lucky girl. The "characters" in *A Dream Play* remind one not a little of what Strindberg had said in the Preface to *Lady Julie:* "My minor characters seem abstract to some people because everyday people are to a certain extent abstract in performing their work; that is to say not individualized, showing only one side while they are doing their work."

The point about the "characters" in *A Dream Play* is twofold, it seems to me. All of them are synthetically perceived in what might be called flashes of insight. Ugly Edith, for example, can be understood by sympathetic sensing; one does not need an analysis of Edith. Various characters may very well be different aspects of Strindberg or of Everyman. For example, the Officer, the Lawyer, and the Poet may, as many students of Strindberg have noted, be three Strindbergs and, by extension, three manifestations of Everyman. As Strindberg says, "Human beings appear at several points and are sketched, the sketches flow together; the same person splits into several persons only to form into one again."

That flow applies to narrative and ideational content as well. As Strindberg says, "But one consciousness [*medvetande*] remains above all of them [the characters]: the dreamer's; for him there are no secrets, no inconsequence, no scruples, no law." In terms of that one consciousness, one can speak justifiably of Strindberg's use of the flow of consciousness which throws light on the essence of the dreamer's life experience.

In his selection and arrangement of material for this play, whose form imitates that of a dream, Strindberg has, of course, made use of symbols, distortion, synthesis, antithesis, the lyric, and music.

The interpretation of major symbols may well concentrate on the growing castle with its chrysanthemumlike bud on top, the clover-leaf opening in the corridor door, the shawl the Doorkeeper wears, and even Victoria as symbols, say, of earthly living and the release of the human soul or spirit through death, the riddle of this life, the accumulation of the burden of human suffering, and the ideal mate. Each of these and many more in *A Dream Play* can provide any sensitive reader with material for speculation.

The symbols, the many illustrations of distortion, the synthetic rather than the analytic approach, antithesis (Fairhaven vs. Foul-strand, for example), and the subjectivity of the whole play fit in nicely with the lyrical-musical elements which dominate from the prologue to the bursting of the flower bud into a gigantic chrysanthemum as the castle burns.

The essential lyrical-musical quality of *A Dream Play* is not restricted to the beautiful lyrics in free verse. The nature of the quality is perhaps best suggested by part of Strindberg's reply to the question: How do you write creatively?

> Well, how? Let him explain who can! It begins with a sort of ferment or a kind of pleasant fever, which becomes ecstasy or intoxication. Sometimes it's like a seed, that sprouts, attracts all interest to itself, consumes everything ever experienced, but still selects and rejects. Sometimes I believe I am some kind of medium, because the writing goes so easily, half unconsciously, [is] only slightly calculated! *

* Quoted in August Falck's *Fem år med Strindberg* (Five Years with Strindberg) (Stockholm: Wahlström and Widstrand, 1935), p. 80.

The subjectivity involves the revelation of personal feelings and intuitions, the revelation of experiences tidied up in recollection in bearable form, the revelation of the very human tendency to see everything in terms of light and dark, and the revelation of sudden insights into oneself, one's fellows, and one's world. A close reading will, moreover, reveal the use of parallelisms, rhythm and cadence, and recurrences, all of which are typical of the lyric.

One can profitably speculate on the musical nature of *A Dream Play* and consider Strindberg's own list of actual music, proposed for the Intimate Theater production of the play. The list is available in various books, among them August Falck's *Fem år med August Strindberg* (p. 274), but as far as I have been able to determine no production of the play has ever made use of Strindberg's suggestions. The play's musical nature is suggested by Strindberg's division into three parts—indicated by roman numerals in the present translation —each of which may be regarded as a musical movement.

A comparison of *A Dream Play* with a largely objective play such as *The Father* (1887) may help to clarify the nature of Strindberg's dream plays, called by many expressionistic dramas. Certainly it will become abundantly clear that *A Dream Play* synthesizes human experience instead of analyzing human beings and their experience, throws light on human existence without having to be seriously limited by the senses, concentrates primarily on the inner life of modern man, accepts the concept of a moral world, presents people as very much alike in their egotism and its results, and attempts to put into visible form what happens within man. But since Strindberg, who called himself "a naturalistic occultist," wrote the play, there is never a total loss of contact with reality; the realistic details in the "insignificant basis of reality" are numerous and telling.

Every reading of *A Dream Play* and certainly every performance one may be fortunate enough to see and hear can give new insights into the magic of this seminal play. In a time such as ours it has served and probably will continue to serve as a commentary on man and the world in which he lives, and as a stimulant to literary artists, dramatic and nondramatic, who set out to interpret for themselves and others what they have observed and sensed of the human condition.

A Dream Play

An Explanatory Note

IN THIS DREAM PLAY as in his earlier dream plays *To Damascus,*[1] the author has tried to imitate the disconnected but apparently logical form of a dream. Everything can happen; everything is possible and likely. Time and space do not exist; on an insignificant basis of reality the imagination spins and weaves new patterns: a blending of memories, experiences, free inventions, absurdities, and improvisations.

The characters split, double, redouble, evaporate, condense, scatter, and converge. But one consciousness remains above all of them: the dreamer's; for him there are no secrets, no inconsequence, no scruples, no law. He does not judge, does not acquit, simply relates; and as the dream is usually painful, less frequently cheerful, a note of sadness and sympathy for every living creature runs through the swaying story. Sleep, the liberator, appears often as painful, but, when the torture is at its very peak, waking comes reconciling suffering with reality, which however painful it may be still at this moment is a delight compared with the tormenting dream.

Prologue

Cloud formations resembling castles and citadels in ruins on crumbling slate hills form the backdrop.

The constellations Leo, Virgo, and Libra can be seen, and among them is the planet Jupiter shining brightly.

INDRA'S DAUGHTER *is standing on the uppermost cloud.*

INDRA'S VOICE (*from above*): Where are you, Daughter? Where?

INDRA'S DAUGHTER'S VOICE: Here, Father, here!

INDRA'S VOICE: You have gone astray, my child; take care, you're sinking . . . How did you get here?

INDRA'S DAUGHTER:

I followed the flash of lightning from high Ether
and took a cloud as my coach . . .
But the cloud sank, and I'm headed down . . .
Tell me, Father Indra,[2] what regions have I come to?
Why is it so close, so hard to breathe?

INDRA'S VOICE:

You have left the second world and gone into the third
from Çukra;[3] the morning star
you have departed and are entering
the dusty atmosphere of Earth;
note the seventh house of the Sun called the Scales[4]
where the morning star stands in autumn
when Day and Night weigh the same . . .

INDRA'S DAUGHTER:

You spoke of Earth . . . Is that this dark
and heavy world lighted by the Moon?

INDRA'S VOICE:

It is the densest and heaviest
of the spheres wandering in space.

INDRA'S DAUGHTER:

Doesn't the sun ever shine here?

INDRA'S VOICE:

Of course, it does, but not always . . .

INDRA'S DAUGHTER:

The cloud is parting, and I can see the earth . . .

INDRA'S VOICE:

What do you see, my child?

INDRA'S DAUGHTER:

I see . . . it's beautiful . . . with green forests,
blue waters, white mountains, and yellow fields . . .

INDRA'S VOICE:

Yes, it's beautiful as everything Brahma [5] created . . .
but it was still more beautiful in the dawn of time;
then something happened, a breakdown in its orbit,
perhaps something else, a rebellion
accompanied by crimes that had to be suppressed . . .

INDRA'S DAUGHTER:

I hear sounds from there . . .
What creatures dwell down there?

INDRA'S VOICE:

Descend and see . . . I will not slander the Creator's children,
but what you hear is their language.

INDRA'S DAUGHTER:

It sounds like . . . it does not have a happy ring.

INDRA'S VOICE:

I imagine! For their mother tongue
is complaint. Yes! The earthlings
are a dissatisfied, ungrateful lot . . .

INDRA'S DAUGHTER:

Don't say that; now I hear shouts of joy,
and shots and booms; I see the lightning flash—
Bells are ringing, fires lighted,
and thousand times thousand voices
sing out in praise and thanks to heaven . . . (*Pause*)
you judge them too severely, Father . . .

INDRA'S VOICE:

Descend and see and hear . . .
then come back and tell me
if their complaints and laments are justified . . .

INDRA'S DAUGHTER:

I will descend, but come with me, Father!

INDRA'S VOICE:

No, I cannot breathe down there . . .

INDRA'S DAUGHTER:

The cloud is sinking . . . it's getting stifling . . .
I'm suffocating . . .
It isn't air but smoke and water I'm breathing . . .
so heavy, it pulls me down, down . . .
and now I already feel its sway . . .
the third world is not the best . . .

INDRA'S VOICE:

No, not the best, but not the worst;
It is Dust, it revolves as all the others do . . .
that's why the earthlings at times get dizzy,
on the verge between folly and madness.
Have courage, my child! It is but a test.

INDRA'S DAUGHTER (*on her knees as the cloud sinks*):

I'm sinking!

I

The backdrop represents a mass of gigantic white, pink, scarlet, sulphur yellow, and violet hollyhocks in bloom; over their tops can be seen the gilded roof of a castle[6] *with a flower bud resembling a crown uppermost. Along the bottom of the castle walls, heaps of straw covering cleaned-out stable litter. The side wings which remain throughout the play are stylized wall paintings, at the same time rooms, architecture, and landscapes.*

The GLAZIER *and* INDRA'S DAUGHTER *come on stage.*

DAUGHTER: The castle's still growing out of the earth . . . Do you see how much it has grown since last year?

GLAZIER (*to himself*): I've never seen that castle before . . . I've never heard that a castle grows . . . but (*to the* DAUGHTER *with firm conviction*)—yes, it has grown four feet, but that's because they've manured it . . . and if you'll look, you'll see a wing has shot out on the sunny side.

DAUGHTER: It really ought to bloom soon . . . it's past midsummer . . .

GLAZIER: Don't you see the flower up there?

DAUGHTER: Yes, I do! (*Claps her hands*) Tell me, Father, why do flowers grow out of the dirt?

GLAZIER (*devoutly*): They don't thrive in dirt; they hurry as fast as they can up into the light to bloom and die!

DAUGHTER: Do you know who lives in that castle?

GLAZIER: I did know, but I've forgotten.

DAUGHTER: I think there's a prisoner in there . . . and he's waiting for me to set him free.

GLAZIER: But at what price?

DAUGHTER: You don't bargain about your duty. Let's go into the castle! . . .

GLAZIER: Yes, let's!

*

They go toward the back, which slowly opens to the sides.

The setting is now a plain, bare room with a table and some chairs. An OFFICER *in an extremely unusual contemporary uniform is sitting on one chair. He is rocking the chair and striking his sword against the table.*

DAUGHTER (*goes up to the* OFFICER *and takes the sword gently out of his hand*): No, no! Don't do that!

OFFICER: Agnes, let me keep my sword!

DAUGHTER: No, you'll ruin the table! (*To the* GLAZIER) Go down into the harness room and put in the pane. I'll see you later! (GLAZIER *goes.*)

*

DAUGHTER: You're a prisoner in your rooms; I've come to set you free!

OFFICER: I've been waiting for that, but I wasn't sure you'd want to.

DAUGHTER: The castle is strong, it has seven walls, but—I'll manage! . . . Do you want to or don't you?

OFFICER: Frankly: I don't know . . . either way I'll be hurt! Every joy in life has to be paid for doubly in sorrow. It's difficult here, but if I'm to purchase freedom, I'll have to suffer threefold. Agnes,[7] I'd rather put up with it—if only I get to see you!

DAUGHTER: What do you see in me?

OFFICER: The beauty which is the harmony in the universe. There are lines in your figure the like of which I can find only in the course of the solar system, in the beautiful melody of strings, in the vibrations of light. You're a child of heaven . . .

DAUGHTER: So are you!

OFFICER: Why then should I tend horses? Look after stables and have litter hauled out?

DAUGHTER: So you'll long to get away from here.

OFFICER: I do long, but it's very hard to get out of this.

DAUGHTER: But it's your duty to seek freedom in light!

OFFICER: Duty? Life has never admitted having any duties toward me.

DAUGHTER: You feel unjustly treated by life, do you?

OFFICER: Yes! It has been unjust!

*

Voices can now be heard behind the screen, which is immediately drawn aside. The OFFICER *and the* DAUGHTER *look in that direction, then stop, their gestures and expressions frozen.*

The MOTHER, *who is ill, is sitting by a table. In front of her is burning a candle which she trims now and then with snuffers. Piles of newly sewn undershirts, which she marks with marking ink and quill pen. A brown wardrobe-cupboard to the left.*

FATHER (*gently, handing her a silk mantilla*): Don't you want it?

MOTHER: A silk mantilla for me, dear! What's the use—I'm soon going to die!

FATHER: Do you believe what the doctor says?

MOTHER: Even what he says, but most of all I believe what my inner voice says.

FATHER (*sadly*): So it is serious! . . . And you think of your children, first and last!

MOTHER: Why, they were my life, my justification . . . my joy, and my sorrow . . .

FATHER: Kristina, forgive me . . . for everything!

MOTHER: For what? Forgive me, dear; we've tortured each other. Why? We don't know! We couldn't do anything else! . . . But here are the children's new undershirts . . . See to it they change twice a week, on Wednesday and Sunday, and that Lovisa washes them . . . all over . . . Are you going out?

FATHER: I have to be at a staff meeting. At eleven o'clock.

MOTHER: Ask Alfred to come in before you leave.

FATHER (*points at the* OFFICER): Why, he's here, dear!

MOTHER: Imagine . . . I'm beginning to lose my eyesight, too . . . Yes, it's getting dark . . . (*Trims the candle*) Alfred! Come!
    (FATHER, *nodding good-bye, goes out right through the wall. The* OFFICER *goes up to the mother.*)

MOTHER: Who's the girl over there?

OFFICER (*whispering*): It's Agnes!

MOTHER: Oh, it's Agnes? You know what they say? . . . That she's the god Indra's daughter, who has asked to come down to Earth to learn how human beings really have it . . . But don't say anything! . . .

OFFICER: She is a child of god!

MOTHER (*out loud*): Alfred, I'm leaving you and your brothers and sisters soon . . . Let me tell you one thing that will help you through life.

OFFICER (*sad*): Tell me, Mother!

MOTHER: Just this: Never quarrel with God!

OFFICER: What do you mean, Mother?

MOTHER: Don't go about feeling mistreated by life.

OFFICER: But when I am mistreated?

MOTHER: You're thinking about the time you were unfairly punished for taking a coin that was later found.

OFFICER: Yes! And that wrong has given a warped twist to my life ever since . . .

MOTHER: Yes. But go over to that cupboard . . .

OFFICER (*ashamed*): So you know! It's . . .

MOTHER: *Swiss Family Robinson* [8] . . . which . . .

OFFICER: Don't say any more . . .

MOTHER: Which your brother was punished for . . . and which you had torn to pieces and hidden!

OFFICER: Imagine—that cupboard's still there after twenty years . . . Why, we've moved many times, and my mother died ten years ago!

MOTHER: Well, so what? You always have to question everything, and so you ruin the best in life for yourself . . . Look, there's Lina.

LINA (*enters*): Ma'am, thank you very much, but I can't go to the christening . . .

MOTHER: Why not, child?

LINA: I haven't anything to wear.

MOTHER: You may borrow my mantilla.

LINA: Goodness no, that won't do!

MOTHER: I don't understand. I'll never go to any party again . . .

*

OFFICER: What will Father say? It was a present from him . . .

MOTHER: How small-minded . . .

*

FATHER (*sticks his head in*): Are you going to lend my present to the maid?

MOTHER: Don't say that . . . Remember, I was a servant, too . . . Why do you hurt an innocent person?

FATHER: Why do you hurt me, your husband . . .

MOTHER: This life! When you do something nice, there's always someone to whom it's ugly . . . If you do something good for someone, you hurt someone else. Ugh, this life! (*She trims the candle so that it goes out. The stage becomes dark, and the screen is replaced.*)

*

DAUGHTER: Human beings are to be pitied!

OFFICER: You've found that out!

DAUGHTER: Yes, life is hard, but love conquers all. Come and see! (*They go toward the back.*)

*

The backdrop is drawn up; a new one can now be seen, representing an old shabby fire wall. In the middle of the wall is a gate opening on a path which ends in a bright green plot in which is a gigantic blue monkshood (aconite). To the left by the gate sits the DOORKEEPER *with a shawl over her head. She is crocheting a bedspread with a star pattern. To the right is a bulletin board which the* BILLPOSTER *is cleaning; next to him is a dip net with a green handle. Still farther to the right is a door with an air hole in the shape of a four-leaf clover. To the left of the gate is a slim linden with a coal-black trunk and a few pale green leaves; next to it a cellar opening.*

DAUGHTER (*goes up to the* DOORKEEPER): Isn't the bedspread finished yet?

DOORKEEPER: No, my dear; twenty-six years aren't enough for a project like this!

DAUGHTER: And your fiancé never came back?

DOORKEEPER: No, but that wasn't his fault. He *had* to leave . . . poor fellow . . . thirty years ago!

DAUGHTER (*to the* BILLPOSTER): Wasn't she in the ballet? Up there in the opera?

BILLPOSTER: Yes, she was number one . . . but when *he* left, he sort of took her dancing along . . . so she didn't get any more roles . . .

DAUGHTER: All of you complain, at least with your eyes, and with your voices . . .

BILLPOSTER: I'm not complaining much . . . not now when I've got a dip net and a green box!

DAUGHTER: That makes you happy?

BILLPOSTER: Yes, very happy, very . . . that was my childhood dream, and now it has come true. I'm past fifty, of course . . .

DAUGHTER: Fifty years for a dip net and a box . . . .

BILLPOSTER: A *green* box, a *green* one . . .

DAUGHTER (*to the* DOORKEEPER): Give me the shawl now so I may sit here observing human beings! But stand behind me to tell me what I need to know. (*The* DAUGHTER *puts on the shawl and sits down by the gate.*)

DOORKEEPER: Today's the last day of the opera season . . . they're finding out if they're engaged for next year . . .

DAUGHTER: What about those who aren't?

DOORKEEPER: Yes, Good Lord, that's something to see . . . Well, I draw the shawl over my head . . .

DAUGHTER: Poor human beings!

DOORKEEPER: Look, there comes one! . . . She's not among the chosen . . . Look, how she's crying . . .

*

The SINGER *rushes in from the right out through the gate with her handkerchief over her eyes. Stops for a moment on the path outside the gate, leans her head against the wall, and then rushes out.*

DAUGHTER: Human beings are to be pitied! . . .

DOORKEEPER: But look at him: that's how a happy human being looks!

(*The* OFFICER *enters through the gate; he is dressed in frock coat and a top hat and is carrying a bouquet of roses. Radiantly happy*)

He's going to marry Miss Victoria! [9] . . .

OFFICER (*downstage; looks up, sings*): Victoria!

DOORKEEPER: She's coming right away!

OFFICER: Fine! The carriage is waiting, the table has been set, the champagne's on ice . . . May I? (*Embraces both the* DAUGHTER *and the* DOORKEEPER. *Sings*) Victoria!

WOMAN'S VOICE (*From above. Sings*): I'm here!

OFFICER (*begins to walk back and forth*): Fine! I'm waiting!

*

DAUGHTER: Do you know me?

OFFICER: No, I know only one woman . . . Victoria! I've been here for seven years waiting for her [10] . . . at noon when the sun hits the chimneys and in the evening when darkness begins to fall . . . Look at the pavement there—you can see traces of the faithful lover! Hurrah, she's mine! (*Sings*) Victoria! (*He gets no answer.*) Well, she's getting dressed! (*To the* BILLPOSTER) There's your dip net, I see! Everybody at the opera's wild about dip nets . . . or about fish, rather! The silent fish—because they can't sing . . . What does a thing like that cost?

BILLPOSTER: It's quite expensive!

OFFICER (*sings*): Victoria! . . . (*Shakes the linden*) Look, it's budding again. The eighth time! . . . (*Sings*) Victoria! . . . now she's combing her hair . . . (*To the* DAUGHTER) Ma'am, let me go up to fetch my bride.

DOORKEEPER: No one's admitted on stage.

OFFICER: I've walked about here seven years! Seven times three hundred and sixty-five make two thousand five hundred fifty-five! (*Stops; pokes at the door with the four-leaf hole*) . . . And I've looked at that door two thousand five hundred fifty-five times without knowing where it leads to! And that four-leaf hole that's to let in light . . . For whom is it to let in light? Is there someone on the other side? Does someone live there?

DOORKEEPER: I don't know. I've never seen it opened . . .

OFFICER: It looks like a pantry door I saw when I was four and went with the maid on Sunday afternoon visits. Visits with other maids, but I never got beyond the kitchens, and I sat between the water barrel and the salt container; I've seen so many kitchens in my day, and the pantries were always in the entrance with round holes and a four-leaf clover in the door . . . But surely the opera doesn't have any pantry since they don't have any kitchen. (*Sings*) Victoria! . . . She'll surely not go out some other way, ma'am?

DOORKEEPER: No, there isn't any other way.

OFFICER: Fine, then I'll see her! (*Theater people rush out and are looked over by the* OFFICER.)

*

OFFICER: She'll have to be here soon! . . . Ma'am! That blue monks-hood out there. I've seen it since I was a child . . . Is it the same one? . . . I remember it in a parsonage when I was seven . . . there are two doves, blue doves under that hood . . . but that time a bee went into the hood . . . I thought: now I've got you! so I grabbed the flower; but the bee stung me, and I cried . . . but the pastor's wife came and put mud on it . . . then we got wild strawberries and milk for dinner! . . . I think it's already getting dark. (*To the* BILLPOSTER) Where are you going?

BILLPOSTER: I'm going home to eat dinner. (*Goes*)

OFFICER (*puts his hand to his eyes*): Dinner? At this time of day? Please! . . . May I just go in to telephone to "the growing castle"?

DAUGHTER: Why, what do you have in mind?

OFFICER: I'm going to tell the glazier to put in double panes—it'll soon be winter, and I'm so terribly cold! (*Goes in*)

*

DAUGHTER (*to the* DOORKEEPER): Who is Miss Victoria?

DOORKEEPER: The woman he loves!

DAUGHTER: Right! He doesn't care what she is to us and others. She *is* only what she is for *him*! . . . (*It grows dark suddenly.*)

DOORKEEPER (*lighting her lantern*): It's growing dark quickly today.

DAUGHTER: To the gods a year is as a minute!

DOORKEEPER: And to human beings a minute can be long as a year!

OFFICER (*comes out again. He looks worn; the roses have withered*):
She hasn't come yet?

DOORKEEPER: No.

OFFICER: She'll *come!* . . . She'll surely come! (*Pacing*) . . . That's
right—I'd probably be wise if I canceled dinner anyway . . . since
it's evening . . . Yes, yes, I'll do that! (*Goes in to telephone*)

*

DOORKEEPER (*to the* DAUGHTER): May I have my shawl now?

DAUGHTER: No, dear, I'll relieve you; I'll do your job . . . I want to
know human beings and life to find out if it's as hard as they say.

DOORKEEPER: But you mustn't fall asleep on this job, never fall asleep,
neither night nor day . . .

DAUGHTER: Not sleep at night?

DOORKEEPER: Yes, you can, if you have the bell cord tied to your arm
. . . for there are night watchmen on the stage, and they're replaced every third hour . . .

DAUGHTER: Why, that's torture . . .

DOORKEEPER: So it seems to you, but we others are glad to get a job
like this, and if you knew how envied I am . . .

DAUGHTER: Envied? They envy someone who's tortured?

DOORKEEPER: Yes! . . . But you see what's harder than keeping awake
at night and drudgery, drafts, and cold, and damp is to have, as I
do, all the unhappy ones up there confide in me . . . They come
to me. Why? Probably they see in the lines of my face the in-
scription carved by suffering which invites confiding . . . In that
shawl, dear, is the agony of thirty years, my own and others! . . .

DAUGHTER: It is heavy, and it burns like nettles . . .

DOORKEEPER: Put it on since you want to . . . When it gets too
heavy, call me, and I'll come and relieve you.

DAUGHTER: Farewell. What you can do, I surely can.

DOORKEEPER: We'll see! . . . But be kind to my young friends and
don't weary of their complaints. (*Goes out by way of the path. It
becomes pitch black on stage. The scenery is changed so that the
linden is stripped of leaves. The blue monkshood has withered;*

and when it turns light again, the green at the end of the path is autumn brown. The OFFICER *comes out when it turns light. His hair and his beard are now gray. His clothes are shabby, his collar dirty and limp. Only the stems of the bouquet of roses remain. He paces back and forth.*)

OFFICER: To judge by all the signs, summer's past and fall's almost here. I can tell by looking at the linden and the monkshood . . . (*Walks about*) But fall is *my* spring, for then the theater opens again! And then she has to come! Dear lady, may I sit on this chair for a while?

DAUGHTER: Yes, my friend—I'll stand.

OFFICER (*sits down*): If I could only sleep a little, it would be better . . . (*He falls asleep for a moment, then rushes up to start walking about, stops in front of the door with the four-leaf hole, and pokes at it.*) This door that doesn't give me any peace . . . What's back of it? There has to be something! (*From up above can be heard soft music in dance measure.*) There! Now they've started rehearsing! (*The stage is lighted intermittently as if by a lighthouse beam.*) What's that? (*Speaks in time with the blinking light*) Light and dark; light and dark?

DAUGHTER (*imitating him*): Day and night; day and night! . . . A kindly providence wants to shorten your waiting. So the days flee, pursuing the nights. (*The light on stage becomes steady. The* BILLPOSTER *enters with his dip net and billposting equipment.*)

OFFICER: It's the billposter with the dip net . . . Was the fishing good?

BILLPOSTER: Oh, yes! The summer was warm and a bit long . . . the dip net was good enough, but not *just* the way I'd wanted it . . .

OFFICER (*emphasizing*): Not just the way I'd wanted it . . . That's marvelously put! Nothing is the way I'd wanted it . . . because the idea is greater than the act—superior to the object. (*Walks about striking the rose bouquet on the walls so that the last leaves and petals fall*)

BILLPOSTER: Hasn't she come down yet?

OFFICER: No, not yet, but she'll come soon . . . Do you know what's back of that door?

BILLPOSTER: No, I've never seen it open.

OFFICER: I'll telephone for a locksmith to open it! (*Goes in to telephone. The* BILLPOSTER *puts up a poster and then is going out to the right.*)

DAUGHTER: What was wrong with the dip net?

BILLPOSTER: Wrong? Well, there wasn't anything really wrong . . . but it wasn't just what I'd wanted, so I didn't enjoy it so much . . .

DAUGHTER: How had you wanted it?

BILLPOSTER: How? . . . I can't say . . .

DAUGHTER: Let me say it . . . You had wanted it as it wasn't. Green, yes, but not *that* green.

BILLPOSTER: You do understand! You know everything—that's why all of them come to you with their troubles . . . Would you listen to mine, too . . .

DAUGHTER: Gladly . . . Come in here and tell me . . . (*Goes into* the DOORKEEPER'S *cage. The* BILLPOSTER *stands outside the window speaking.*)

*

It becomes pitch dark again; then it turns light, and the linden gets green leaves again, and the monkshood blooms; the sun illuminates the foliage along the path. The OFFICER *comes out; he is old and white-haired; he is ragged, his shoes are worn out; he is carrying the remains of the bouquet. He walks back and forth slowly, like an old man. He reads the playbill. A* BALLET GIRL *comes in from the right.*

OFFICER: Has Miss Victoria gone?

GIRL: No, she hasn't.

OFFICER: Then I'll wait. She'll come soon, I hope?

GIRL (*seriously*): She's sure to.

OFFICER: Don't go—then you'll see what's back of this door—I've sent for the locksmith.

GIRL: It'll really be fun to see that door opened. That door and the growing castle. Do you know the growing castle?

OFFICER: Do I? Why, I was a prisoner in it.

GIRL: Well, were you the one? But why did they have so many horses there?

OFFICER: It was a stable castle, of course . . .

GIRL (*hurt*): How stupid I am! not able to understand that! (*Goes*)

*

A MEMBER OF THE CHORUS *enters from the right.*

OFFICER: Has Miss Victoria gone?

CHORUS GIRL: No, she hasn't. She never goes.

OFFICER: That's because she loves me! . . . You mustn't go before the locksmith who's going to open the door comes.

CHORUS GIRL: Oh, is the door going to be opened? What fun! . . . I just want to ask the doorkeeper something.

(*The* PROMPTER *enters from the right.*)

OFFICER: Has Miss Victoria gone?

PROMPTER: No, not that I know.

OFFICER: There, you see! Didn't I say she's waiting for me! Don't go—the door's going to be opened.

PROMPTER: What door?

OFFICER: Is there more than one door?

PROMPTER: Oh, I know—the one with the four-leaf opening . . . Then I'll certainly stay! I'm just going to talk with the doorkeeper a little.

*

The BALLET GIRL, *the* CHORUS GIRL, *and the* PROMPTER *station themselves next to the* BILLPOSTER *outside the* DOORKEEPER'S *window. They all talk to the* DAUGHTER *in turn. The* GLAZIER *enters through the gate.*

OFFICER: Are you the locksmith?

GLAZIER: No, he had calls to make, and a glazier will do just as well.

OFFICER: Yes, of course . . . of course, but do you have your diamond?

GLAZIER: Naturally! What's a glazier without a diamond?

OFFICER: Nothing! So let's go to work. (*Strikes his hands together. All of the rest gather with him in a circle about the door. Chorus members dressed as* Meistersinger,[11] *and supers as dancers in* Aida *join the group from the right.*

*

OFFICER: Locksmith—or glazier—do your duty!

(*The* GLAZIER *comes forward with his diamond.*)

OFFICER: A moment like this seldom recurs in a lifetime, so, my friends, I beg you . . . to consider carefully . . .

POLICEMAN (*comes up*): In the name of the law I forbid the opening of this door!

OFFICER: Oh lord, what a fuss when we want to do something new and great . . . But we'll take it to court . . . To the lawyer, then! We'll find out if the laws will hold up! To the lawyer!

*

The scene changes into a LAWYER's *office without lowering the curtain thus: the gate remains functioning as the gate to the office railing, which extends directly across the stage. The* DOORKEEPER's *room remains as the* LAWYER's *writing nook but is open to the front of the stage; the linden stripped of leaves is a combination hat- and clotheshanger; the bulletin board is covered with official notices and judgments in legal cases; the door with the four-leaf hole is now part of a cupboard containing documents.*

The LAWYER *in tails and white tie is sitting to the left inside the gate at a desk covered with papers. His appearance testifies to extremely great suffering: his face is chalk-white and heavily lined, the shadows on it verge on violet; he is ugly, and his face reflects all the sorts of crimes and vices with which his profession has forced him to deal.*

One of his two CLERKS *has only one arm, the other is one-eyed.*

The people who have gathered to see "the opening of the door" remain, but now as if they were clients waiting to see the LAWYER. *They look as if they had been standing there forever.*

The DAUGHTER *(wearing the shawl) and the* OFFICER *are on the level closest to the audience.*

LAWYER *(going up to the* DAUGHTER*)*: May I have the shawl, my dear . . . I'll hang it up in here until I get the fire in the tile stove going; then I'll burn it with all its sorrows and miseries . . .

DAUGHTER: Not yet . . . I want it really full . . . first . . . and above all I want to gather in it your afflictions, all you have received in confidence about crimes, vices, thefts, backbiting, slander, libel . . .

LAWYER: Your shawl wouldn't do for all that, my friend! Look at these walls. Isn't it as if all sins have soiled the wallpaper? Look at these papers on which I record the accounts of wrongdoing . . . look at me . . . Never does a person who smiles come here—only evil looks, bared teeth, shaking fists . . . And all of them spray their evil, their envy, their suspicions over me . . . See! My hands are black, and can never be washed. Do you see how cracked and bleeding they are? . . . I can never wear clothes for more than a few days, for they smell of other people's crimes . . . Sometimes I fumigate with sulphur in here, but that doesn't help. I sleep in the next room, and dream only about crime . . . Just now I have a murder trial going in court . . . That's bearable, I suppose, but do you know what's worse than everything else? . . . Separating husband and wife! Then it's as if earth itself and heaven above cried out . . . cried treason against the source of life, the spring of what is good, against love . . . And, you see, when reams of paper have been filled with their accusations against each other, and a sympathetic person takes one of them aside in private, takes him by his ear, and smiling asks the simple question: What do you really have against your husband—or your wife?—he—or she—stands there without an answer and doesn't know! Once—well, it had to do with a green salad, I think, and another time with a word, usually with nothing. But the pangs, the suffering! I have to hear them . . . Look at me! Do you think I could win a woman's love when I look like a criminal? And do you think

anyone wants to be my friend when I have to collect the debts, the
financial debts, of everyone in town? . . . It's hard to be a human
being!

DAUGHTER: Human beings are to be pitied!

LAWYER: That's right. And what people live on is a puzzle to me.
They get married on an income of two thousand when they need
four thousand . . . They borrow, of course; all of them borrow!
So they walk a sort of tightrope until they die . . . then the estate
is never clear of debt. Who finally has to pay up? I don't know.

DAUGHTER: The One who feeds the birds!

LAWYER: Yes! But if the One who feeds the birds would descend to
His earth to see how the poor children of man have it, He'd probably pity us . . .

DAUGHTER: Human beings are to be pitied!

LAWYER: Yes, that's the truth! (*To the* OFFICER) What do you wish?

OFFICER: I only wanted to ask if Miss Victoria had gone.

LAWYER: No, she hasn't, you can be absolutely sure . . . Why are
you poking at my cupboard?

OFFICER: I thought the door was so like . . .

LAWYER: Oh no, no, no!

(*Church bells can be heard ringing.*)

OFFICER: Is there a funeral?

LAWYER: No, it's commencement [12]—the candidates are receiving
their doctor's degrees. I was just about to go up to get my doctor
of laws' degree. Perhaps you'd like to graduate and get a laurel
wreath?

OFFICER: Well-l-l, why not? That would always be a little break
from monotony . . .

LAWYER: Perhaps we should proceed to the solemn rites at once?—
Just go and change your clothes.

The OFFICER *goes out; the stage becomes dark—the following
changes take place: the railing remains and now serves as the bal-
ustrade for the sanctuary in a church; the billboard becomes a
bulletin board listing psalms; the linden-clotheshanger becomes*

a candelabra; the LAWYER's *desk the* CHANCELLOR's *lectern; the door with the four-leaf opening now leads into the sacristy. The singers from* Die Meistersinger *become* HERALDS *carrying scepters, and the* DANCERS *carry the laurel wreaths.*[13]

The rest of the people comprise the audience.

The backdrop is raised. The new one represents a single large organ with keyboard below and a mirror above.

Music is heard. To the sides the four faculties—philosophy [arts and sciences], theology, medicine, and law. The stage is empty for a moment. The HERALDS *enter from the right.*

The DANCERS *follow with laurel wreaths in their outstretched hands.*

Three CANDIDATES *enter, one after the other, from the left and are crowned by the* DANCERS *and then go out to the right.*

The LAWYER *comes forward to be crowned.*

The DANCERS *turn away, refusing to crown him, and go out.*

The LAWYER, *shaken, leans against a pillar. Everyone else leaves. The* LAWYER *is alone.*

DAUGHTER (*enters with a white veil over her head and shoulders*): Look, I've washed the shawl . . . But why are you standing here? Didn't you get the wreath?

LAWYER: No, I wasn't worthy.

DAUGHTER: Why? Because you've defended the poor, put in a good word for the criminal, lightened the burden for the guilty, got respite for the condemned . . . Poor human beings . . . They aren't angels; but they're to be pitied.

LAWYER: Don't say anything bad about human beings; why, I'm to plead their case . . .

DAUGHTER (*leaning on the organ*): Why do they slap their friends in the face?

LAWYER: They don't know any better.

DAUGHTER: Let's teach them! Do you want to? With me!

LAWYER: They won't learn! . . . If only our complaint could reach the gods in heaven . . .

DAUGHTER: It will reach the throne! (*Places herself by the organ*) Do you know what I see in this mirror? . . . The world right side to! . . . Yes, since it's reversed in itself!

LAWYER: How did it get reversed?

DAUGHTER: When the copy was made . . .

LAWYER: That's it! The copy . . . I always sensed it was an imperfect copy . . . and when I began to remember the original, I became dissatisfied with everything . . . People called that dissatisfaction the devil's fragments of glass in my eye . . . and other things . . .

DAUGHTER: It's certainly mad! Look at the four faculties! The government that's to preserve the community pays all four of them: theology, the doctrine about God, which is always attacked and ridiculed by philosophy, which says it's wisdom itself! And medicine, which always questions the validity of philosophy and doesn't consider theology one of the sciences but calls it superstition . . . And they sit in the same council which is to teach the students respect—for the university. Why, it's an insane asylum! And pity the poor soul who gets sane first!

LAWYER: Those who learn that first are the theologians. As preliminary studies they get philosophy, which teaches them theology is nonsense; then they learn in theology that philosophy is nonsense. Madmen, aren't they?

DAUGHTER: And law, the servant of all, except the servants!

LAWYER: Justice, which when it wants to be just, becomes the death of the just! . . . The court of justice, which often is unjust!

DAUGHTER: What a mess you've made for yourselves, children of man! Child!—Come here; I'll give you a wreath . . . that will be more becoming for you! (*Places a crown of thorns*[14] *on his head*) Now I'll play for you! (*She sits down at the piano and plays a Kyrie,*[15] *but instead of organ music human voices are heard.*)

CHILDREN'S VOICES: Eternal Lord! (*The last note is extended.*)

WOMEN'S VOICES: Have mercy on us! (*The last note is extended.*)

MEN'S VOICES (*tenors*): Save us, for the sake of Thy mercy! (*The last note is extended.*)

MEN'S VOICES (*basses*): Spare Thy children, oh Lord, and be not angry with us!

*

ALL: Have mercy! Hear us! Pity us mortals!—Eternal God, why art Thou so far away? . . . Out of the depths we cry: Mercy, oh God! Do not make Thy children's burden too heavy! Hear us! Hear us!

*

The stage becomes dark. The DAUGHTER *gets up, approaches the* LAWYER. *Through a change in lighting the organ becomes Fingal's Cave.*[16] *The sea dashes in swells under the basalt pillars and produces a harmonious sound of waves and wind.*

LAWYER: Where are we?

DAUGHTER: What do you hear?

LAWYER: I hear drops falling . . .

DAUGHTER: They are the tears when human beings weep . . . What else do you hear?

LAWYER: Sighs . . . cries . . . moans . . .

DAUGHTER: Mortals' laments have come this far . . . not farther. But why this eternal grumbling? Hasn't life anything to be happy about?

LAWYER: Yes, the most delightful which is also the most bitter: love! Mate and home! The highest and the lowest!

DAUGHTER: Let me try it!

LAWYER: With me?

DAUGHTER: With you! You know the rocks, the stumbling blocks. Let's avoid them!

LAWYER: I'm poor!

DAUGHTER: What difference does that make if we love each other? And a little beauty doesn't cost anything.

LAWYER: I have dislikes which you probably don't have.

DAUGHTER: We'll have to compromise.

LAWYER: If we weary?

DAUGHTER: Then our child will come and give us a diversion that's always new!

LAWYER: You want to marry me—poverty-stricken and ugly, despised, rejected?

DAUGHTER: Yes! Let's join our destinies!

LAWYER: So be it!

II

A very simple room next to the LAWYER's *office. To the right a large double bed with a canopy; next to it a window. To the left a sheet-iron stove with cooking utensils on it.* KRISTIN *is pasting strips along the inner windows. At the back an open door to the office; poor people waiting to be heard can be seen out there.*

KRISTIN: I paste! I paste! [17]

DAUGHTER (*pale and worn, is sitting by the stove*): You're shutting out the air! I'm suffocating! . . .

KRISTIN: Now there's only one little crack left!

DAUGHTER: Air, air! I can't breathe!

KRISTIN: I paste, I paste!

LAWYER: That's right, Kristin! Heat is expensive!

DAUGHTER: It's as if you were gluing my mouth shut!

LAWYER (*stands in the door with a document in his hand*): Is the baby asleep?

DAUGHTER: Yes, at last!

LAWYER (*gently*): His crying frightens my clients away.

DAUGHTER (*friendly*): What can we do about it?

LAWYER: Nothing.

DAUGHTER: We'll have to get a larger apartment.

LAWYER: We haven't any money.

DAUGHTER: May I open the window? This bad air is suffocating me!

LAWYER: Then the heat will go out, and we'll have to freeze.

DAUGHTER: That's terrible! . . . May we scrub out there then?

LAWYER: You're not strong enough to scrub, nor am I, and Kristin has to paste; she has to paste the whole house, every last crack—in the ceiling, the floors, the walls.

DAUGHTER: I was prepared for poverty, not for dirt!

LAWYER: Poverty is always relatively dirty.

DAUGHTER: This is worse than I imagined!

LAWYER: We're not the worst off. We still have food in our pot!

DAUGHTER: But what food! . . .

LAWYER: Cabbage is inexpensive, nourishing, and good.

DAUGHTER: For the one who likes cabbage. I can't stand it!

LAWYER: Why didn't you say so?

DAUGHTER: Because I loved you! I wanted to sacrifice my taste!

LAWYER: Then I'll have to sacrifice my taste for cabbage. The sacrifices have to be mutual.

DAUGHTER: What shall we eat then? Fish? But you hate fish.

LAWYER: And it's expensive.

DAUGHTER: This is harder than I thought.

LAWYER (*friendly*): Yes, you see how hard it is . . . And our child, who was to be our bond and blessing . . . becomes our ruin!

DAUGHTER: Darling! I'm dying in this air, in this room with its view of the backyard, with endless hours of our child's crying—without sleep, with those people out there, and their complaining, squabbling, and accusations . . . I'll die in here!

LAWYER: Poor little flower, without light, without air . . .

DAUGHTER: And you say there are people who are worse off.

LAWYER: I'm one of those who are envied in this neighborhood.

DAUGHTER: Everything would be all right if I could only have a bit of beauty in our home.

LAWYER: I know you mean a flower, a heliotrope especially, but that costs one and a half—that's the price of six quarts of milk or two pecks of potatoes.

DAUGHTER: I'd gladly go without food if I could only get my flower!

LAWYER: There's a kind of beauty that doesn't cost anything, and the lack of which in his home is the biggest torture for a man with a sense of beauty.

DAUGHTER: What's that?

LAWYER: If I tell you, you'll get angry!

DAUGHTER: We've agreed not to get angry!

LAWYER: We've agreed . . . Everything will do, Agnes, except the short, hard accents . . . Do you know them? Not yet.

DAUGHTER: We'll never hear them!

LAWYER: Not so far as I'm concerned.

DAUGHTER: So tell me!

LAWYER: Well: when I come into a home, I first see how the curtains hang . . . (*Goes up to the window and straightens the curtain*) . . . If it hangs like a rope or a rag . . . then I leave pretty soon . . . Then I look at the chairs . . . if they're in their places, I stay! (*Moves a chair into its proper place against the wall*) Then I look at the candles in their holders . . . If they lean, the house is off base. (*Straightens a candle on the bureau*) . . . It's this bit of beauty, my dear, that doesn't cost anything.

DAUGHTER (*inclines her head downward*): Not the short accents, Axel.

LAWYER: They weren't short!

DAUGHTER: Yes, they were!

LAWYER: What the hell! . . .

DAUGHTER: What sort of language is that?

LAWYER: Forgive me, Agnes. But I have suffered from your slovenliness as you suffer from dirt. And I haven't dared to put things into their places myself, for you'd get as angry then as if I scolded you . . . Ugh! Shall we stop?

DAUGHTER: It's terribly hard to be married . . . it's harder than anything else. One has to be an angel, I think.

LAWYER: Yes, I think so.

DAUGHTER: I think I'm beginning to hate you!

LAWYER: Too bad for us if you do! . . . But let's prevent hate. I promise never to criticize your housekeeping . . . though it's torture to me.

DAUGHTER: And I'll eat cabbage, though it's agony for me.

LAWYER: So, a life together in agony. The one's pleasure, the other's pain!

DAUGHTER: Human beings are to be pitied!

LAWYER: You do understand that?

DAUGHTER: Yes, but in God's name let's avoid the rocks now that we know them so well!

LAWYER: Let's. Why, we're humane and enlightened people; we can forgive and overlook!

DAUGHTER: Why, we can smile at trifles!

LAWYER: We, only we, can! . . . Do you know I read in the *Morning News!* . . . by the way—where is the paper?

DAUGHTER (*embarrassed*): What paper?

LAWYER (*harshly*): Do I take more than one?

DAUGHTER: Smile and don't speak harshly now . . . I started the fire with your paper . . .

LAWYER (*violently*): What the hell!

DAUGHTER: Smile! . . . I burned it because it made fun of what I consider sacred . . .

LAWYER: Which isn't sacred for me. Huh . . . (*Hits his fist into his other hand, beside himself*) I'll smile, I'll smile so my molars show . . . I'll be humane, and conceal my thoughts and say yes to everything, and evade and play the hypocrite! So you burned my paper! So-o! (*Rearranges the curtain on the bed*) There! Now I'll straighten up so you'll be angry . . . Agnes, this is simply impossible!

DAUGHTER: It certainly is!

LAWYER: And just the same we have to stick it out, not because of our vows but for the sake of our child.

DAUGHTER: That's true. For the child's . . . (*Sighs*) We must stick it out!

LAWYER: And now I have to go out to my clients. Listen to them—they're buzzing with impatience to tear at each other, to get each other fined and imprisoned . . . lost souls . . .

DAUGHTER: Poor, poor human beings. And this pasting! (*She bows her head in silent despair.*)

KRISTIN: I paste, I paste!

  (*The* LAWYER *stands at the door, fingering the doorknob nervously.*)

DAUGHTER: How that lock squeaks; it's as if you were crushing my heart . . .

LAWYER: I crush, I crush . . .

DAUGHTER: Don't do it!

LAWYER: I crush . . .

DAUGHTER: No!

LAWYER: I . . .

OFFICER (*enters from the office, takes hold of the knob*): Permit me!

LAWYER (*lets go the knob*): Go ahead. Since you got your degree!

OFFICER: Everything in life is mine now! All careers are open to me, Parnassus [18] has been climbed, the laurel wreath has been won, immortality, honor, everything's mine!

LAWYER: How are you going to support yourself?

OFFICER: Support myself?

LAWYER: You'll need food, shelter, and clothing, I suspect.

OFFICER: There'll always be a way, just so one has someone who loves one.

LAWYER: I can imagine . . . Yes, imagine . . . Paste, Kristin! Paste! Until they can't breathe! (*Goes out backward, nodding*)

KRISTIN: I paste, I paste! Until they can't breathe!

OFFICER: Are you coming along now?

DAUGHTER: Right away. But where?

OFFICER: To Fairhaven! [19] It's summer there, the sun is shining there, youth is there and children and flowers; singing and dancing, parties and rejoicing!

DAUGHTER: Then I want to go there!

OFFICER: Come!

*

LAWYER (*comes in again*): I'm returning to my first hell . . this was the second . . . and the greatest! The most delightful is the greatest hell . . . Look at that—she has dropped hairpins on the floor again! . . . (*Picks one up*)

OFFICER: Imagine, he has discovered the hairpins, too!

LAWYER: Too? . . . Look at this one. It has two prongs but is one pin! There are two, but it's one! If I straighten it out, there's only one! If I bend it, there are two without ceasing to be one. That means: the two are one! But if I break it—here! Then they're two! Two! (*Breaks the hairpin and throws the pieces away*)

OFFICER: You've seen all this . . . But before you can break them off, the prongs have to diverge. If they converge, it holds up.

LAWYER: And if they're parallel—they never meet—it's neither one nor two.

OFFICER: The hairpin is the most perfect of all created things! A straight line that equals two parallel ones.

LAWYER: A lock that closes when it's open!

OFFICER: Open, closes—a braid of hair that remains open when it's bound . . .

LAWYER: It's like this door. When I shut it, I open the way out for you, Agnes! (*Goes out, shutting the door*)

*

DAUGHTER: So?

(*Change on stage: the bed with its canopy becomes a tent; the stove remains; the backdrop is raised; to the right in the foreground one sees burned-over mountains with red heather and stumps black and white after a forest fire; red pigpens and outhouses. Below, an open gymnasium in which people are exercised on machines resembling instruments of torture. To the left in the foreground, part of the quarantine building's open shed with hearths, furnace walls, and plumbing pipes. The middle area is a sound. The back of the stage is a beautiful shore with trees in foliage, piers (decorated with flags) to which white boats are tied; some of them have their sails hoisted, some not. Small Italian villas, pavilions, kiosks, marble statues can be seen among the foliage.)* [20]

QUARANTINE MASTER, *in blackface, is walking on the shore.*

OFFICER (*comes up to him and shakes his hand*): Well, if it isn't Ordström! [21] So you've landed here?

MASTER: Yes, I'm here.

OFFICER: Is this Fairhaven?

MASTER: No, that's over there. This is Foulstrand!

OFFICER: Then we've come to the wrong place!

MASTER: We?—Aren't you going to introduce me?

OFFICER: No, it's not proper. (*Softly*) It's Indra's own daughter, you see.

MASTER: Indra's? I thought it was Waruna [the supreme god] himself! . . . Well, aren't you amazed my face is black?

OFFICER: My boy, I'm over fifty—at that age one doesn't get amazed any more—I assumed right away you were going to a masquerade this afternoon.

MASTER: Absolutely right! I hope you'll come along.

OFFICER: Most likely, for it . . . it doesn't look too attractive here . . . What sort of people live here?

MASTER: The sick live here; those who are healthy live over there.

OFFICER: I suppose there are only poor people here.

MASTER: No, old man, the rich are here. Look at the man on that rack! He has eaten too much goose liver with truffles and drunk so much burgundy that his feet have become malformed!

OFFICER: Malformed?

MASTER: Yes! . . . And the one lying on the guillotine over there; he has consumed so much Hennessy [22] that his backbone has to be ironed out!

OFFICER: That can't be good either!

MASTER: In general the ones who live on this side all have some form of misery to hide. Look at the one who's coming, for example!

(*An older* FOP *is wheeled in in a wheelchair, accompanied by a sixty-year-old coquette, dressed in the latest fashion and attended by* HER FRIEND, *who is forty.*)

OFFICER: It's the major! Our schoolmate!

MASTER: Don Juan! You see, he's still in love with the old wreck by his side. He doesn't see she has aged, that she's ugly, faithless, cruel!

OFFICER: Well, that's love! I'd never have believed that flighty soul capable of loving so profoundly and seriously.

MASTER: You do have a nice attitude!

OFFICER: I've been in love—with Victoria . . . yes, I still haunt the corridor waiting for her . . .

MASTER: Are you the one in the corridor?

OFFICER: Yes, I am.

MASTER: Well, have you got the door opened yet?

OFFICER: No, we're still in court about it . . . The billposter is out with his dip net, of course, so hearing testimony has been delayed . . . in the meanwhile the glazier has put in panes in the castle which has grown a half story . . . It has been an unusually good year this year . . . warm and wet.

MASTER: But you still haven't had it as warm as I have!

OFFICER: How warm do you keep the ovens?

MASTER: When we disinfect people who may have cholera, we keep them at 144 degrees.

OFFICER: Is cholera raging again?

MASTER: Didn't you know? . . .

OFFICER: Of course I knew, but I so often forget what I know!

MASTER: I often wish I could forget, myself mostly; that's why I like masquerades, dressing up, and amateur theatricals.

OFFICER: What have you been up to?

MASTER: If I tell, they say I'm bragging; if I keep still, I'm called a hypocrite!

OFFICER: Is that why you've blackened your face?

MASTER: Yes! A little blacker than I am!

OFFICER: Who's that coming?

MASTER: Oh, he's a poet. Who's going to have his mudbath! (*The* POET *enters with his eyes directed toward the sky and a pail of mud in his hand.*)

OFFICER: Heavens, you'd think he'd need a bath in light and air!

MASTER: No, he's always way up there in the heights so he gets homesick for mud . . . wallowing in dirt makes his skin as hard as a pig's. He doesn't feel the gadflies' stings after that!

OFFICER: What a strange world of contradictions this is!

*

POET (*ecstatically*): Of clay the god Ptah [23] created man on a potter's wheel, a lathe—(*skeptically*)—or what the hell have you!—(*Ecstatically*) Of clay the sculptor creates his more or less immortal masterpieces—(*skeptically*)—which most often are pure junk! (*Ecstatically*) Of clay are created these vessels so needed in the pantry, which have the name dishes in common, plates—(*skeptically*)—as far as that goes I don't care much what they're called! (*Ecstatically*) This is the clay! When it's mixed with water and flows, it's called mud—*C'est mon affaire!* (*Calls*) Lina!

*

LINA *enters with a pail.*

POET: Lina, let Miss Agnes see you! She knew you ten years ago when you were a young, happy, let's say pretty girl . . . [*To the* DAUGHTER] See what she looks like now! Five children, drudgery, yelling, starving, beatings! See how her beauty has perished, how her joy has disappeared, while she has been doing her duty, which should have given her the inner satisfaction that reflects itself in the harmonious lines of a face and in the quiet glow of the eyes . . .

MASTER (*places his hand over the* POET's *mouth*): Keep still! Keep still!

POET: That's what they all say! And if one keeps still, they say: speak! Perverse human beings!

*

DAUGHTER (*goes up to* LINA): Tell me your complaints!

LINA: No, I don't dare to—then I'd have it still worse!

DAUGHTER: Who is that cruel?

LINA: I don't dare to say—then I'll get a beating!

POET: That's how it can be! But I will tell you even if that black fellow wants to knock my teeth out! . . . I'll tell you that there is injustice sometimes . . . Agnes, daughter of God! . . . Do you hear music and dancing up there on the hillside? Fine! . . . It's Lina's sister, who has come home from the city where she went astray . . . you understand . . . Now they're butchering the fatted calf,[24] but Lina who stayed at home has to carry the pail to feed the pigs! . . .

DAUGHTER: There's rejoicing in her home because the one who has gone astray has given up her wickedness—not only because she has come home! Remember that!

POET: But then put on a dinner and ball every evening for this blameless woman who has never gone astray! Do that! . . . But people don't . . . instead when Lina has a little leisure, she has to go to church and get scolded because she isn't perfect. Is that justice?

DAUGHTER: Your questions are so hard to answer because . . . there are so many unknowns . . .

POET: The caliph Harun the Just [25] understood that, too! He sat quietly on his throne and never saw how they had it down below. The complaints finally reached his noble ear. Then one fine day he stepped down, disguised himself, and went about unrecognized among the crowds of people to see how it was with justice.

DAUGHTER: You surely don't think I'm Harun the Just?

OFFICER: Let's talk about something else . . . Company's coming!

(*A white dragon-shaped boat with a light blue silk sail with a golden yard and golden mast with a rose-red pennant glides forward on the sound from the left. At the helm with their arms about each other sit* HE *and* SHE.)

OFFICER: Look at that—perfect happiness, total bliss, the ecstasy of young love!

(*The stage becomes lighter.*)

HE (*stands up in the boat and sings*):

Hail thee, lovely bay,

where I spent my early years

where I dreamt my first dreams of love,

here you have me once again,

but not alone as then!

Groves and bays,

skies and sea,

hail her!

My true love, my bride!

My sun, my life!

(*The flags on the docks at Fairhaven dip in greeting, white handkerchiefs from villas and shores wave, and a chord played by harps and violins sounds over the water.*)

POET: See how they radiate light! Listen to the melody from across the water! Eros!

OFFICER: It is Victoria!

MASTER: What?

OFFICER: It's his Victoria; I have mine! And mine, no one else may see! . . . Raise the quarantine flag now; I'm going to pull in the net.

(MASTER *waves a yellow flag.*)

OFFICER (*pulls on a line so that the boat turns toward Foulstrand*): Hold it there!

(HE *and* SHE *now notice the ghastly landscape and express their horror.*)

MASTER: Yes, yes! It's hard. But everyone, every last one who comes from an infected area has to come here.

POET: Imagine, being able to talk like that, being able to do that when one sees two human beings who have met in love. Don't touch them! Don't touch love! That's the greatest crime! . . . Poor souls! Everything beautiful has to go down, down into the mud!

(HE *and* SHE *step ashore, sorrow-stricken and ashamed.*)

HE: What have we done?

MASTER: You don't have to have done anything to be hit by the small discomforts of life.

SHE: That's how short happiness and joy are!

HE: How long do we have to stay here?

MASTER: Forty days and nights! [26]

SHE: Then we'd rather drown ourselves!

HE: Live here, among the scorched hills and the pigpens?

POET: Love conquers all, even sulphur fumes and carbolic acid!

*

QUARANTINE MASTER (*lights the stove; blue sulphur vapors rise*): Now I'm lighting the sulphur. Please step in!

SHE: My blue dress will lose its color!

MASTER: Yes, it'll turn white! Your red roses will turn white, too!

HE: And your cheeks as well! In forty days!

SHE (*to* OFFICER): *That will please you!*

OFFICER: No, it won't! . . . Your happiness did cause my suffering, but . . . that doesn't matter—I now have my degree and am tutoring over there . . . [*sighs*] . . . and this fall I'll have a place in a school . . . teaching boys the same lessons I had in all of my childhood, in all of my youth, and now I'm going to do the same lessons through all my years of maturity and finally through all of my old age . . . the same lessons: How much is two times two? How many times does two go into four? . . . Until I'm retired with a pension and have to go—without anything to do, waiting for my meals and the papers—until at last they bring me to the crematory and burn me up . . . Don't you have anyone who's ready to be pensioned out here? I suspect that's the worst next to two times two is four. Starting school again just when one has received his degree; asking the same questions until he dies . . . (*An older man walks by with his hands behind his back.*) There goes a pensioner waiting to die! Probably a captain who didn't become a major or a law clerk who didn't get to be a judge—many are called, but few are chosen . . . He's waiting and waiting for breakfast . . .

PENSIONER: No, for the paper! The morning paper!

OFFICER: And he's only fifty-four years old; he can live for twenty-five more years waiting for his meals and his paper . . . Isn't that terrible?

PENSIONER: What isn't terrible? Tell me that!

OFFICER: Yes, let him who can tell us that! . . . Now I'm going to teach boys two times two is four: How many times does two go into four? (*He puts his hands to his head in despair.*) And Victoria, whom I love and for whom I wished the greatest happiness on earth . . . Now she has happiness, the greatest she knows, and I suffer . . . suffer . . . suffer!

SHE: Do you think I can be happy when I see you suffer? How can you think that? Maybe my being a prisoner here for forty days and nights will relieve your suffering a little. Does it?

OFFICER: Yes, and no. I can't be happy when you're suffering!

HE: And do you think my happiness can be built on your agony?

OFFICER: We are to be pitied—all of us!

(ALL *raise their hands toward heaven and utter a cry of pain resembling a dissonant chord.*)

DAUGHTER: Eternal God, hear them! Life is evil! Human beings are to be pitied!

(ALL *cry out as before.*)

*

The stage becomes pitch black for a moment, during which the actors leave or change places. When the lights come on again, the shore of Foulstrand [27] can be seen at the back in shadow. The sound lies in the middle area, and Fairhaven in the foreground, both fully lighted up. To the right, a corner of the clubhouse with its windows open; couples can be seen dancing inside. On an empty box outside stand three MAIDS, their arms about each other, looking in at the dance. On the porch is a bench on which UGLY EDITH is sitting, bareheaded, depressed, with her heavy head of hair disheveled. In front of her an open piano.

To the left a yellow wooden house.

Two lightly clad CHILDREN are tossing a ball back and forth outside the clubhouse.

In the foreground a dock with white boats and flagpoles with flags waving. Out on the sound a warship rigged with cannon openings is anchored.

But the whole landscape is in its winter dress with snow on leafless trees and the ground.

The DAUGHTER and the OFFICER enter.

*

DAUGHTER: Here there's peace and happiness during vacation time. Work is over, there's a party every day; people are dressed in their holiday clothes; music and dancing even in the forenoon. (To the MAIDS) Why don't you go in and dance, children?

MAIDS: We?

OFFICER: Why, they're servants!

DAUGHTER: That's true! . . . But why is Edith sitting there instead of dancing?

(EDITH hides her face in her hands.)

OFFICER: Don't ask her! She has been sitting there for three hours without being asked . . . (He goes into the yellow house to the left.)

DAUGHTER: What a cruel pleasure!

MOTHER (comes out, wearing a low-cut dress, goes up to EDITH): Why don't you go in as I've told you?

EDITH: Because . . . I can't ask for a dance. I know I'm ugly . . .

that's why no one wants to dance with me, but you could quit reminding me about that! (EDITH *begins to play Johann Sebastian Bach's Toccata and Fugue No. 10 on the piano.*)

(*The waltz from the dance indoors can be heard softly at first, but then becomes louder as if competing with Bach's Toccata.* EDITH *plays the waltz down, however, and brings it to silence. Dancers appear in the door and listen to her music; everyone on stage stands listening with rapt attention.*)

A NAVAL OFFICER (*puts his arm about* ALICE, *one of the dancers, and leads her down to the dock*): Come quickly!

(EDITH *breaks off playing, stands up, and looks at the* NAVAL OFFICER *and* ALICE *with despair. Remains standing as if turned to stone*)

*

The wall of the yellow house is lifted away. One can see three schoolbenches with boys on them; among them sits the OFFICER, *looking uneasy and troubled. The* SCHOOLMASTER *with glasses, chalk, and cane is standing in front of them.*

SCHOOLMASTER (*to the* OFFICER): Well, my boy, can you tell me how much two times two is?

(OFFICER *remains seated, searching painfully in his memory without finding the answer.*)

SCHOOLMASTER: You should stand up when a question is put to you.

OFFICER (*tortured, gets up*): Two . . . times two . . . Let me see! . . . It's two twos!

MASTER: So! You haven't studied your lesson!

OFFICER (*ashamed*): Yes, I have, but . . . I know the answer, but I can't say it . . .

MASTER: You're trying to get out of it! You know but *can't* say it. Maybe I can help you! (*Pulls the* OFFICER's *hair*)

OFFICER: It's terrible, it is terrible!

MASTER: Yes, it's terrible a big boy hasn't the ambition . . .

OFFICER (*humiliated*): A *big* boy! Yes, I am big, much bigger than these boys; I'm grown up; I've finished school—(*As if awakening*) Why, I have my degree . . . Why am I sitting here? Didn't I get my degree?

SCHOOLMASTER: Yes, you did, but you're to sit here maturing, you see . . . you're to mature . . . Isn't that right?

OFFICER (*his hand to his forehead*): Yes, that's right . . . One should mature . . . Two times two . . . is two . . . and I'll prove it by analogy, the highest form of proof! Listen . . . One times one is one, so two times two is two. What applies to the one applies to the other!

SCHOOLMASTER: The proof is absolutely correct according to the laws of logic, but the answer is wrong!

OFFICER: What's in keeping with the laws of logic can't be wrong! Let's test it! One goes into one once, so two goes into two twice.

SCHOOLMASTER: Absolutely correct by analogy. But how much is one times three?

OFFICER: Three!

SCHOOLMASTER: So two times three is also three!

OFFICER (*thoughtfully*): No, that can't be right . . . it can't . . . or . . . (*Sits down, in despair*) No, I'm not mature yet.

SCHOOLMASTER: No, you're not mature by a long shot . . .

OFFICER: But how long will I have to sit here?

SCHOOLMASTER: How long? Do you think time and space exist? . . . Assume that time exists. Then you should be able to say what time is! What is time?

OFFICER: Time . . . (*Considers*) I can't say it, but I know what it is: ergo, I can know how much two times two is without my being able to say it! Can you say what time is, sir?

SCHOOLMASTER: Of course I can!

ALL THE BOYS: Go on—tell us!

SCHOOLMASTER: Time? . . . Let me see! (*Stands motionless with his finger to his nose*) While we're speaking, time flies. So time is something that flies while I speak!

ONE BOY (*gets up*): You're talking now, sir, and while you're talking, I fly, so I'm time! (*Flees*)

SCHOOLMASTER: That's absolutely right according to the laws of logic!

OFFICER: But then the laws of logic are crazy, for Nils who fled can't be time!

SCHOOLMASTER: That, too, is absolutely right according to the laws of logic, though it is crazy.

OFFICER: Then logic is crazy!

SCHOOLMASTER: It really looks like it! But if logic is crazy, the whole world is crazy . . . Then to hell with sitting here teaching you nonsense! . . . If anyone offers to treat us to a drink, we'll go swimming!

OFFICER: That is a *posterus prius,* or the world turned backside to, because usually one goes swimming first and then has a drink! You old fogey!

SCHOOLMASTER: Don't be arrogant, Doctor!

OFFICER: Use my military title, please! I'm an officer, and I don't understand why I'm sitting here among schoolboys being scolded . . .

SCHOOLMASTER (*lifts his finger*): We should mature!

*

QUARANTINE MASTER (*enters*): The quarantine's beginning!

OFFICER: There you are! Can you imagine that fellow has me sitting on the school bench though I have my degree?

QUARANTINE MASTER: Well, why don't you leave?

OFFICER: Why not? . . . Leave? That's not so easy!

SCHOOLMASTER: No, I imagine not. Try!

OFFICER (*to the* QUARANTINE MASTER): Save me! Save me from his eyes!

QUARANTINE MASTER: Come along! . . . Just come and help us dance . . . We have to dance before the epidemic breaks out. We have to!

OFFICER: Is the ship leaving then?

QUARANTINE MASTER: The ship is to leave first! . . . There'll be weeping then, of course!

OFFICER: Always weeping: when it comes, and when it leaves . . . Let's go!

(*They go out. The* SCHOOLMASTER *silently continues teaching.*)

*

The MAIDS, *who have been standing at the dance-hall window, move sadly toward the dock;* EDITH, *who has stood as if turned to stone by the piano follows them slowly.*

DAUGHTER (*to the* OFFICER): Isn't there a single happy human being in this paradise?

OFFICER: Yes, there are two newlyweds over there. Listen to them!

*

The newlyweds enter.

HUSBAND (*to the* WIFE): My happiness is so great I could wish to die . . .

WIFE: Why die?

HUSBAND: Because in the midst of happiness grows the seed of unhappiness; it consumes itself as the flame of fire . . . it can't burn forever but must go out; this presentiment of the end destroys bliss while at its very height.

WIFE: Let's die together, right now!

HUSBAND: Die? All right! For I fear happiness! It's deceitful! (*They go toward the water.*)

*

DAUGHTER (*to the* OFFICER): Life is evil! Human beings are to be pitied!

OFFICER: Look at that fellow who's coming! He's the most envied of all the mortals in this place! (*The* BLINDMAN *is led in.*) He owns these hundred Italian villas; he owns all these firths, bays, shores, forests, the fish in the water, the birds in the air, and the wildlife in the forest. These thousand people are his paying guests, and the sun rises on his sea and sets on his lands . . .

DAUGHTER: Well, does he complain, too?

OFFICER: Yes, and with good reason—he can't see!

QUARANTINE MASTER: He's blind! . . .

DAUGHTER: The one most envied of all!

OFFICER: Now he's to see the ship sail—his son is on board.

*

BLINDMAN: I don't see, but I hear! I hear how the anchor tears the bottom as when one pulls a fishhook out of a fish and its heart comes along through its throat! . . . My son, my only child, is going to foreign countries by way of the wide sea; I can follow him only with my thoughts . . . now I hear the anchor chain grating . . . and . . . there's something fluttering and crackling like washing on a clothesline . . . wet handkerchiefs probably . . . and I hear sobbing and sighing as when people are crying . . . if it's the washing of the waves against the ship or girls on the shore . . . the deserted and the ones who can't be comforted . . . I once asked a child why the sea was salt, and the child, whose father was on a long journey, answered at once: The sea is salt because the sailors weep so much. Why do the sailors weep so much, then? . . . Well, he answered, because they're always going away . . . and therefore they always dry their handkerchiefs up on the masts! . . . Why does a human being weep when he's sad? I then asked . . . Well, said the child, his glasses have to be washed occasionally so he can see more clearly! . . .

(*The ship has hoisted its sails and is gliding away; the girls on shore wave their handkerchiefs and, alternately, dry their tears. Now the signal "yes" is hoisted on the topmast—a red ball on a white field.* ALICE *waves jubilantly by way of answer.*)

DAUGHTER (*to the* OFFICER): What does that flag mean?

OFFICER: It means "yes." It's the lieutenant's "yes" in red—the red blood of his heart—inscribed on the blue cloth of the sky!

DAUGHTER: What does "no" look like then?

OFFICER: It's blue as the tainted blood in blue veins . . . but do you see how Alice is rejoicing?

DAUGHTER: And how Edith is weeping! . . .

BLINDMAN: Meeting and parting! Parting and meeting! That is life! I met his mother. And she's gone! I still had my son. And now he has gone!

DAUGHTER: He'll surely come back.

BLINDMAN: Who is it talking to me? I've heard that voice before, in my dreams, in my youth, when summer vacation began, when I was just married, when my child was born. Every time life smiled, I heard that voice like the sighing of the south wind, like music on a harp above, as I imagine the chorus of angels greeting Christmas night . . .

(LAWYER *enters, goes up to the* BLINDMAN, *and whispers to him.*)

BLINDMAN: Really!

LAWYER: Yes, that's how it is! (*Goes up to the* DAUGHTER) Now you've seen most things, but you haven't tried the worst.

DAUGHTER: What can that be?

LAWYER: Repetition . . . doing the same thing again and again! . . . Going back! Redoing one's lessons! . . . Come!

DAUGHTER: Where?

LAWYER: To your duties!

DAUGHTER: What are they?

LAWYER: They're everything you loathe! Everything you don't want to do but have to do! They're doing without, giving up, forsaking, and leaving . . . everything unpleasant, repulsive, painful . . .

DAUGHTER: Aren't there any pleasant duties?

LAWYER: They become pleasant when they're fulfilled . . .

DAUGHTER: When they don't exist any more . . . So duty is everything unpleasant! What's pleasant, then?

LAWYER: What's pleasant is sin.

DAUGHTER: Sin?

LAWYER: Which is to be punished, yes! If I've had a pleasant day and evening, I have the pangs of hell and a bad conscience the next day!

DAUGHTER: How strange!

LAWYER: Yes, I wake up in the morning with a headache, and the repetition begins . . . in reverse. In such a way that everything that last night was beautiful, pleasant, clever, memory today presents as evil, vile, stupid. Pleasure sort of rots, and joy goes to pieces. What human beings call success always becomes the cause of the next defeat. The successes I've had in life became my ruination. You see, human beings have an instinctive horror of other people's success; they think fate is unjust to favor one person, so they try to restore the balance by rolling stones in one's way. Being talented is extremely dangerous, for you can easily starve to death! . . . In the meanwhile, return to your duties or I'll sue you, and we'll go through all three courts—one, two, three!

DAUGHTER: Return? To the stove, with the pot filled with cabbage, the baby's clothes . . .

LAWYER: Yes, indeed! We have a big washing today; we're going to wash all the handkerchiefs, you see . . .

DAUGHTER [sighs]: Am I going to do it over again?

LAWYER: All of life is only repetitions . . . Look at the teacher in there . . . He got his doctor's degree yesterday, was crowned with the laurel wreath, they fired cannon shots in his honor, he climbed Parnassus, and was embraced by the king . . . and today he begins school over again, asks how much is two times two, and will be doing that until he dies . . . However, come back . . . to your home!

DAUGHTER: I'd rather die!

LAWYER: Die? You mayn't! First, it's so disgraceful your body'll be outraged, and afterward . . . you're damned! . . . It's a mortal sin!

DAUGHTER: It isn't easy to be a human being!

*

ALL: Right!

*

DAUGHTER: I'll not return to degradation and dirt with you! . . . I want to return to where I came from, but . . . first the door must be opened so I learn the secret . . . I want the door opened!

LAWYER: Then you must retrace your steps, go back the same way, and bear all the horrors of the process, the repetitions, the circumlocutions, the reiterations . . .

DAUGHTER: So be it, but I'll go alone into the wilderness to find myself again. We'll meet again! (*To the* POET) Come with me! (*Cries of agony from the back, in the distance*)

DAUGHTER: What was that?

LAWYER: The damned at Foulstrand!

DAUGHTER: Why do they complain more than usual today?

LAWYER: Because the sun is shining here, because there's music here, dancing here, youth here. Then they feel their agony so much more deeply.

DAUGHTER: We must set them free!

LAWYER: Try! A liberator did come once, but He was hanged on a cross!

DAUGHTER: By whom?

LAWYER: By all the right-thinking people!

DAUGHTER: Who are they?

LAWYER: Don't you know all the right-thinking? Then you're going to get to know them.

DAUGHTER: Were they the ones who refused to grant you your degree?

LAWYER: Yes.

DAUGHTER: Then I know them!

*

A shore on the Mediterranean. To the left in the foreground can be seen a white wall, over which branches of fruit-bearing orange trees are hanging. At the back, villas and a casino with a terrace. To the right, a large pile of coal with two wheelbarrows. At the back to the right, a strip of the blue sea.

Two COALHEAVERS, *naked to their waists, black on their faces, on their hands, and on the other exposed parts of their bodies, are sitting, hopeless, each on a wheelbarrow. The* DAUGHTER *and the* LAWYER *come in at the back.*

DAUGHTER: This is paradise!

FIRST COALHEAVER: This is hell!

SECOND COALHEAVER: Over 115 degrees in the shade!

FIRST COALHEAVER: Shall we take a dip?

SECOND COALHEAVER: Then the police will come. Bathing's forbidden here.

FIRST COALHEAVER: Can't we take an orange from the tree?

SECOND COALHEAVER: No, then the police will come.

FIRST COALHEAVER: But I can't work in this heat; I'll give up the whole thing.

SECOND COALHEAVER: Then the police will come and take you! . . . (*Pause*) And besides you'll have nothing to eat . . .

FIRST COALHEAVER: Nothing to eat? We who work the most get to eat the least; and the rich who don't do anything have the most! . . . Shouldn't one—without getting too close to the truth—say it's unjust? . . . What does that daughter of the gods over there say?

*

DAUGHTER: I haven't the answer! . . . But tell me: what have you done to be so black and to have so hard a lot?

FIRST COALHEAVER: What have we done? We were born to poor and rather worthless parents . . . Probably punished a couple of times!

DAUGHTER: Punished?

FIRST COALHEAVER: Yes! The unpunished sit up there in the casino eating seven courses with wine.

DAUGHTER (*to the* LAWYER): Can that be true?

LAWYER: For the most part, yes! . . .

DAUGHTER: You mean every human being at some time or other has deserved imprisonment?

LAWYER: Yes!

DAUGHTER: Even you?

LAWYER: Yes!

*

DAUGHTER: Is it true the poor can't bathe in the sea here?

LAWYER: Yes, not even with their clothes on. Only the ones who intend to drown themselves get out of paying. But they're likely to get beaten up at the police station!

DAUGHTER: Couldn't they go outside the city limits, out into the country, to bathe?

LAWYER: There isn't any free land—it's all fenced in.

DAUGHTER: Out in the open, I mean.

LAWYER: There isn't any open . . . it's all taken.

DAUGHTER: Even the sea, the great, wide sea . . .

LAWYER: Everything! You can't go on a boat at sea and land anywhere without its being recorded and paid for. Lovely, isn't it!

DAUGHTER: This isn't paradise!

LAWYER: No, I assure you it isn't!

DAUGHTER: Why don't human beings do something to improve their situation . . .

LAWYER: They do, of course, but all reformers end up either in prison or in the insane asylum . . .

DAUGHTER: Who puts them in prison?

LAWYER: All the right-thinking, all the decent . . .

DAUGHTER: Who puts them in the insane asylum?

LAWYER: Their own despair over seeing how hopeless their efforts are.

DAUGHTER: Hasn't anyone thought there are secret reasons for its being as it is?

LAWYER: Yes, those who are well off always think that!

DAUGHTER: That it's fine as it is? . . .

*

FIRST COALHEAVER: And all the same we're the foundations of society; if you don't get any coal, the fire in the kitchen stove goes out, the fire in the fireplace, the machine in the factory; the lights go out on the street, in the stores, in the homes; darkness and cold fall upon you . . . And that's why we sweat like hell to carry the black coal . . . What do you give in return?

LAWYER (*to the* DAUGHTER): Help them . . . (*Pause*) That it can't be absolutely equal for all, I understand, but how can it be so unequal?

*

A GENTLEMAN *and a* LADY *walk across the stage.*

LADY: Are you coming to play a game?

GENTLEMAN: No, I have to take a little walk so I can eat dinner.

*

FIRST COALHEAVER: So he *can* eat dinner?

SECOND COALHEAVER: So he *can?* . . .

(*The* CHILDREN *enter; scream with horror when they see the black laborers.*)

FIRST COALHEAVER: They scream when they see us! They scream . . .

SECOND COALHEAVER: Damn it! . . . I suppose we'll have to bring out the scaffolds soon and go to work on this rotten body . . .

FIRST COALHEAVER: Damn it! I say, too! Ugh!

*

LAWYER (*to the* DAUGHTER): Of course it's crazy! People aren't so bad . . . but . . .

DAUGHTER: But? . . .

LAWYER: But the administration . . .

DAUGHTER (*covers her face and goes*): This is not paradise!

COALHEAVERS: No, it's hell. That's what it is!

III

Fingal's Cave. Long, green waves roll slowly into the cave; in the foreground a red sounding buoy rocks on the waves. The buoy sounds only at indicated places.

The music of the winds. The music of the waves.

POET: Where have you brought me?

DAUGHTER: Far from the noise and wailing of human beings, to the end of the sea, to this cave we call the Ear of Indra, since they say the Lord of Heaven listens here to the complaints of mortals!

POET: What? Here?

DAUGHTER: Do you see how this cave is shaped like a seashell? Yes, you do. Don't you know your ear is shaped like a shell? You know, but you haven't thought about it. (*She picks up a seashell from the shore.*) As a child, didn't you hold a shell to your ear and listen . . . heard your lifeblood flow, the throbbing of your brain, the breaking of a thousand worn-out little tissues in the web of your body . . . You hear that in the little shell; imagine what can be heard in this big one! . . .

POET (*listening*): I can't hear anything but the sighing of the wind . . .

DAUGHTER: Then I'll be its interpreter. Listen! The lamentation of the winds!

(*Recites to soft music*)

Born under the clouds of heaven

we were chased by the bolts of Indra
down unto the dusty earth . . .
The litter on the fields soiled our feet;
the dust of the highways,
the smoke of the cities,
vile human breaths,
the smell of food and wine
we had to bear . . .
Out on the wide sea we fled
to give our lungs air,
to shake our wings,
and wash our feet.
Indra, Lord of Heaven,
hear us!
Hear when we sigh!
The earth is not clean,
life is not good,
human beings not evil,
nor are they good.
They live as they can,
one day at a time.
The sons of dust wander in dust,
born of dust
they return to dust.
They have feet to walk,
but not wings.
They become dusty.
Is the blame theirs
or yours?

*

POET: That's what I heard once . . .
DAUGHTER: Sh-h! The winds are still singing!
    (*Recites to soft music*)
We, the winds, children of the air,

carry the laments of mankind.
If you heard us
in the chimney on autumn evenings,
in the openings of the stove,
in the cracks by the windows,
when the rain wept on the roofs,
or on a winter evening
in a snowy fir forest
on the stormy sea
if you heard moans and sighs
in sails and rigging . . .
It was we, the winds,
children of the air,
who from human hearts
through which we've passed
have learned these melodies of torment . . .
in sickrooms, on battlefields,
most in children's rooms
where the newborn whimper,
wailing, screaming
over the pain of existence.
It is we, we, the winds
who whine and moan!

*

POET: It seems to me I've . . .
DAUGHTER: Sh-h! The waves are singing.
    (Recites to soft music)
It is we, we, the waves,
that rock the winds
to rest!
Green cradles, we the waves.
We are wet and salt;
we are like flames of fire,
we are wet flames.

Quenching, burning,
washing, bathing,
breeding, bearing.
We, we the waves
that rock the winds
to sleep!

*

DAUGHTER: False and faithless waves: everything that isn't burned on earth is drowned—in the waves. Look at that! (*Points to a rubbish heap*) See what the sea has stolen and crushed . . . Only the figureheads of sunken ships remain . . . and their names: *Justice, Friendship, The Golden Peace, Hope*—that's all that's left of *Hope* . . . deceitful *Hope!* . . . Beams, oarlocks, bailers! And look, the lifebuoy . . . it saves itself, but lets the man in distress perish!

POET (*searching in the rubbish heap*): The nameboard of the ship *Justice* is here. That was the one that left Fairhaven with the blindman's son aboard. So it sank! And on board was Alice's fiancé, Edith's hopeless love.

DAUGHTER: The blindman? Fairhaven? I must have dreamed that! And Alice's fiancé, ugly Edith, Foulstrand, and the quarantine, sulphur and carbolic acid, the commencement in the church, the lawyer's office, the corridor and Victoria, the growing castle, and the officer . . . I've dreamed that . . .

POET: I put it into poetry once . . .

DAUGHTER: Then you know what poetry is . . .

POET: Then I know what dreaming is . . . What is poetry?

DAUGHTER: Not reality, but more than reality . . . not dreaming, but waking dreams . . .

POET: And the children of man think we poets only play . . . invent and make up!

DAUGHTER: And that is good, my friend; otherwise the world would be laid waste for lack of encouragement. Everyone would lie on his back looking at the sky; no one would put his hand to the plow and spade, plane or hoe.

POET: And this you say, Daughter of Indra, you who by half belong up there . . .

DAUGHTER: You may well reproach me; I've been too long down here bathing in mud as you do . . . My thoughts cannot fly any more; there's clay on my wings . . . soil on my feet . . . and I myself—(*lifts her arms*)—I'm sinking, sinking . . . Help me, Father, God of Heaven! (*Silence*) I don't hear His answer any more! Ether won't carry the sound from His lips to the shell of my ear . . . the silver thread has broken . . . (*Sighs*) I am earthbound!

POET: Do you intend to ascend . . . soon?

DAUGHTER: As soon as I have burned my body . . . for the waters of the sea cannot cleanse me. Why do you ask?

POET: Because . . . I have a prayer . . . a petition . . .

DAUGHTER: What sort of petition . . .

POET: A petition from mankind to the ruler of the world, put together by a dreamer!

DAUGHTER: To be delivered by . . .

POET: Indra's daughter . . .

DAUGHTER: Can you recite your poem?

POET: Yes, I can.

DAUGHTER: Say it then.

POET: Better you do it!

DAUGHTER: Where will I read it?

POET: In my thoughts, or here! (*Hands her a roll of paper*)

DAUGHTER: Fine! Then I'll recite it!

    (*Accepts the paper but reads by heart*)

"Why were you born with pain,
why do you torment your mother,
child of man, when you are giving
her the joy of becoming a mother,
the joy above all joys?
Why do you awaken to life,
why do you greet light,

with a cry of anger and of pain?
Why don't you smile at life,
child of man, when the gift of life
is happiness itself?
Why are we born like beasts,
we who are divine and human?
The spirit would want a garment
other than this of blood and filth!
Is the image of God to cut its teeth . . ."
Sh-h! . . . the creature blames not the Creator!
No one has yet solved the riddle of life! . . .
"And so begins the wandering
over thorns, thistles, stones;
if you walk on a beaten path
they say at once it's forbidden;
if you pick a flower, you
learn at once it's someone else's;
if your way is through a field
and you have to go directly,
you're tramping down another's crop;
others will tramp on yours
to make the difference less!
Every joy which you enjoy
brings sorrow to all others,
but your sorrow makes no one happy,
because sorrow is heaped on sorrow!
So goes the journey until your death,
which becomes another's bread." . . .
Is that how you intend to approach,
son of dust, the highest god? . . .

POET:

How shall the son of dust find
words bright, pure, light enough
to be able to rise from earth . . .

Child of God, will you convert
our lamentation into the speech
the Immortals grasp best?

DAUGHTER: I will!

POET (*pointing at the buoy*): What's that floating there? . . . A buoy?

DAUGHTER: Yes.

POET: It looks like a lung with a voice box!

DAUGHTER: It's the watchman of the sea. When danger threatens, it sings.

POET: It seems to me the sea is rising and the waves are beginning to roll . . .

DAUGHTER: Most likely!

POET [*sighs*]: What do I see? A ship . . . outside the reef.

DAUGHTER: What ship can it be?

POET: I think it's the ghost ship.[28]

DAUGHTER: What's that?

POET: *The Flying Dutchman.*

DAUGHTER: That one? Why is he punished so severely, and why doesn't he ever land?

POET: Because he had seven faithless wives.

DAUGHTER: Should he be punished for that?

POET: Yes! All right-thinking people condemned him . . .

DAUGHTER: Strange world! . . . How can he be freed from his sentence?

POET: Freed? Better watch out for setting free . . .

DAUGHTER: Why?

POET: Because . . . No, it isn't the *Dutchman.* It's an ordinary ship in distress . . . Why doesn't the buoy sing? . . . See, the sea's rising, the waves are high; soon we'll be shut up in the cave! . . . Now the ship's bell's ringing! We'll soon get another figurehead . . . Scream, buoy; do your duty, watchman . . . (*The buoy sings a four-part chord in fifths and sixths resembling fog-*

horns.) . . . The crew is waving to us . . . but we ourselves are
perishing!

DAUGHTER: Don't you want to be set free?

POET: Yes, of course, I do, but not now . . . and not in water!

CREW (*sings in four-part*): Christ Kyrie!

Christ Ky - ri - e!

POET: Now they're calling, and the sea's calling. But no one hears!

CREW (*as before*): Christ Kyrie!

DAUGHTER: Who's coming out there?

POET: Walking on the water? There's only one who walks on water.
It isn't Peter,[29] the rock, for he sank like a stone . . .

(*A white glow can be seen on the water.*)

CREW: Christ Kyrie!

DAUGHTER: Is it He?

POET: It is He, the crucified one . . .

DAUGHTER: Why—tell me, why was He crucified?

POET: Because He wanted to set free . . .

DAUGHTER: Who—I've forgotten—who crucified Him?

POET: All the right-thinking.

DAUGHTER: What a strange world!

POET: The sea's rising! Darkness is upon us! . . . The storm's getting worse . . .

*

CREW *scream.*

POET: The members of the crew are screaming with terror when they see their redeemer . . . And . . . they're jumping overboard out of fear of their savior . . . (*The* CREWMEN *scream again.*) Now they're screaming because they have to die! Scream when they're born, and scream when they die! (*The rising waves threaten to drown them in the cave.*)

DAUGHTER: If I were sure it is a ship . . .

POET: Honestly . . . I don't think it is. . . . It's a two-story house with trees outside . . . and a telephone tower . . . a tower that reaches up into the skies . . . It's the modern tower of Babel [30] which sends lines up there . . . to inform those above . . .

DAUGHTER: Child, human thought doesn't need any metal wire to get there . . . The prayer of the devout makes its way through all the worlds . . . It's certainly no tower of Babel, for if you want to take heaven by storm you must do it by means of your prayers.

POET: No, it's not a house . . . not a telephone tower . . . Do you see that?

DAUGHTER: What do you see?

POET: I see a snow-covered heath, a training field . . . the winter sun shines behind a church on the hill, and the tower casts its long shadow on the snow . . . a troop of soldiers is marching onto the field; they march on the tower, up the spire; now they're on the cross, but I sense that the first one who steps on the cock must die . . . now they're getting close . . . the corporal's in the van . . . (*laughs*) . . . a cloud is rolling across the heath, past the sun, of course . . . now it's all gone . . . the water in the cloud put out the fire in the sun! The sunlight created the dark image of the tower, but the cloud's dark image choked the tower's . . .

(*While the above was being said, the stage has again become the theater corridor.*)

DAUGHTER (*to the* DOORKEEPER): Has the lord chancellor arrived yet?

DOORKEEPER: No.

DAUGHTER: Have the deans?

DOORKEEPER: No.

DAUGHTER: Summon them at once, then—the door's to be opened . . .

DOORKEEPER: Is that so urgent?

DAUGHTER: Yes, it is! For there's a suspicion that the solution to the puzzle of the world is kept in there . . . So summon the deans of the four faculties and the lord chancellor!

(*The* DOORKEEPER *blows a whistle.*)

DAUGHTER: And don't forget the glazier and his diamond, or nothing will get done!

*

Theater people enter from the left as early in the play.

*

OFFICER (*comes in from the back dressed in frock coat and top hat and carrying a bouquet of roses. He is radiantly happy*): Victoria!

DOORKEEPER: She'll soon be here!

OFFICER: Fine! The carriage is ready, the table's set, the champagne's on ice . . . May I embrace you, ma'am?

WOMAN'S VOICE (*from above, sings*): I'm here!

OFFICER (*walking about*): Fine! I'm waiting.

*

POET: I seem to have lived through this before . . .

DAUGHTER: I, too.

POET: Perhaps I dreamt it?

DAUGHTER: Or composed it, perhaps?

POET: Or composed it.

DAUGHTER: Then you know what poetry is.

POET: Then I know what dreaming is.

DAUGHTER: It seems to me we've stood elsewhere saying these words before.

POET: Then you can soon determine what reality is!

DAUGHTER: Or dreaming!

POET: Or poetry!

*

The LORD CHANCELLOR *and the* DEANS *of theology, philosophy, medicine, and law, respectively, enter.*[31]

CHANCELLOR: It's the question of the door, of course! What do you, dean of the theological faculty, think?

DEAN OF THEOLOGY: I don't think, I believe . . . credo . . .

DEAN OF PHILOSOPHY: I think . . .

DEAN OF MEDICINE: I know . . .

DEAN OF LAW: I doubt until I have evidence and witnesses.

CHANCELLOR: Now they're going to squabble again! . . . What do you, dean of theology, believe?

DEAN OF THEOLOGY: I believe this door must not be opened, because it conceals dangerous truths . . .

DEAN OF PHILOSOPHY: The truth is never dangerous.

DEAN OF MEDICINE: What is truth?

DEAN OF LAW: What can be proved by two witnesses!

DEAN OF THEOLOGY: Anything and everything can be proved with two false witnesses—by a perverter of the law.

DEAN OF PHILOSOPHY: Truth is wisdom, and knowledge is philosophy itself . . . Philosophy is the science of sciences, the knowledge of all knowledge, and all the other sciences are the servants of philosophy.

DEAN OF MEDICINE: The only science is natural science—philosophy isn't a science. It's merely empty speculations.

DEAN OF THEOLOGY: Bravo!

DEAN OF PHILOSOPHY (*to* DEAN OF THEOLOGY): You say bravo! What are you really? You're the eternal enemy of all knowledge, you're the opposite of science, you're ignorance and darkness . . .

DEAN OF MEDICINE: Bravo!

DEAN OF THEOLOGY (*to* DEAN OF MEDICINE): You say bravo, you who don't see farther than your nose in your magnifying glass, you who only believe in your deceptive senses, in your eye, for example, which can be farsighted, shortsighted, blind, dimsighted, cross-eyed, one-eyed, color blind, blind to red, blind to green . . .

DEAN OF MEDICINE: Fool!

DEAN OF THEOLOGY: Ass! (*They rush at each other.*)

CHANCELLOR: Quiet! One raven shouldn't hack out the eyes of the other!

DEAN OF PHILOSOPHY: If I were to select between those two, theology and medicine, I'd select—neither!

DEAN OF LAW: And if I were to judge you three, I'd convict—all of you! . . . You can't agree on a single point, and never have been able to. But back to the matter at hand! What are your views on this door and its opening, lord chancellor?

CHANCELLOR: Views? I haven't any views. The government has simply appointed me to see you don't break each other's arms and legs in council . . . while you're bringing up young people. Views? No, I watch out for views. I once had a few, but they were immediately disproved; views are immediately disproved— by one's opponent, of course! . . . Perhaps we may now open the door even at the risk that it conceals dangerous truths?

DEAN OF LAW: What is truth? Where is truth?

DEAN OF THEOLOGY: I am the truth and the life . . .

DEAN OF PHILOSOPHY: I am the knowledge of all knowledge . . .

DEAN OF MEDICINE: I am exact knowledge . . .

DEAN OF LAW: I doubt! (*They rush at each other.*)

*

DAUGHTER: Teachers of youth, blush for shame!

DEAN OF LAW: Lord chancellor, representative of the government, head of our faculty, punish this woman for her offence. She has told you to blush for shame. That is an insult, and she has called you teachers of youth in a contemptuous, ironic sense, and that is libelous!

DAUGHTER: Poor young people!

DEAN OF LAW: She pities the young—that amounts to accusing us, lord chancellor. Punish her for her offence!

DAUGHTER: Yes, I accuse you, all of you for sowing doubt and dissension in the minds of the young.

DEAN OF LAW: Listen: she is making the young doubt our authority, and she accuses us of causing doubt. Isn't that a criminal act? I ask all right-thinking people.

ALL THE RIGHT-THINKING: Yes, it's criminal!

DEAN OF LAW: All right-thinking people have condemned you! Go in peace with your gain! Or—

DAUGHTER: My gain? Or? Or what?

DEAN OF LAW: Or you'll be stoned.

POET: Or crucified.

DAUGHTER: I am going. Come with me, and you'll get the answer to the riddle!

POET: Which riddle?

DAUGHTER: What does he mean by "my gain"?

POET: Probably nothing. It's what we call talk. He was just talking.

DAUGHTER: But he hurt me deeply by saying that!

POET: That's probably why he said it . . . People are like that.

*

ALL RIGHT-THINKING: Hurrah! The door has been opened!

*

CHANCELLOR: What was hidden back of the door?

GLAZIER: I can't see anything.

CHANCELLOR: He can't see anything! No, I can believe that! . . . Deans! What was concealed back of the door?

DEAN OF THEOLOGY: Nothing! That's the solution to the riddle of the world . . . In the beginning God created heaven and earth out of nothing.

DEAN OF PHILOSOPHY: Out of nothing comes nothing.

DEAN OF MEDICINE: Bosh! That's nothing.

DEAN OF LAW: I doubt. And here there's a fraud. I appeal to all right-thinking people!

DAUGHTER (to POET): Who are the right-thinking?

POET: Let him say who can. Usually all the right-thinking are just

one person. Today it's I and mine, tomorrow it's you and yours.
A person's labeled that, or, more accurately, a person labels himself that.

*

ALL RIGHT-THINKING: They've deceived us!

CHANCELLOR: Who has deceived you?

ALL RIGHT-THINKING: The daughter!

CHANCELLOR (*to the* DAUGHTER): Will you please tell us what you intended by the opening of this door?

DAUGHTER: No, my friends! If I told you, you wouldn't believe it.

DEAN OF MEDICINE: Why, there's nothing there.

DAUGHTER: As you say! But you didn't understand that nothing!

DEAN OF MEDICINE: It's nonsense what she's saying.

ALL: Bosh!

DAUGHTER (*to the* POET): They're to be pitied.

POET: Are you serious?

DAUGHTER: I'm always serious.

POET: Do you pity the right-thinking, too?

DAUGHTER: Them perhaps most of all.

POET: And the deans, too?

DAUGHTER: Even them, and not least! Four heads, four minds in one
body! Who created that monster?

ALL: She doesn't answer!

CHANCELLOR: Strike her, then!

DAUGHTER: I have answered.

CHANCELLOR: Listen, she's answering.

ALL: Strike her! She's answering.

DAUGHTER: "Either she answers, or she doesn't answer: strike her!"
. . . Come, seer [*to the* POET], I'm going—far away from here!—
to tell you the riddle—but out in the wilderness, where no one can
hear us, no one can see us! Because . . .

*

LAWYER (*comes forward, takes the* DAUGHTER *by her arm*): Have you
forgotten your duties?

DAUGHTER: Goodness no! But I have higher duties.

LAWYER: And your child?

DAUGHTER: My child! So?

LAWYER: Your child is calling for you.

DAUGHTER: My child! (*sadly*) I am earthbound! . . . And this torment in my heart, this anguish . . . What is it?

LAWYER: Don't you know?

DAUGHTER: No!

LAWYER: They're pangs of conscience.

DAUGHTER: Pangs of conscience?

LAWYER: Yes! And they appear after every neglected duty, after every pleasure, even the most innocent—if there are any innocent pleasures, which I rather doubt; and after every suffering one has caused his neighbor.

DAUGHTER: And there's no cure?

LAWYER: Yes, but only one! That's to do one's duty right away . . .

DAUGHTER: You look like a demon when you utter the word *duty!* But when one has—as I do—two duties to fulfill?

LAWYER: One fulfills first one, then the other!

DAUGHTER: The highest first . . . so you look after my child, then I'll do my duty . . .

LAWYER: Your child suffers from missing you . . . Can you understand that someone suffers because of you?

DAUGHTER: Now my soul is disturbed . . . it split into two, and I'm torn in two directions!

LAWYER: Those are life's little difficulties, you see!

DAUGHTER: Oh, how it tears!

*

POET: If you had any idea how I've spread sorrow and destruction through fulfilling my calling—note "calling"—which is the highest duty, you wouldn't want to take me by the hand!

DAUGHTER: What do you mean?

POET: My father had built his hopes on me—his only son, who would carry on his business . . . I ran away from the college of

business administration . . . My father died of grief. My mother
wanted me to become a minister . . . I couldn't become a minister . . . she disowned me . . . I had a friend who had stood by
me in my most difficult times . . . My friend behaved like a
tyrant against those I spoke for and sang for. I had to strike down
my friend and benefactor to save my own soul. Since then I don't
have inner peace any more; people call me an infamous scoundrel;
it doesn't help that my conscience says: You did the right thing,
for the next minute my conscience says: You did wrong! Life is
like that!

DAUGHTER: Come with me into the wilderness!

LAWYER: But your child!

DAUGHTER (*pointing at all those present*): These are my children!
Each one by himself is good, but all you have to do to turn them
into demons is to bring them together . . . Farewell!

   (*Outside the castle; the same scenery as in the first tableau in
   the first act. But the ground at the base of the castle is now covered with flowers (blue monkshood, Aconite). At the very peak
   on the tower of the castle roof is a chrysanthemum bud ready to
   burst. The castle windows are illuminated with candlelight.*)

*

DAUGHTER: The moment isn't far off when with the help of fire I
will ascend to Ether again . . . That is what you mortals call
death, and what you approach with fear.

POET: Fear of the unknown.

DAUGHTER: Which you know.

POET: Who does?

DAUGHTER: Everyone! Why don't you believe your prophets?

POET: Prophets have never been believed. How does that happen?
And "if God has spoken, why don't human beings believe?" His
convincing power ought to be irresistible!

DAUGHTER: Have you always doubted?

POET: No. I've had certainty many times, but after a while, it has
gone its way as a dream does when one awakens.

DAUGHTER: It isn't easy to be a human being!

POET: You understand and admit that?

DAUGHTER: Yes!

POET: Wait! Wasn't it Indra who once sent His son down here to hear the complaints of mankind?

DAUGHTER: Yes, it was. How was He received?

POET: How did He carry out His mission? To answer with a question.

DAUGHTER: To answer with another . . . Wasn't the lot of man better after His stay on earth? Tell me truthfully!

POET: Better? . . . Yes, a little. Very little! . . . But instead of asking questions, won't you explain the riddle?

DAUGHTER: Yes. But to what point? You'll not believe me.

POET: I'll believe you, for I know who you are!

DAUGHTER: Well, then, I will tell you. In the morning of time before the sun shone, Brahma, the primordial divine force, let Maja,[32] mother of the world, seduce him in order to increase and multiply. This, the union of the divine and the earthly, was heaven's fall from grace. The world, life, and human beings are therefore only phantoms, appearances, visions . . .

POET: My vision!

DAUGHTER: A true vision! . . . But to free themselves from the earthly, Brahma's descendants seek self-denial and suffering . . . There you have suffering as the savior . . . But this longing for suffering is in conflict with the instinct to enjoy or love . . . Do you yet understand what love is with its greatest pleasure in the greatest suffering, the most pleasant in the most bitter? Do you understand what woman is? Woman, through whom sin and death entered into life?

POET: I understand . . . And the end? . . .

DAUGHTER: What you feel . . . The struggle between the pain of joy and the joy of suffering . . . the penitent's anguish and the voluptuary's pleasures . . .

POET: A struggle, then?

DAUGHTER: Struggle between opposites generates power, just as fire and water produce steam . . .

POET: But peace? And rest?

DAUGHTER: Sh-h! You may not ask any more, and I may not answer! . . . The altar is adorned for the sacrifice . . . the flowers keep watch . . . the candles are lighted . . . white sheets are at the windows . . . pine boughs [33] in the entrance . . .

POET: You say this as calmly as if suffering no longer existed for you!

DAUGHTER: No! . . . I have suffered all your sufferings, but a hundredfold, for my perceptions are finer . . .

POET: Tell me your sorrows!

DAUGHTER: Poet, could you tell me yours so there wouldn't be an extra word, could your words for once really express your thoughts?

POET: No, you're right! I seemed like someone deaf and dumb to myself, and when the crowd listened with admiration to my song, I thought it only words . . . that's why, you see, I always blushed with shame when they praised me

DAUGHTER: So you want me to? Look me in the eye!

POET: I can't bear your look . . .

DAUGHTER: How could you bear my words if I were to speak my language? . . .

POET: Tell me, though, before you leave: what caused you most suffering here on earth?

DAUGHTER: Existing—being alive; feeling my sight weakened by an eye, my hearing dulled by an ear, and my thought, my airy light thought bound in the labyrinths of layers of fat. Why, you've seen a brain . . . what twisted, creeping ways . . .

POET: Yes, and that's why the thinking of all right-thinking people is twisted.

DAUGHTER: Malicious, always malicious, but all of you are . . .

POET: How can one be anything else?

DAUGHTER: Now I shake the dust from my feet . . . the earth, the clay . . .

(*She takes off her shoes and puts them into the fire.*)

DOORKEEPER (*enters, puts her shawl into the fire*): Perhaps I may burn up my shawl, too? (*Exits*)

OFFICER (*enters*): And I my roses—only the thorns remain! (*Exits*)

BILLPOSTER (*enters*): The posters may go, but never the dip net! (*Exits*)

GLAZIER (*enters*): The diamond that opened the door! Farewell! (*Exits*)

LAWYER (*enters*): The documents in the big case concerning the pope's beard or the decrease in water in the sources of the Ganges! (*Exits*)

QUARANTINE MASTER (*enters*): A little contribution—the black mask that made me a black man against my will! (*Exits*)

VICTORIA (*enters*): My beauty, my sorrow! (*Exits*)

EDITH (*enters*): My ugliness, my sorrow! (*Exits*)

BLINDMAN (*enters; sticks his hand into the fire*): I give my hand for my eye! (*Exits*)

DON JUAN (*enters in his wheelchair, accompanied by* HIS MISTRESS *and* HER FRIEND): Hurry up, hurry up, life is short! (*The three exit.*)

*

POET: I read that when life comes close to its end, everything and everyone rushes by in a single procession . . . Is this the end?

DAUGHTER: Yes, it's mine! Farewell!

POET: Give me a parting word!

DAUGHTER: No, I can't! Do you think your words could express our thoughts?

*

THEOLOGIAN (*enters, raging*): I'm disavowed by God, I'm persecuted by people, I'm deserted by the government and ridiculed by my colleagues! How can I believe when no one else believes . . . how can I defend a god who doesn't defend his own? It's all nonsense! (*Throws a book on the fire and exits*)

POET (*grabs the book from the fire*): Do you know what that was?

. . . A book of martyrs, a calendar with a martyr for each day in the year.

DAUGHTER: Martyr?

POET: Yes, someone who has been tortured for his faith! Tell me why! Do you think everyone who's tortured suffers, and everyone who's killed feels pain? Why, suffering is redemption, and death release.

KRISTIN (*with strips of paper*): I paste, I paste until there isn't anything more to paste . . .

POET: And if heaven itself were rent, you'd try to paste it together . . . Go!

KRISTIN: Aren't there any inner windows over there in the castle?

POET: No, not there.

KRISTIN (*going*): Then I'll go!

*

DAUGHTER:
Our parting comes, and the end as well;
farewell, child of man, you the dreamer,
you the poet who best understands living;
on wings hovering above the earth,
you dive at times into the dust
not to stay in it but to touch it!
. . . .
. . . .
Now when I'm going . . . in the moment of parting
When one must part from a friend, a place,
how our longing for what one has loved rises
and regret over what one has broken . . .
Now I feel all the agony of being,
that's how it's to be a human being . . .
One misses even what one has not valued,
one regrets even what one has not broken . . .
One wants to leave, and one wants to stay . . .
So the halves of the heart are torn apart,

and feelings are torn as between horses
by contradiction, indecision, disharmony . . .
. . . .
. . . .
Farewell! Tell your fellows I remember them,
where I'm now going, and in your name
I shall bear their complaints to the throne.
Farewell!

   (*She goes into the castle. Music in heard. The backdrop is
lighted by the burning castle and shows a wall of human faces,
asking, sorrowing, despairing . . . When the castle burns, the
flower bud on the roof bursts into a gigantic chrysanthemum.*)

[CURTAIN]

Notes on

'A Dream Play'

1. The three parts of the trilogy *Till Damaskus* were written in 1898, 1898, and 1904, respectively. Extremely subjective, they deal with Strindberg's conversion during his Inferno period (1894–97) from what may be called agnosticism to a confessionless Strindbergian Christianity or syncretism. In the three plays he makes extensive use of various forms of the dream experience.

2. Indra, one of the eight gods keeping watch over the world, a hero in battle and love and the god of thunder, is the most popular of Vedic gods. For a brief account of Indra, see A. A. Macdonell's *The Vedic Mythology* (Varanasi, India: Indological Book House, 1963). Strindberg's great interest in oriental as well as occidental religions from the Inferno period on; his syncretism; his infatuation with Harriet Bosse who, he thought, looked oriental; and his conviction that only through a woman could he be reconciled with life may account for his making his major Christ figure the daughter of an oriental god.

3. The morning star is Venus. The sequence is apparently high Ether, the morning star, and Earth.

4. The Scales (Virgo and Scorpio) = the seventh house of the Sun. Libra (Latin for "scales") is defined in *Webster's Collegiate Dictionary* as "a southern zodiacal constellation between Virgo and Scorpio, represented as a pair of scales."

5. Strindberg presents Brahma, the first in the Hindu trinity of Brahma, Vishnu, and Siva, as the creator of the world. The concept of a golden age, a paradise in the dawn of time, was not restricted, of course, to Strindberg's most immediate source—the Old Testament account of the rebellion of Lucifer and other angels, their expulsion from heaven, the fall of man, and his expulsion from the Garden of Eden.

6. "The gilded roof of a castle" refers to the cavalry barracks

(*Hästgardekasernen*) topped by a golden budlike crown and visible from Strindberg's window when he lived at Karlavägen 40, Stockholm. What it looked like to him can easily be seen by examining his sketch for a possible set for *A Dream Play* (see illustration section). He called the building, which he considered one of the most beautiful in the city, the growing castle; the implication of horses and manure in terms of growth is obvious. What may not be so obvious to present-day readers is the old custom of placing stable litter next to the foundations of buildings to help preserve warmth in winter.

7. The reason for the choice of the name Agnes for Indra's daughter is uncertain. The name may have been suggested by that of the prominent Vedic god Agni, personification of sacrificial fire and mediator between gods and men. Its appropriateness in the play is certain: the name itself means purity. Since Strindberg was highly interested in hagiography, there may also be some connection with St. Agnes, patroness of young, innocent girls.

8. *Der Schweizerische Robinson,* translated into English as *The Swiss Family Robinson* and into Swedish as *Den Schweiziske Robinson,* was written in 1813 by Johann Rudolf Wyss and was for many generations a favorite novel for children. It was, as the title suggests, inspired by Daniel Defoe's *Robinson Crusoe* (1719).

9. Interestingly enough, the name Victoria has the same meaning as the name Siri (the diminutive form of Sigrid). Strindberg's first wife was baptized Sigrid Sofia Matilda Elisabet. Victoria = the ideal woman.

10. Two of Strindberg's wives were actresses, and on occasion he had waited for one or the other in the corridor of the old royal dramatic theater, which did have a door with a clover-leaf opening. The seven years of waiting may well be reminiscent of Jacob's waiting for Rachel (see Genesis 29 and 30).

11. Wagner's opera *Die Meistersinger von Nürnberg* (1868) was first performed in Stockholm in 1887. The *Meistersinger* or Mastersingers were trained male singers who were members of German crafts guilds during the fourteenth, fifteenth, and sixteenth centuries. *Aïda* is Verdi's opera (1869), which is set in "ancient" Egypt.

12. A traditional Swedish university commencement is a highly formal occasion restricted to the awarding of doctors' degrees. The parts of the ceremony emphasized in the play are, appropriately, the crowning of

each successful candidate with a laurel wreath (see following note) in the midst of elaborate dignity and general impressiveness.

13. The laurel wreath, which has been used since Greek and Roman times as a symbol of victory and achievement, has for many generations been important in Swedish life. For another illustration, see Strindberg's *Dance of Death,* in which Alice's two withered and dusty laurel wreaths are, symbolically, highly important.

14. See the illustration section. The lawyer is given a crown of thorns as a symbol of vicarious suffering; the placement of such a crown on Christ's head was a cruel and cynical gesture. See Matthew 27:29 and John 19:5.

15. The petition, "Lord, have mercy upon us," in the church service and its musical setting.

16. Fingal's Cave, on the island of Staffa in the Hebrides west of Scotland, has six-sided basalt pillars and a roof of basalt. The opening faces the sea, and the bottom of the cave lies below the surface of the sea. It is interesting that Fingal's Cave has been called the Cave of Music. See James Macpherson's *Fragments of Poetry Translated from Gaelic and Erse Languages* (1760), *Fingal* (1762), and *Temora* (1763) for accounts of Fingal, Ossian's father and the leading hero of the Ossianic poems. Compare also Felix Mendelssohn's *Fingal's Cave Overture.*

17. Pasting strips of paper along the windows and putting up double windows were until a generation or so ago common practices designed to keep houses warm during winter in Sweden and other countries with cold climates. See also note 6.

18. Parnassus, the mountain in Greece sacred to Apollo and the Muses, here represents intellectual achievement. See notes 13 and 14.

19. Fairhaven is *Fagervik* (Fair or Beautiful Bay) in the original, and contrasts with Foulstrand (*Skamsund* = Shame Sound).

20. Both the quarantine and the coalheaver scenes are echoes of Strindberg's trip to Italy in 1884. Used to a country in which everyone could easily have access to water, open spaces, and wooded areas, Strindberg found Italy, with its privileged wealthy and landed aristocracy and underprivileged workers and peasantry, anything but a perfect state.

21. Ordström, literally translated, means wordstream, that is, stream of words. The implication is obviously that the man is talkative.

22. Hennessy cognac.

23. Ptah, the Egyptian god who was regarded as the creator of the world and the progenitor of other gods and men.

24. For an account of the prodigal son and the fatted calf slaughtered for him, see Luke 15.

25. Harun the Just, caliph in the eighth century, is celebrated in the *Arabian Nights* and elsewhere as a model of integrity. See Pär Lagerkvist's *The King* for a more recent treatment on a much more extensive scale of the same motif.

26. See the seventh chapter of Genesis for the account of the flood that lasted forty days and nights. Note, too, that Jesus fasted forty days and forty nights in the wilderness (see Matthew 4).

27. See note 19.

28. The sixteenth- or seventeenth-century legend about the Flying Dutchman, a sea captain condemned to sail the seas on a ghost ship forever because of his godlessness, has various versions. Shortly after writing *A Dream Play,* Strindberg wrote the dramatic fragment *Holländarn,* one of his most remarkable treatments of the relationship between man and woman.

29. See Matthew 14 for the account of how Jesus walked on the water and Peter ("the rock") failed to do so because of little faith.

30. See Genesis 11:4–19 for the account of the Tower of Babel, the erection of which led to God's anger and consequent punishment of the builders by making their speech mutually unintelligible.

31. The Swedish universities still maintain the traditional division into four faculties: philosophy (arts and sciences), theology, law, and medicine.

32. Maja is the earth goddess in the Vedic religion.

33. Hanging white sheets before the windows and strewing evergreen boughs on the walk out to the road are, along with flowers and lighted candles, common elements of traditional Swedish funeral customs.

Introduction to

'Stormy Weather'

ANYONE WHO HAS READ Strindberg's autobiographical volumes such as *The Son of a Servant, Inferno, Legends, Alone,* and *The Occult Diary* knows that he was intensely aware of the houses in which he and his family (parental and personal) had tried to make homes, and that he was every whit as interested in what people who were not members of his family were making of the places in which they lived. Strindberg's accounts of his daily walks, his observation of the people he met on these walks and what he saw through windows and doorways, his descriptions of what he heard or thought he heard going on next door or in the apartment above or below and what he imagined was going on behind walls separating him from others are clear indications of his interest in other people and their "homes"—not least, apparently, because they could provide him with excellent material for his creative writing. Strindberg, it should be added, was not a Peeping Tom in any vulgar sense; while he was intensely curious, he was at the same time compassionate.

The double implication of what has been said above is revealed, I believe, very clearly in the five plays in this volume. As I said in my Introduction to *A Dream Play,* that play is, among other things, a study of man and the world in which he must try to make his home. The four other plays have many close bonds with *A Dream Play,* one of which is particularly pertinent here. *Stormy Weather* could have been entitled "The Silent House"; the people living in it call it that. *The House That Burned* is the revelation of much of the truth about one family "home"; it burns, figuratively as well as literally. *The Ghost Sonata* is in a very real sense the exposure of a dwelling that seems to be "the home of beauty and refinement." *The Pelican* is the study of a home that was not a home in any idealistic or even rational sense. All four plays have in common a concentration on individual human dwellings and on the people who live in them.

The last four plays are linked with each other by their classification as chamber plays. A number of factors account for Strindberg's interest in creating plays that would be parallels, in dramatic form, to chamber music. Perhaps the oldest factor was his dream of having a theater of his own, most likely because of the facts of his personal economy, a small and intimate one. His interest in writing plays for such a theater was intense in the late 1880's and early 1890's. Plays such as *Creditors* (1888) and *The Stronger* (1889) are proof of that, and a careful rereading of the Preface to *Lady Julie* (1888) will reveal that he not only was interested in writing such plays but was very much aware of the little theaters that were beginning to appear in Paris, Berlin, and other continental cities. Another factor was his intensified interest in music, which found one kind of expression in his Beethoven evenings and another in all of the plays in this volume. His use of music to supplement and complement dialogue and stage action was carefully considered and applied in all of his major plays after his Inferno years (1894–97); the music could, he believe, help to reveal his new insights into God, man, and the universe. Music did, moreover, provide him with ideas for new structural devices for drama.

In *Open Letters to the Intimate Theater,* he says:

> Last year Reinhardt went the whole way by opening the Kammar-spiel-Haus [in 1906], which by its very name indicates its real program: the concept of chamber music transferred to drama. The intimate action, the highly significant motif, the sophisticated treatment. . . .
>
> If anyone asks what it is an intimate theater wants to achieve and what is meant by chamber plays, I can answer like this: in drama

we seek the strong, highly significant motif, but with limitations. We try to avoid in the treatment all frivolity, all calculated effects, places for applause, star roles, solo numbers. No predetermined form is to limit the author, because the motif determines the form. Consequently: freedom in treatment, which is limited only by the unity of the concept and the feeling for style.

Of the other statements Strindberg made about his chamber plays an excerpt from a January, 1907, letter to his friend Adolf Paul is useful as a supplement to the above quotation: "Seek the intimate in the form; the little motif, thoroughly developed; few characters; broad points of view; free play of the imagination but based on observation, experience, carefully studied, simply but not too simply, no large apparatus. . . ." As he suggests in these quotations and elsewhere, particularly in the first of the open letters to the Intimate Theater, he was writing plays that called for ensemble playing by comradely and enthusiastic colleagues, a new style of acting, and experiments in staging through simplification and suggestion.

Stormy Weather (*Oväder,* Opus 1) is a particularly fine application of what Strindberg himself said about the chamber play. The plot has been reduced to minor importance; characterization is left to suggestion rather than to analysis in depth; there is no star role; every one of the characters has his or her contribution to make to the commentary on life and the silent house; and the atmosphere and mood are highly important.

The plot is slight: the Gentleman, an aging survivor of professional and particularly marital storms, has sought and found refuge in solitude and withdrawal from the struggles of life (marriage, paternity, friends, calling) in the Silent House. His life, restricted to bearable and unavoidable essentials, permits him to be an observer of a limited human scene until his peace is interrupted by stormy weather (heat lightning, not ordinary lightning) in the form of a reappearance of his younger ex-wife and her second husband. When the "heat lightning" has passed, literally and figuratively, the gentleman can resume his life of resignation and withdrawal that will prepare him for the final move—by implication, perhaps, to the grave.

The Gentleman has the greatest number of lines, but what every one of the other characters has to do and say is equally important in establishing the central theme of human loneliness. Not one of them has succeeded in breaking through the walls of the isolation of the individual human being. All the inhabitants of the house live in seclusion: they act as if they were in hiding, the members of the various households do not know each other, it is as if they felt safe and secure only in isolation, they never show curiosity openly and stoop to gossip rarely, and they avoid getting involved with each other.

> I think there are ten households if you count the other side, too; but they don't know each other—there's usually very little gossiping in this house; it's more as if they were in hiding. I've lived here for ten years, and the first two years I had as neighbors next door an unknown couple who were silent all day, but came out at night when carriages came to fetch something. At the end of the second year I learned it was a nursing home and what was fetched were dead people.

The brothers treat each other with tact and consideration; and the confectioner and his wife live out their days doing what has to be done to sustain life; Louise enjoys her life in quiet and peace; Agnes hovers about, restless and groping for something more than the silent house has to offer; the Iceman and the Mailman come and go on their business: "I'm settling my accounts with life and people, and I've already started packing for the journey. Living alone is so-so, of course, but when no one else has any claims on one, one does have freedom. Freedom to go and come, think and act, eat and sleep as one wants to." Only when the Fischers move in are the peace and the silence disturbed. They provide the heat lightning, the stormy weather; they have not yet achieved acceptance of life as it is and the resignation that brings peace and freedom from disturbing involvement.

What sensitive Stockholmers and others who know Stockholm well must appreciate in this play is the remarkably fine atmosphere and mood Strindberg has managed to convey: a quiet residential district in eastern Stockholm in August, when the midnight sun no longer provides continuous light and the street lamps have to be lighted for the first time, is the setting. As every Stockholmer knows, the city is practically empty of Stockholmers in the summer. Hence, the quiet and peacefulness in the midst of which the Gentleman and his brother can take their evening walk, play chess, and live in the past with its touched-up memories. And dusk does conceal; it even conceals flaws in the human condition, literally and figuratively.

The whole play is a personal and highly subjective twilight piece. Even though it is based on Strindberg's own experiences and observation in his last post-divorce period, it has its interest and application for everyone who is alive to what human loneliness implies, particularly to the aging: "After a certain age, nothing changes, everything stops, but moves ahead only as a toboggan on a hillside . . . No love, no friends, only a little company in one's loneliness; and then human beings become human without the right to possess one's feelings and sympathies; so one loosens like an old tooth and falls out without pain and regret."

Staged with scrupulous attention to such matters as Strindberg's intention, his emphasis on ensemble playing, his clearly indicated and telling pauses, and simplified but suggestive staging, *Stormy Weather* can—as occasional productions in Sweden have demonstrated—be well worth seeing as an illuminating study of the aloneness and loneliness of human beings. It requires an ensemble performance in which every instrument (every voice, every "character") will have its contribution to make simply and effectively. *Stormy Weather* calls for "the suspension of disbelief"; certainly the play can best be understood and enjoyed if one gives oneself to it in the spirit Strindberg wrote it.

Opus 1

Stormy Weather:
The Silent House

Characters

THE GENTLEMAN, *a pensioned civil servant*
HIS BROTHER, *the consul (Karl Fredrik)*
STARCK, *confectioner*
AGNES, *his daughter*
LOUISE, *the gentleman's relative*
GERDA, *the gentleman's divorced wife*
FISCHER, *Gerda's new husband (has no speaking part)*
A BOY
THE ICEMAN
THE MAILMAN
THE LAMPLIGHTER

Settings

1. The façade of the house
2. Its interior
3. The façade of the house

A modern house façade, the lower part granite, the upper part brick with yellow facing; windowsills and ornamentation of sandstone; in the middle of the granite portion a low entrance to the courtyard and an entrance to the confectioner's shop; the façade ends with its corner to the right where a planted area with climbing roses and other flowers can be seen; there is a mailbox at the corner; above the granite portion is the ground floor with large open windows; four of these belong to an elegantly furnished dining room; above this can be seen the apartment on the floor above; this apartment has drawn red shades which are lighted up from within.

In front of the façade is a sidewalk lined with trees; in the foreground are a green bench and a gas street lamp.

Scene i

CONFECTIONER *comes out with a chair, places it on the sidewalk, and sits down.*

GENTLEMAN *can be seen at the table in the dining room; behind his back is a green tiled stove, with a ledge on which stands a large photograph between two candelabras and flower vases; a young girl in light-colored clothes is finishing serving him the last course.*

BROTHER (*comes on stage outside from the left; taps with his cane on the windowsill*): Will you be through soon?

GENTLEMAN: I'll be there right away.

99

BROTHER (*greets the* CONFECTIONER): Good evening, Mr. Starck! It's still warm . . . (*Sits down on the bench*)

CONFECTIONER: Good evening, Consul; it's August heat, and we've been making jam all day . . .

BROTHER: Oh . . . Is it a good year for fruit?

CONFECTIONER: Good enough; spring was cold, but summer unbearably hot; those of us who stayed in town have really found that out . . .

BROTHER: I came back from the country yesterday; when evenings begin to get dark, I long to get back . . .

CONFECTIONER: Neither my wife nor I got beyond the city limits—there wasn't much doing, but one has to be on the job to get ready for winter; first one has strawberries and wild ones, too; then come the cherries, then the raspberries, and then the gooseberries, melons, and the whole fall harvest . .

BROTHER: Tell me something, Mr. Starck: are they going to sell this house?

CONFECTIONER: No, not that I've heard.

BROTHER: Are a lot of people living in it?

CONFECTIONER: I think there are ten households if you count the other side, too; but they don't know each other—there's usually very little gossiping in this house; it's more as if they were in hiding. I've lived here for ten years, and the first two years I had as neighbors next door an unknown couple who were silent all day, but came out at night when carriages came to fetch something. At the end of the second year I learned it was a nursing home and what was fetched were dead people.

BROTHER: That was nasty!

CONFECTIONER: And it's called the silent house

BROTHER: But they surely talk a little.

CONFECTIONER: They've put on fireworks occasionally . . .

BROTHER: Tell me, Mr. Starck, who lives right above my brother?

CONFECTIONER: Well, up there where the red shades glow, the renter died last summer; then it was empty for a month, and eight days

ago a couple I haven't seen moved in . . . I don't know their
names; I don't think they even go out. Why do you ask?

BROTHER: Ta . . . I don't know! The four red shades look like
curtains, behind which they're rehearsing bloody dramas . . .
that's what I imagine; there's a phoenix palm with branches like
iron throwing its shadow on a window shade . . . if one could
only see some people . . .

CONFECTIONER: I've seen a lot, but only late at night!

BROTHER: Women or men?

CONFECTIONER: Both, of course . . . but now I'll have to get down
to my kettles . . . (*goes in through the entrance*)

GENTLEMAN (*has got up and lit a cigar; he's now at the window
talking to his* BROTHER): I'm almost done. Louise is going to sew
a button on my glove.

BROTHER: Are you thinking of walking downtown?

GENTLEMAN: Maybe we'll do that for a while . . . Whom were you
talking to?

BROTHER: Just the confectioner . . .

GENTLEMAN: Oh! Well, he's a decent fellow . . . my only company
here this summer, as far as that goes . . .

BROTHER: Have you actually stayed in there every evening—never
been out?

GENTLEMAN: Never! These bright evenings make me shy—it's
beautiful out in the country, no doubt, but in town it's as if everything were against the order of nature, almost ghastly; when it's
time to turn on the lights again, I feel calm again and can take my
evening walk. Then I get tired and sleep better . . . (LOUISE
hands him his glove.) Thank you, child . . . The windows might
as well be open—there aren't any mosquitoes here . . . Now I'm
coming. (*In a moment the* GENTLEMAN *appears from the planted
area and slips a letter into the mailbox; then he comes forward
and sits down beside his* BROTHER *on the bench.*)

BROTHER: But tell me: *why* are you in town when you *could* be out
in the country?

GENTLEMAN: I don't know. I can't leave; I'm bound to this apartment by memories . . . It's only in there I feel calm and secure. Yes, in there! It's interesting to see one's home from outside; I imagine it's someone else who's living in there . . . think of it . . . I've been living there for ten years . . .

BROTHER: Ten years?

GENTLEMAN: Yes, time goes fast when one looks back, but drags—when it's going . . . The house was new then; I saw how they put in the parquet floor, how they painted panels and doors, and *she* was allowed to choose the wallpapers that are still there . . . Well, that's that! The confectioner and I were the first to move in, and he has had his troubles, he, too . . . He's the sort of person who never succeeds, who always has difficulties. I've sort of lived his life and borne his burden along with my own.

BROTHER: Does he drink?

GENTLEMAN: No. Doesn't neglect his work but doesn't get ahead . . . But he and I know the history of this house: they've come in wedding carriages and have moved out in hearses, and that mailbox on the corner has received their secrets . . .

BROTHER: Someone did die here this summer?

GENTLEMAN: Yes, from typhoid fever . . . he was a banker; his apartment was empty for a month; first they took out the coffin, then the widow, the children, and last of all the furniture . . .

BROTHER: That was one flight up, wasn't it?

GENTLEMAN: Up there where the lights are on . . . I don't know the new tenants yet.

BROTHER: Haven't you seen them either?

GENTLEMAN: I never ask about other tenants; what I happen to hear, I listen to without misusing it or getting involved, for I want peace in my old age . . .

BROTHER: Old age, yes! I think it's nice to get old—then one doesn't have so much left on the account.

GENTLEMAN: Yes, of course, it's nice. I'm settling my accounts with life and people, and I've already started packing for the journey. Living alone is so-so-, of course, but when no one else has any claims on one, one does have freedom. Freedom to go and come, think and act, eat and sleep as one wants to.

(*A shade is raised in the apartment above but only far enough so that one can see a woman's dress; then the shade is hastily lowered again.*)

BROTHER: They're up and about, up there! Did you see?

GENTLEMAN: Yes, it's very strange, especially at night. Sometimes there's music—poor music; sometimes they play cards, I think, and long after midnight carriages come and fetch . . . I never complain about fellow tenants, for they avenge themselves, and no one does as I wish . . . It's best not to know anything.

(*A bareheaded gentleman in a tuxedo comes out and puts a great many letters into the mailbox. He then disappears.*)

BROTHER: That fellow certainly had a lot of mail!

GENTLEMAN: They seemed to be circulars.

BROTHER: But who can he be?

GENTLEMAN: Why, he can't be anyone but the tenant one flight up . . .

BROTHER: Was it he? What might he be, do you think?

GENTLEMAN: I don't know. A musician, a director, someone out of an operetta, on the verge of a vaudeville show, a card shark, an Adonis, a little of this and that . . .

BROTHER: His face was extremely white so his hair should have been black, but it was brown, so it's either dyed or a wig; a tuxedo at home suggests he hasn't anything else to wear, and the way his hands moved when he put the letters in looked as if he were mixing, cutting, and dealing . . . (*They hear a waltz played very softly one flight up.*) Always waltzes . . . maybe they teach dancing, but almost always the same waltz. What's it called?

GENTLEMAN: My word I think . . . it's "Pluie d'Or" . . . I know it by heart . . .

BROTHER: So you've heard it in your home?

GENTLEMAN: Yes. That and "Alcazar" . . . (LOUISE *can be seen arranging glasses she has dried on the buffet.*)

BROTHER: You're still satisfied with Louise?

GENTLEMAN: Very much!

BROTHER: Isn't she going to get married?

GENTLEMAN: Not that I know.

BROTHER: Doesn't she have a boy friend?

GENTLEMAN: Why do you ask?

BROTHER: Maybe you're speculating?

GENTLEMAN: I? No thanks! When I got married last time I wasn't too old since we got a child in due course . . . but I'm too old now, and I want to grow old in peace . . . Do you think I'd want a boss in *my* home to take over my life, honor, and property?

BROTHER: You did get to keep your life and your property . . .

GENTLEMAN: Was there a flaw in my honor, then?

BROTHER: Didn't you know?

GENTLEMAN: What are you trying to tell me?

BROTHER: She killed your honor when she left . . .

GENTLEMAN: So I've been murdered for five years without knowing it!

BROTHER: Didn't you know?

GENTLEMAN: No, but now you're going to find out what really happened . . . When I, a fifty-year-old, married a relatively young girl, whose heart I had won and who without fear or necessity gave me her hand, I promised her that when my age became too great for her youth, I'd leave, restoring her freedom. Since our child was born at the proper time, and neither of us wanted any more and since our daughter had begun to grow away from me, and I felt superfluous, I left. That's to say: I took a boat since we lived on an island, and so the story was over. I had kept my promise and saved my honor. So?

BROTHER: Yes, but she considered herself dishonored, for she herself had wanted to leave. So she murdered you by quiet accusations which you never got to hear.

GENTLEMAN: Did she accuse herself, too?

BROTHER: No, she had no reason to.

GENTLEMAN: Well, then there's no danger.

BROTHER: Do you know anything about what's happened to her and the child since then?

GENTLEMAN: I don't want to know anything! Since I lived through all the horror of missing them, I thought the matter was settled, and since only pleasant memories have remained in the apartment, I've stayed on. Thank you, though, for that precious bit of information . . .

BROTHER: Which one?

GENTLEMAN: That she hadn't anything to blame herself for . . . that would have been an accusation against me . . .

BROTHER: I think you're living in a great illusion . . .

GENTLEMAN: Let me live in it! A clear conscience, relatively clear, has always been my diver's suit with which I plumbed the depths without suffocating. (*Gets up*) Think of it, I got out of that alive! And now it's past. Shall we take a walk down the avenue?

BROTHER: Yes, then we'll see how they light the first lamp.

GENTLEMAN: But there'll surely be moonlight tonight, August moon light?

BROTHER: I think there'll be a full moon at that . . .

GENTLEMAN (*goes up to the window, addresses* LOUISE): Louise, please give me my cane. The light summer cane, just to hold in my hand.

LOUISE (*hands him a Spanish cane*): Here you are, sir.

GENTLEMAN: Thank you, child. Put out the lights in the living room if you've nothing to do in there . . . we'll be gone for a while . . . I don't know how long . . .

(*The* GENTLEMAN *and his* BROTHER *go out to the left.* LOUISE *appears at the window.*)

CONFECTIONER (*out through the entrance*): Good evening, Miss; it's pretty warm . . . Have your gentlemen gone?

LOUISE: Yes, they're taking a walk up the avenue . . . it's the first evening my master's been out this summer.

CONFECTIONER: We old people love the dusk—it conceals so many flaws in ourselves and others . . . you know my wife's getting blind, but she doesn't want an operation. There's nothing to look at, she says, and sometimes she wishes she were deaf, too.

LOUISE: I can understand that—sometimes!

CONFECTIONER: You people lead such a quiet beautiful life in there, well off, without worries; I never hear a voice raised or a door slammed. Probably a little too calm for a young woman like you?

LOUISE: Goodness, no! I love the calm and the dignified, pleasant, careful manner, everything's not blurted out, and my master feels he has to overlook the less pleasant details of daily life . .

CONFECTIONER: And you never have company either?

LOUISE: No, only the consul comes. I've never seen the like by way of brotherly love.

CONFECTIONER: Who is the older of those two?

LOUISE: I don't know . . . If there's a year between them or two or if they're twins, I don't know, for they treat each other with mutual respect as if they both were the elder brother.

(AGNES *comes out, tries to steal by the* CONFECTIONER.)

CONFECTIONER: Where are you going, my girl?

AGNES: I'm only going to take a little walk.

CONFECTIONER: That's fine, but come back soon! (AGNES *goes.*)

CONFECTIONER: Do you think your master still mourns for his loved ones?

LOUISE: He doesn't mourn, doesn't miss them either, for he doesn't want them back, but he lives with them in his memory, where he has only what's attractive . . .

CONFECTIONER: But his daughter's fate does disturb him occasionally . . .

LOUISE: Yes, he had to put up with her mother's getting remarried, and then it all depended on who became her stepfather . . .

CONFECTIONER: They've told me his wife rejected alimony at first, but five years later sent a lawyer with a long bill amounting to several thousand . . .

LOUISE (*avoiding the matter*): I don't know about that . . .

CONFECTIONER: But I think his wife's most beautiful—in his memory . . .

RESTAURANT BOY (*enters with a basket containing wine bottles*): Excuse me. Does Mr. Fischer live here?

LOUISE: Mr. Fischer? Not that I know.

CONFECTIONER: Probably the fellow one flight up is Fischer! Go up one flight, around the corner.

BOY (*going toward the planted area*): One flight up. Thank you.

LOUISE: Now it'll be a sleepless night again since they're getting bottles.

CONFECTIONER: What kind of people are they? Why doesn't one ever see them?

LOUISE: I think they use the back entrance. I've never seen them. But I hear them!

CONFECTIONER: I, too, have heard doors slamming and corks popping, probably other noises, too . . .

LOUISE: They never open their windows, in this heat . . . they must be southerners . . . Look, flashes of lightning! One, two, three . . . It's only heat lightning! For there's no thunder!

VOICE (*from the basement*): Starck, dear, come down and help with the syrup!

CONFECTIONER: I'm coming, old girl!—I'm coming . . . We're putting up jam, you see . . . I'm coming, I'm coming . . . (*Goes down to his place.* LOUISE *remains at the window. The* BROTHER *walks slowly in from the right.*)

BROTHER: Hasn't my brother come back?

LOUISE: No, sir.

BROTHER: He went in to telephone, and I was to go on ahead. Well, he'll be here soon . . . what's this? (*Bends down and picks up*

a card) What does it say?—"The Boston Club after midnight
. . . Fischers."—Who are Fischers? Do you know, Louise? Who
was looking for Fischers, one flight up?

LOUISE: A man was just here with wine looking for Fischers, one
flight up!

BROTHER: One flight up, Fischers! The red shade that glows like a
lantern at night; I think you've got undesirable people in the
house!

LOUISE: What is a Boston club?

BROTHER: It can be something quite innocent, but in this case, I
don't know . . . But the card! He was the one who dropped it
a while ago; I'll put it in the box . . . Fischer? I've heard that
name before, in connection with something I've forgotten . . .
Miss Louise, may I ask you something? Doesn't my brother ever
talk about . . . the past?

LOUISE: Never with me.

BROTHER: Miss Louise . . . may I ask you . . .

LOUISE: Excuse me, the milk's being delivered, and I have to get
it . . .

(*She leaves, the girl delivering milk can be seen to the right.
She goes in over the planted area.*)

CONFECTIONER (*comes out again, takes off his white cap and puffs*):
Out and in like a badger out of its hole . . . It's damnably hot
down there by the stoves . . . and not even evening coolness . . .

BROTHER: It's going to rain, since the lightning's flashing . . . It
isn't pleasant in town, but up here it's peaceful—never a carriage
that rumbles, still less a streetcar—why, it's like the country!

CONFECTIONER: It's calm all right, but for my business it's too calm;
I know my job, but I'm a poor salesman, always have been, and
can't learn, or there's something else wrong . . . I probably don't
have the manner; if a buyer treats me like a cheat, I just get embarrassed, and then as angry as I can get—I can't get really angry
any more; it wears out, everything wears out.

BROTHER: Why don't you get another job?

CONFECTIONER: No one wants me!

BROTHER: Have you tried?

CONFECTIONER: What good would it do?

BROTHER: Well—so?

(*Now a long extended cry is heard from the apartment one flight up.*)

CONFECTIONER: What in heaven's name are they up to up there? Are they killing each other?

BROTHER: I don't like this unknown factor that's come into the house. It's like a red thundercloud over one. What sort of people are they? Where did they come from? What do they want?

CONFECTIONER: It's dangerous to dig into other people's business . . . one just gets involved . . .

BROTHER: Do you know anything about them?

CONFECTIONER: No, I don't . . .

BROTHER: Now they screamed again, on the stairs . . .

CONFECTIONER (*slowly withdraws*): I don't want to be in on this . . .

(GERDA, *the* GENTLEMAN'S *divorced wife, comes out on the planted area, bareheaded with her hair undone, excited; the* BROTHER *goes toward her; they recognize each other. She shrinks back.*)

BROTHER: So it's you, my former sister-in-law?

GERDA: Yes!

BROTHER: How did you get into this house? Why couldn't you let my brother enjoy his peace and quiet?

GERDA (*beside herself*): They gave us the wrong name—I thought he had moved; it's not my fault . . .

BROTHER: Don't be afraid of me. You mustn't be afraid of me, Gerda . . . Can I help you? What's happening up there?

GERDA: He hit me!

BROTHER: Is your little girl here, too?

GERDA: Yes!

BROTHER: So she has a stepfather?

GERDA: Yes!

BROTHER: Put up your hair and calm yourself . . . I'll try to straighten this out, but spare my brother . . .

GERDA: I suppose he hates me?

BROTHER: No! Don't you see how he looks after your flowers and your flower beds here? He carried the soil in himself, you remember, in a basket. Don't you know your blue gentians and mignonettes, your roses, Malmaison and Merveille de Lyon, which he grafted himself? Don't you understand how he has tended his memories of you and your daughter?

GERDA: Where is he now?

BROTHER: He's taking a walk, he'll soon be here with the evening paper, and when he comes from the left, he'll take the other entrance, and sit down in his living room to read. Stand still and he won't notice you!—But you must go up to your own apartment.

GERDA: I can't; I can't return to that man . . .

BROTHER: Who is he? And what?

GERDA: He . . . has been a singer!

BROTHER: Has been and is now? A swindler!

GERDA: Yes!

BROTHER: Keeps a gambling joint?

GERDA: Yes!

BROTHER: And your child? Decoy? Bait?

GERDA: Don't say that!

BROTHER: That's terrible!

GERDA: You're taking it too seriously.

BROTHER: One should take filth lightly, very nicely! But one should pile filth on a just case! Why did you ruin his honor? Why did you fool me into becoming your accomplice? I suppose I was childish enough to believe you, and I defended your unjust case against his!

GERDA: You forget he was too old.

BROTHER: No, he wasn't then, since you got pregnant right away. And when he proposed, he asked you if you wanted to have a child with him. Besides, he promised to restore your freedom when he had fulfilled his promise and when old age began to make itself felt.

GERDA: He deserted me—that was an insult.

BROTHER: Not for you! Your youth protected you from the shame!

GERDA: He should have let me leave!

BROTHER: Why? Why did you want to dishonor him?

GERDA: Well, one person has to have the dishonor!

BROTHER: How strangely you think! But you've destroyed his reputation and fooled me into doing it, too! How can we restore it?

GERDA: If his is restored, it will be at my expense.

BROTHER: I can't follow your thinking, which is based on hate. But if we forget restoring his good name and consider saving his daughter, what should we do?

GERDA: She's my child; the court awarded her to me; and my husband is her father . . .

BROTHER: You're overemphasizing that! And you've become coarse . . . Sh-h, he's coming!

(*The* GENTLEMAN *enters from the left with a newspaper in his hand and goes thoughtfully in through the other entrance while the* BROTHER *and* GERDA *stand motionless, concealed by the corner next to the planted area.*)

(*The* BROTHER *and* GERDA *come forward. Then the* GENTLEMAN *can be seen sitting down in his living room to read the paper.*)

GERDA: It was he!

BROTHER: Come over here, take a look at your home! See how he has kept everything as your taste arranged it!—Don't be afraid— he doesn't see us out here in the dusk—the light blinds him, you see.

GERDA: Imagine, how he lied to me . . .

BROTHER: How?

GERDA: He certainly hasn't aged! He got tired of me, that's all. Look —what a collar he's wearing, and the tie—the latest fashion; I'm sure he has a mistress!

BROTHER: You can see her portrait on the tile stove between the candelabras.

GERDA: It's I, and our child? Does he still love me?

BROTHER: His memory of you!

GERDA: That's strange.

(*The* GENTLEMAN *quits reading, stares out through the window.*)

GERDA: He's looking at us!

BROTHER: Stand still!

GERDA: He's looking me right in the eyes.

BROTHER: Stand still! He doesn't see you.

GERDA: He looks like a dead man . . .

BROTHER: Well, he was killed!

GERDA: Why do you say that?

(*The* BROTHER *and* GERDA *are lighted up by a flash of heat lightning. The* GENTLEMAN *shudders with horror and gets up.* GERDA *flees behind the corner of the planted area.*)

GENTLEMAN: Karl Fredrik! (*At the window*) Are you alone? I thought . . . Are you really alone?

BROTHER: As you see.

GENTLEMAN: It's so sultry, and the flowers give me a headache . . . I'm going to finish the paper. (*Resumes his seat*)

BROTHER (*at* GERDA's *side*): Now to your business. Do you want me to go up with you?

GERDA: Perhaps. But there'll be trouble!

BROTHER: But the child has to be saved. And I am a lawyer.

GERDA: Well, then, for the child's sake. Come along! (*They go.*)

GENTLEMAN (*from within*): Karl Fredrik! Come and play chess!— Karl Fredrik!

[CURTAIN]

SCENE 2

In the living room. At the back, the tile stove; to the left of the stove a door open to the dining room; to the right a door open to the hall. To the left a buffet with a telephone; to the right a piano and a clock. A door on the left wall, another door on the right wall. LOUISE *enters.*

GENTLEMAN: Where did my brother go?

LOUISE (*uneasy*): He was outside a while ago, and can't be far away.

GENTLEMAN: There's a terrible commotion in the apartment up there; it's as if they were tramping on my head; now they're pulling out bureau drawers as if they intended to take a trip, perhaps run away . . . If you could only play chess, Louise!

LOUISE: Well, I can play a little . . .

GENTLEMAN: Well, if you only know how the pieces go, you'll no doubt manage . . . Sit down, child! (*He sets up the game.*) They're making such a commotion up there that the light fixtures are rattling, and the confectioner has the fire going downstairs . . . I think I'll move soon.

LOUISE: You ought to anyway, sir—I've thought so for a long time.

GENTLEMAN: Anyway?

LOUISE: It isn't good to live with old memories too long.

GENTLEMAN: Why not? After a while, all memories are beautiful.

LOUISE: But you could live for twenty more years, sir, and that will be too long to live with memories . . . they'll fade, and maybe one fine day change color.

GENTLEMAN: How much you know, child!—Start out now by moving a pawn. But not the queen's; then you'd be checkmated in two moves!

LOUISE: Then I'll begin with the knight . . .

GENTLEMAN: Just as dangerous . . .

LOUISE: But I think I'll begin with the knight anyway!

GENTLEMAN: Fine! Then I'll move my bishop . . .

(CONFECTIONER *can be seen with a tray in the hall.*)

LOUISE: There's Mr. Starck with the tea cakes. He walks as quietly as a little rat! (LOUISE *gets up, goes into the hall, takes the tray, and then goes into the dining room.*)

GENTLEMAN: Well, Mr. Starck, how's your wife?

CONFECTIONER: Thank you, her eyes are bothering her as usual.

GENTLEMAN: Have you seen my brother?

CONFECTIONER: I think he's strolling out there.

GENTLEMAN: Is someone with him?

CONFECTIONER: No. I don't think so.

GENTLEMAN: It's a long time since you saw this apartment, Mr. Starck.

CONFECTIONER: Yes, it's exactly ten years . . .

GENTLEMAN: When you came with the wedding cake . . . Has it changed?

CONFECTIONER: Not at all . . . The palms have grown a little, of course; yes, it's very much the same . . .

GENTLEMAN: And will be until you come with the funeral cake. After a certain age, nothing changes, everything stops, but moves ahead only like a toboggan on a hillside . . .

CONFECTIONER: Yes, that's how it is.

GENTLEMAN: And it's calm like this . . . No love, no friends, only a little company in one's loneliness; and then human beings become human without the right to possess feelings and sympathies; so one loosens like an old tooth and falls out without pain and regret. Louise, for example, is a beautiful young girl—from seeing her I get a pleasure as from a work of art I don't ask to possess; nothing disturbs our relationship. My brother and I associate like two old gentlemen who never get too close to each other or too inquisitive about each other. By keeping neutral about people, one gets a certain perspective, and at a distance we show up better. In a word, I'm satisfied with old age and its quiet peace. (*Calls out*) Louise!

LOUISE (*shows up in the left door, friendly as always*): The laundry
has come, and I have to count it . . .

GENTLEMAN: Well, Mr. Starck, won't you sit down and talk? Maybe
you play chess?

CONFECTIONER: I can't be away from my kettles, and at eleven
o'clock I have to get the oven going . . . Thanks all the same . . .

GENTLEMAN: If you see my brother, ask him to come in to keep me
company . . .

CONFECTIONER: I certainly will . . . I certainly will. (*Goes*)

GENTLEMAN (*alone; moves the chess pieces for a couple of seconds,
then gets up and walks about*): The peace of old age, yes! (*Sits
down at the piano, strikes a couple of chords, gets up, and walks
about again*) Louise! Can't you postpone that . . . with the
laundry?

LOUISE (*in the left door*): It's impossible—the laundress is in a
hurry, and she has a husband and children who are waiting for
her . . .

GENTLEMAN: Huh! (*Sits down by the table and taps it with his
fingers; tries to read the newspaper but gets tired of that; lights
matches and blows them out; looks at the clock. Noise in the
hall*) Is that you, Karl Fredrik?

MAILMAN (*appears*): It's the mailman. Excuse me for coming right
in, but the doors were open.

GENTLEMAN: Are there letters for me?

MAILMAN: Just a card. (*Hands it over and leaves*)

GENTLEMAN (*reads the card*): Mr. Fischer again! The Boston Club!
That's the fellow upstairs. The one with white hands in a tuxedo.
And addressed to me! Shameless! I have to move!—Fischer!
(*Tears the card to pieces. Noise in the hall*) Is that you, Karl
Fredrik?

ICEMAN: It's the iceman!

GENTLEMAN: It's nice we're getting ice in this heat. But be careful
about the bottles in the icebox! And put the piece on edge so I

can hear it melting and the drops of water falling—that's my water clock, which measures time, the long, long time . . . Say, where do you get the ice?—Has he gone?—All of them go . . . home to hear their own voices and get company . . . (*Pause*) . . . Is that you, Karl Fredrik?

From the apartment above can now be heard Chopin's Fantaisie Impromptu, *Op. 66, on the piano, but only the first part.*)

GENTLEMAN (*listens, becomes alert, looks at the ceiling*): Who is playing? My impromptu? (*He covers his eyes with one hand and listens. His* BROTHER *enters from the hall.*) Is that you, Karl Fredrik? (*The music is interrupted.*)

BROTHER: It's I!

GENTLEMAN: Where have you been so long?

BROTHER: I had some business to take care of. Have you been lonely?

GENTLEMAN: Of course! Come and play chess now.

BROTHER: I'd rather talk. And you probably need to hear the sound of your voice.

GENTLEMAN: True enough, but we drift so easily into talking about the past . . .

BROTHER: Then one forgets the present . . .

GENTLEMAN: There isn't any present—what's right now is empty nothingness; ahead or behind—preferably ahead, for that's where hope lies!

BROTHER (*at the table*): Hope, for what?

GENTLEMAN: A change!

BROTHER: Fine! So you're saying you've had enough of the peace of old age?

GENTLEMAN: Perhaps.

BROTHER: Certainly, you mean! And if you could choose between loneliness and the past . . .

GENTLEMAN: No ghosts, though!

BROTHER: What about your memories?

GENTLEMAN: They don't haunt me; they're my poems about certain facts; but if the dead were to walk again, they would be ghosts.

BROTHER: In any case, in your memory, which of the two gives you the most beautiful illusion, your wife or your child?

GENTLEMAN: Both! I can't separate them, so I never tried to keep the child.

BROTHER: But did you do the right thing then? Didn't you think about the possibility of a stepfather?

GENTLEMAN: I didn't think that far ahead, but since then I've certainly—thought—about—that possibility.

BROTHER: A stepfather, who mistreated, probably degraded your daughter!

GENTLEMAN: Sh-h!

BROTHER: What did you hear?

GENTLEMAN: I thought I heard "her little steps," her little tripping steps in the corridor when she came along to find me . . . It was probably the child who was best. Seeing that fearless little being, who feared nothing, who suspected nothing about the treachery of life, who had no secrets. I remember her first experience of human evil. She caught sight of a beautiful child down in the park, and with open arms she went up to the stranger in order to kiss her; the beautiful child responded to her friendliness by biting her cheek and then sticking out her tongue. You should have seen my little Anne-Charlotte then: she stood as if turned to stone, not from pain, but from the horror of seeing this whole abyss which is called the human heart opening itself. I saw it once: behind the most beautiful of eyes two strange stares like those of an evil animal suddenly showed themselves; I became so afraid, literally, that I looked to see if someone were standing behind her face, which looked like a mask. But why are we sitting talking about this? Is it the heat and the stormy weather, or what?

BROTHER: Loneliness brings on heavy thoughts, and you should have company; this summer in town seems to have hit you hard.

GENTLEMAN: It's only these last few weeks; the death up there hit me as if I lived through it myself; the confectioner's sorrows and troubles have become mine, too, so I go about being uneasy about his financial condition, his wife's eye ailment, his future . . . and lastly I dream every night about my little Anne-Charlotte . . . I see her in dangers, unknown, undiscovered, nameless; and before I fall asleep, when my hearing becomes unbelievably sharp, I hear her little steps . . . once I heard her voice . . .

BROTHER: Where is she?

GENTLEMAN: I don't know!

BROTHER: And if you were to meet her on the street . . .

GENTLEMAN: I imagine I'd lose my mind or collapse . . . When my little sister was growing up, I was abroad for quite a long time . . . after several years I came back, found on the steamboat landing a young girl who hugged me. With horror I saw two eyes that forced their way into mine, but with a strange look, which expressed the most ghastly horror over not being recognized. "It's I," she said several times before I recognized my own sister.

That's about how I imagine meeting my daughter would be. At that age, five years make one unrecognizable. Imagine: not recognizing one's own child! The same person, yet a stranger! I wouldn't survive that! No, then I'd rather keep my little four-year-old on the family altar over there; I don't want anyone else . . . (*Pause*)

Is it Louise who's busy in the linen closet? That smells clean, and reminds . . . yes, my wife at the linen closet, the good spirit, who takes care of and renews, the housewife with her iron smoothens out what's uneven and removes the wrinkles . . . Yes, the wrinkles . . . Now—I'm—going—in to write a letter. Will you stay here? I'll be back very soon. (*Goes out to the left. The* BROTHER *coughs.*)

GERDA (*appears in the hall door*): Are you . . . (*The clock strikes.*) Oh God! That sound . . . that I've heard in my ears for ten years! This clock, which never kept time accurately, but measured out five years' long hours, days, and nights. (*Looks about*) My piano . . . my palms . . . the dining-room table; he has really kept it shining as a shield! My buffet! With the knight and Eve,

Eve with the apples in her basket . . . In the right-hand drawer, farthest in, was a thermometer . . . (*Pause*) I wonder if it's still there . . . (*Goes to the buffet, pulls out the right-hand drawer*) Yes, it is!

BROTHER: What does that mean?

GERDA: Well, it finally became a symbol. Of what isn't permanent!— When we set up housekeeping, the thermometer was put down— it should have been outside the window, of course . . . I promised to put it up . . . but forgot . . . he promised to, and forgot. So we nagged at each other, and finally, to get away from it, I hid it in the drawer . . . I got so I hated it—so did he. Do you know what that means?—Well, nobody believed our marriage would last since we immediately took off our masks and showed our antipathies. At the beginning we lived as if we were ready to jump . . . ready to flee at any time. It was the thermometer . . . and here it lies! Up and down, always changeable, like the weather. (*She puts it down and goes over to the chess game.*) My chess game! That he bought to pass the long days of waiting before the baby came! Whom does he play with now?

BROTHER: With me.

GERDA: Where is he?

BROTHER: He's in his study writing a letter.

GERDA: Where?

BROTHER (*pointing to the left*): There!

GERDA (*seemingly on verge of collapse*): And he's lived here for five years?

BROTHER: Ten years, five years alone!

GERDA: But he likes being alone?

BROTHER: I think he's had enough.

GERDA: Will he show me the door?

BROTHER: Find out! You're not risking anything—he's always polite.

GERDA: I didn't make that table runner . . .

BROTHER: That's to say, you're risking his asking about his child . . .

GERDA: But he's the one who's going to help me find her . . .

BROTHER: Where do you think Fischer has gone? And why did he run away?

GERDA: To get out of this uncomfortable neighborhood, in the first place; then to get me to come running after him; he wants to have the girl as a hostage and then bring her up for the ballet since she has really shown both inclination and talent for that.

BROTHER: The ballet? You mustn't tell *her father* that—he hates the stage!

GERDA (*sits down by the chessboard and absentmindedly arranges the pieces*): The stage! I've been there, too!

BROTHER: You!

GERDA: I've accompanied him!

BROTHER: Poor Gerda!

GERDA: Why "poor"? I loved that life, and when I was a prisoner here, it wasn't my keeper's fault but the prison's that I was unhappy.

BROTHER: But you've had enough now?

GERDA: Now I love calm and solitude . . . my child above everything!

BROTHER: Sh-h! He's coming!

GERDA (*gets up as if to flee, but collapses on the chair again*): Oh!

BROTHER: Now I'll go! Don't think about what you're going to say; that will come of itself as the "next move" in a chess game.

GERDA: I'm most afraid of his first look—in that I'll be able to tell if I've changed favorably or not . . . if I've become old and ugly . . .

BROTHER (*goes into a room to the right*): If he thinks you've become older, he'll dare to approach you; if he thinks you're as young as ever, he won't have any hope, and he's far more modest than you think.—Now!

(*The* GENTLEMAN *walks slowly past the open left door leading to the dining room; he has a letter in his hand; he disappears but can be seen again in the hall; he goes out.*)

BROTHER (*in the right door*): He went out to the mailbox!

GERDA: I'll never live through this! How can I ask *him* for help in getting this divorce? I'm going. It's too shameless.

BROTHER: Stay! You know he's unbelievably kind. He'll help you for the sake of the child.

GERDA: No, no!

BROTHER: He's the only one who can help.

GENTLEMAN (*comes in rapidly from the hall, nods to* GERDA, *whom because of his nearsightedness, he takes to be* LOUISE; *goes to the telephone by the buffet and rings; but in passing he throws a word to* GERDA): Already done! Set out the pieces, Louise, and we'll start over! from the beginning . . .

(GERDA, *as if turned to stone, understands nothing.*)

GENTLEMAN (*his back to* GERDA, *telephoning*): Hello!—Good evening. Is that you, Mother?—Fine, thank you. Louise is ready to play chess, but she's a little tired from a little bother she's had.— Yes, it's over now, and everything's fine. Just trivial matters.—If it's hot? The lightning's passed, right over our heads, but didn't strike anything. False alarm! What did you say? Fischers! Yes, but I think they're about to leave.—Why? I don't know anything in particular.—Really? really?—Yes, it leaves at 6:15, takes the outer route through the archipelago, and lands, let me see, at 8:25! —Did you have fun? (*Chuckles*) Yes, he's really too crazy when he's in the mood. What did Maria say about it?—How I've been this summer? Well, Louise and I have been here; she has such an even and good temperament.—Oh, she's very kind, very!—No, thanks. not that! (GERDA *has begun to understand, get up horrified.*) My eyes?—Well, I'm getting nearsighted, but I say, like the confectioner's wife, there's nothing to look at! She wanted to be a little deaf, too. Deaf and blind! The neighbors upstairs are terribly noisy at night . . . they have some sort of gambling club . . . There, they broke the connection in order to listen in! (*He rings again.* LOUISE *appears at the hall door, unseen by the* GENTLEMAN. GERDA *looks at her with admiration and hate.* LOUISE *goes toward the right-hand door. The* GENTLEMAN *at the tele-*

phone) Are you there? Imagine: they broke the connection by picking up the receiver to listen! Tomorrow at 6:15 then!—Thank you very much.—I certainly will. Goodbye, Mother! (*Rings off or hangs up*)

   (LOUISE *has gone out*; GERDA *stands in the middle of the room.*)

GENTLEMAN (*turns around; takes a look at* GERDA *and gradually recognizes her; puts a hand to his heart*): Good Lord, was it you? Wasn't it Louise just now? (GERDA *silent. The* GENTLEMAN *weakly*) How—did you—get here?

GERDA: Excuse me, I'm out traveling, happened to come this way, and wanted to see my old home . . . the windows were open . . . (*Pause*)

GENTLEMAN: Still the same, don't you think?

GERDA: The same, but somehow different . . .

GENTLEMAN (*uncomfortable*): Are you satisfied—with your life?

GERDA: Yes, indeed. I have what I wanted.

GENTLEMAN: And our child?

GERDA: Well, she's growing, and is happy; everything's fine for her.

GENTLEMAN: Then I won't ask any more questions. (*Pause*) Is there anything you want? Can I do anything for you?

GERDA: Thank you, but . . . I don't need anything since I've seen everything's fine for you, too. (*Pause*) Did you want to see Anne-Charlotte? (*Pause*)

GENTLEMAN: I don't think so now that I hear everything's fine for her.—It's so hard to start over again; it's like repeating old lessons that one really knows though the teacher doesn't think so.—I'm so far away from all that—I was on a totally different level—and I can't connect up again with the past.—It's hard for me to be impolite, but I'll not ask you to sit down—you're another man's wife —and you're not the same person I was divorced from.

GERDA: Have I—changed that much?

GENTLEMAN: Yes! Voice, look, manner . . .

GERDA: Have I aged?

GENTLEMAN: I don't know!—They say that in three years' time there isn't one atom left in a human body—in five years everything's re-newed, so you who are standing there are not the person who lived and suffered here—I can hardly say "Gerda," that's how much of a stranger you seem to me. And I suppose it would be the same with my daughter!

GERDA: Don't talk like that; I'd prefer your being angry.

GENTLEMAN: Why should I be angry?

GERDA: Because of all the harm I've done you!

GENTLEMAN: Have you? I don't know about that.

GERDA: Didn't you read the charges?

GENTLEMAN: No, I let the lawyer do that. (*Sits down*)

GERDA: And the decree?

GENTLEMAN: I haven't read that, either. Since I don't intend to re-marry, I didn't need documents like that. (*Pause.* GERDA *sits down*). What did the papers say? That I was too old? (GERDA *nods in agreement.*) Why, it was only the truth, so that shouldn't embarrass you! I wrote exactly the same thing in my reply, and asked that the court restore your freedom.

GERDA: Did you write that . . .

GENTLEMAN: I wrote that I *was* not but was about to become too old for *you!*

GERDA: (*hurt*): For me?

GENTLEMAN: Yes!—I couldn't say I was too old when we got mar-ried, because then our child's origin might have been unpleasantly interpreted. She was *our* child, wasn't she?

GERDA: You know she was!—But . . .

GENTLEMAN: Do you mean I'm to be ashamed of my age? Well, if I were to take up dancing the Boston and playing cards at night, I'd probably soon end up in a wheelchair or on the operating table, and that would be a shame.

GERDA: You don't look so . . .

GENTLEMAN: Did you think the divorce would kill me? (GERDA *am-biguously silent*) There are those who say you murdered me! Do you think I look murdered? (GERDA *embarrassed*) They say your friends caricatured me in minor papers, but I never saw them, and they've been waste paper for five years now. So don't torture your conscience for my sake!

GERDA: Why did you marry me?

GENTLEMAN: You know very well why a man gets married, and you know, too, I didn't need to beg for your love. And you ought to remember how we smiled together at all the wise people who warned you.—But why you played up to me I've never been able to explain . . . After the wedding ceremony you didn't see me but acted as if you were at somebody else's wedding. Then I thought you had kept a wager to murder me. All my underlings hated me, of course, since I was the head of the department, but they became your friends right away. As soon as I got an enemy, he became *your* friend! Which gave me a reason for saying: You shall not hate your enemies, true, but you shall not *love* my enemies!—But when I saw what you were up to, I began to pack up, but I wanted a living witness of your lying first, so I waited until our daughter was born.

GERDA: Think of it: how false you were!

GENTLEMAN: I became secretive, but I never lied!—You slowly changed my friends into detectives, and you seduced my own brother into faithlessness toward me. But worst of all you raised doubt about your child's legitimacy by your thoughtless talk!

GERDA: I've taken that back!

GENTLEMAN: You can't take back a word once you've uttered it. And the worst of all is that the false rumor has reached the child, who considers her mother a . . .

GERDA: Oh, no!

GENTLEMAN: Yes, that's how it is!—You built up a whole tower on a foundation of lies, and now the tower of lies is collapsing on you!

GERDA: That's not true!

GENTLEMAN: Oh, yes! I ran into Anne-Charlotte a little while ago . . .

GERDA: You did?

GENTLEMAN: We met on the stairs, and she said I was her uncle. Do you know what that sort of uncle is? He's an older friend of the family and the mother. And I know that at school I'm considered the uncle, too!—Why, that's terrible for the child.

GERDA: Have you met?

GENTLEMAN: Yes. But I didn't have to tell anyone that. Don't I have the right to keep still? Besides, the meeting was so disturbing I brushed it from my memory as if it had never happened.

GERDA: What can I do to restore your reputation?

GENTLEMAN: You? You certainly can't restore it—I'm the only one who can. (*They fix each other's glances sharply and for a long time.*) That's to say, my reputation has already been restored. (*Pause*)

GERDA: Can't I make up for what I did? Can't I beg you to forgive me and forget . . .

GENTLEMAN: What do you mean?

GERDA: Restore, repair . . .

GENTLEMAN: Do you mean renewing, starting over, making you my master again? No thanks! I don't want you!

GERDA: I'm to hear this!

GENTLEMAN: How does it feel? (*Pause*)

GERDA: That's a lovely table runner . . .

GENTLEMAN: Yes, it is lovely!

GERDA: Where did you get it?

(LOUISE *appears in the dining room with a bill in her hand.*)

GENTLEMAN (*turns around*): Is it a bill?

(GERDA *gets up, pulls on her gloves so the buttons fly off.*)

GENTLEMAN (*takes up money for the bill*): Eighteen seventy-two. That's it exactly.

LOUISE: May I tell you something, sir?

GENTLEMAN (*gets up, goes to the door, where* LOUISE *whispers something to him*): Oh, lord . . . (LOUISE *leaves.*) Poor Gerda!

GERDA: What do you mean? That I should be jealous of your maid?

GENTLEMAN: No, I didn't mean that.

GERDA: Yes, you did, and you meant you were too old for me but not for her. I understand the insult . . . she's pretty—I don't deny that—considered as a maid . . .

GENTLEMAN: Poor Gerda!

GERDA: Why do you say that?

GENTLEMAN: Because you're to be pitied! Jealous of my servant; that's restoration of my reputation . . .

GERDA: I . . . jealous? . . .

GENTLEMAN: Why did you hit out at my decent, quiet, little relative?

GERDA: "More than your relative". . .

GENTLEMAN: No, child, I gave up a long time ago . . . I'm very much satisfied with being alone . . . (*The telephone rings; he goes over to it.*) Mr. Fischer? . . . He's not here . . . Oh, yes, it's I.—He has run away?—With whom did he run away?—The confectioner's daughter! Good God! How old is she?—Eighteen! Just a child!

GERDA: I knew he had run away!—But with a woman!—Now you're glad?

GENTLEMAN: No, I'm not glad; although it does comfort me when I see there's justice in this world. Life passes swiftly, and now you're where I was!

GERDA: Her eighteen years against my twenty-nine—I'm old, too old for him!

GENTLEMAN: Everything is relative, even age!—But another thing. Where's your child?

GERDA: My child! I had forgotten her! My child! Good God! Help me! He has taken the child with him; he loved Anne-Charlotte as if she were his own daughter . . . come with me to the police . . . come with me!

GENTLEMAN: I? Now you're asking too much!

GERDA: Help me!

GENTLEMAN (*goes to the right-hand door*): Karl Fredrik, come and take a taxi! Go with Gerda to the police—Won't you?

BROTHER (*enters*): Of course I will! The Lord knows we're human beings!

GENTLEMAN: Quick! But don't say anything to Mr. Starck! Everything can still be set straight. Poor fellow—and poor Gerda!—Hurry!

GERDA (*looks out the window*): It's beginning to rain; lend me an umbrella . . . Eighteen—only eighteen—quick! (*She and the* BROTHER *go out.*)

GENTLEMAN (*alone*): The peace of old age!—And my child in the hands of a swindler!—Louise! (*She enters.*) Come and play chess with me!

LOUISE: Has the consul? . . .

GENTLEMAN: He has gone out on an errand . . . Is it still raining?

LOUISE: No, not right now.

GENTLEMAN: Then I'll go out and cool off. (*Pause*) You're a good girl, and a sensible one. You know the confectioner's daughter?

LOUISE: Yes, but not well.

GENTLEMAN: Is she pretty?

LOUISE: Yes-s-s!

GENTLEMAN: Do you know the couple upstairs?

LOUISE: I've never seen them.

GENTLEMAN: Avoiding the question!

LOUISE: I've learned to keep still . . . in this house!

GENTLEMAN: I admit pretended deafness can go too far and can become dangerous. Get tea ready while I go out to cool off.—And one thing, child, you see what's happening here, of course, but don't ask me anything.

LOUISE: I? No, sir, I'm not curious.

GENTLEMAN: Thank you!

SCENE 3

The same setting as in Scene 1. The CONFECTIONER's *lights shine from below. The lights one flight up are on, the windows are open, and the shades are pulled up. The* CONFECTIONER *is standing outside his door.*

GENTLEMAN (*on the green bench*): That was a nice little shower we got.

CONFECTIONER: Really welcome, too; the raspberries will perk up.

GENTLEMAN: Then I'm going to order a few liters—we've tired of putting up jam ourselves—it only stands and ferments and gets moldy . . .

CONFECTIONER: Yes, I know about that. You have to watch the jam jars like naughty children; there are some who put in salicylic acid, but's that's just a new trick, which I don't approve of . . .

GENTLEMAN: Salicylic. Well, that's supposed to be antiseptic—that could be a good thing—

CONFECTIONER: Yes, but it affects the taste . . . and it's a trick . . .

GENTLEMAN: Do you have a telephone, Mr. Starck?

CONFECTIONER: No, I don't . . .

GENTLEMAN: Oh.

CONFECTIONER: Why do you ask?

GENTLEMAN: Well, I just happened to think that . . . one needs a telephone sometimes . . . orders . . . important messages . . .

CONFECTIONER: Perhaps, but sometimes it's good not to get—messages.

GENTLEMAN: Right! Right!—Well. My heart always starts pounding when the telephone rings—one never knows what one will get to hear . . . and I want peace . . . peace, above all.

CONFECTIONER: I, too.

GENTLEMAN (*looks at his watch*): They should be lighting the lamp soon.

CONFECTIONER: He has probably forgotten us—the ones on the avenue are already lighted . .

GENTLEMAN: Then he'll soon come. It will really be a pleasure to see the lamp again . . .

(*The telephone in the living room rings;* LOUISE *can be seen answering it; the* GENTLEMAN *gets up, puts his hand to his heart, and tries to hear but fails. Pause.* LOUISE *comes out.*)

GENTLEMAN (*uneasy*): Anything new?

LOUISE: No change.

GENTLEMAN: Was it my brother?

LOUISE: No, it was the lady.

GENTLEMAN: What did she want?

LOUISE: To talk with you, sir.

GENTLEMAN: I don't want to! Should I comfort my executioner? I've done that before, but I'm tired of it!—Look, up there! They've left their lights burning—empty rooms when they're lighted are more terrible than when they're in darkness . . . why, one sees the ghosts. (*Softly*) About the confectioner's Agnes . . . Do you think he knows anything?

LOUISE: That's hard to say, for he doesn't talk about his troubles; neither does anyone else in this silent house.

GENTLEMAN: Should I tell him?

LOUISE: No, for heaven's sake . . .

GENTLEMAN: But it's not the first time she has made him worry, is it?

LOUISE: He never talks about her . . .

GENTLEMAN: That's terrible! Are we going to see the end soon? (*The telephone rings.*) Now it's ringing again. Don't answer it! I don't want to know anything!—My child! With that pair! A swindler and a slut!—It's too much. Poor Gerda!

LOUISE: It's better to know for sure—I'll go in—you have to do something, sir.

GENTLEMAN: I can't move . . . I can take it, but I can't hit back.

LOUISE: But if you try keeping a danger at arm's length, it crowds in on you, and if you don't oppose it, you're crushed!

GENTLEMAN: But if one doesn't get involved, one can stay out of it.

LOUISE: Stay out of it?

GENTLEMAN: Everything goes better if one doesn't complicate it by interfering. How would I be able to control this when so many emotions are involved? I can't curb their passions or change their course.

LOUISE: But the child?

GENTLEMAN: Why, I gave up my rights . . . besides—frankly speaking, I'm not anxious . . . not at all now, since *she* came in and disturbed my memories; she erased everything beautiful I had kept—there's nothing left.

LOUISE: Why, that's being set free!

GENTLEMAN: See how empty it looks in there. As if they had just moved . . . and up there, as if there had been a fire.

LOUISE: Who's that coming?

(AGNES *enters, stirred up, afraid, controls herself, goes toward the entrance where the* CONFECTIONER *is sitting.*)

LOUISE (*to the* GENTLEMAN): It's Agnes! What does this mean?

GENTLEMAN: Agnes!—Then it's beginning to straighten out!

CONFECTIONER (*absolutely calm*): Good evening, dear; where have you been?

AGNES: I've been out walking.

CONFECTIONER: Mother has asked for you several times.

AGNES: Oh! Well, I'm back now.

CONFECTIONER: Please go down to help her keep the fire going in the little oven.

AGNES: Is she angry with me?

CONFECTIONER: She can't get angry with you.

AGNES: Oh, yes, but she doesn't say anything.

CONFECTIONER: Well, it's a good thing, dear, that you get out of a scolding. (AGNES *goes in.*)

GENTLEMAN: Does he know, or doesn't he?

LOUISE: I hope he doesn't find out . . .

GENTLEMAN: But what has happened? Broken up! (*To the* CONFECTIONER) Listen, Mr. Starck.

CONFECTIONER: Was there something?

GENTLEMAN: I wondered . . . Did you see anyone leave the house a while ago?

CONFECTIONER: I saw an iceman and a mailman, I think.

GENTLEMAN: Oh! (*To* LOUISE) Maybe I'm mistaken—that I didn't hear right—I can't explain this . . . Maybe he's fooling! What did the lady say on the telephone?

LOUISE: She wanted to talk with you, sir.

GENTLEMAN: How did she sound? Was she upset?

LOUISE: Yes.

GENTLEMAN: I think it's shameless to appeal to me in a situation like this . . .

LOUISE: But the child!

GENTLEMAN: Imagine—I met my daughter on the stairs, and when I asked her if she recognized me, she called me uncle, and then she told me her father was up there . . . why, he's her stepfather and has all the rights—they've eliminated me, slandered me . . .

LOUISE: A taxi's stopping at the corner! (*The* CONFECTIONER *goes in*.)

GENTLEMAN: I hope they don't come back so I get them on my back— imagine, hearing my child praise her father, the other one—and then begin the old story: "Why did you marry me?"—"You certainly know why. But why did you accept me?"—"You certainly know why"; and so on to the end of the world.

LOUISE: It's the consul who's coming!

GENTLEMAN: How does he look?

LOUISE: He's in no hurry.

GENTLEMAN: Going over what he's going to say. Does he look satisfied?

LOUISE: Hesitant, rather . . .

GENTLEMAN: Oh . . . That's how it always was; if he only got near that woman, he became faithless to me . . . She could charm everybody—but me! With me she was coarse, simple, ugly, stupid, and with others she was nice, charming, beautiful, intelligent! All the hatred my independence awakened about me gathered about her as a boundless sympathy for the one who did me wrong. They tried to control and influence me, hurt me, finally murder me—through her!

LOUISE: I'll go in and wait at the telephone—this stormy weather will surely pass, too.

GENTLEMAN: People can't stand anyone who's independent; they want you to obey them; all my underlings at work, down to the janitors, wanted me to obey them; but when I didn't want to obey, they called me a tyrant. The maids at home wanted me to obey them and eat warmed-up food, but when I didn't want to, they set my wife on me, and finally she wanted me to obey our child, but then I left, and then they conspired against the tyrant—against me! Hurry in now, Louise, so we can set off the mine out here!

(*His* BROTHER *comes in from the left.*)

GENTLEMAN: The result!—No details!

BROTHER: May we sit down? I'm a little tired . . .

GENTLEMAN: It rained a little on the bench, I think . . .

BROTHER: But when you've been sitting there, it can't be dangerous for me.

GENTLEMAN: As you please.—Where's my child?

BROTHER: May I start at the beginning?

GENTLEMAN: Start!

BROTHER (*slowly*): I got down to the station with Gerda—I saw him and Agnes at the ticket window . . .

GENTLEMAN: So Agnes was along?

BROTHER: Yes, and your child!—Gerda stayed back, and I went up to them. Just then he handed Agnes the tickets, but when she saw they were for third class, she threw them in his face and went out to get a taxi.

GENTLEMAN: Ugh!

BROTHER: Just when I was reaching an understanding with the man, Gerda hurried up, took the child, and disappeared in the crowd . . .

GENTLEMAN: What did he say?

BROTHER: Well, you know how it is when one gets to hear the other side and so on!

GENTLEMAN: I want to hear!—Naturally he isn't as bad as we had thought; he has his good points, too . . .

BROTHER: Exactly.

GENTLEMAN: I should have known! But you certainly don't want me to sit here listening to you praise my enemy?

BROTHER: No, not praise, but extenuating circumstances . . .

GENTLEMAN: Did you ever want to listen to me when I explained how things really were? Yes, you heard me and answered with the silence of disapproval, as if I were sitting there lying. You were always on the wrong side, and you believed only lies, and the reason was that—you were enchanted by Gerda. But there was another reason, too . . .

BROTHER: Don't say any more.—You see it only from your point of view!

GENTLEMAN: Do you want me to look at my situation from my enemy's point of view? I certainly can't lift my hand against myself!

BROTHER: I am not your enemy.

GENTLEMAN: Yes, when you're a friend of the one who has done me wrong!—Where is my child?

BROTHER: I don't know.

GENTLEMAN: How did it end at the station?

BROTHER: He went south alone.

GENTLEMAN: And the others?

BROTHER: Disappeared!

GENTLEMAN: Then I can get them on my back again! (*Pause*) Did you see if the others went along?

BROTHER: No, he went alone.

GENTLEMAN: Then we know about that one, at least. Number two.— Remaining: the mother and the child!

BROTHER: Why are the lights on up in their apartment?

GENTLEMAN: Because they forgot to put them out.

BROTHER: I'll go up . . .

GENTLEMAN: No, don't!—Just so they don't come back! Repeat, re-peat, repetition, the whole thing!

BROTHER: But the beginning has straightened out . . .

GENTLEMAN: And the worst remains . . . Do you think they'll come back?

BROTHER: Not Gerda, since she had to restore your reputation in Louise's presence.

GENTLEMAN: I had forgotten that! She really did me the honor of becoming jealous. I believe there's justice in the world!

BROTHER: And she got to know Agnes was younger.

GENTLEMAN: Poor Gerda! But in cases like this we may not tell people that there is justice, a vengeful justice . . . for it just isn't true that they love justice. And one has to touch their filth lightly. And Nemesis—that's only for others! . . . Now it rang! It sounds like a rattlesnake, that telephone. (LOUISE *is seen at the telephone. Pause. Then the* GENTLEMAN *says to her*) Did the snake bite?

LOUISE (*at the window*): May I talk with you, sir?

GENTLEMAN (*up to the window*): Go ahead!

LOUISE: Your former wife has gone to her mother in Dalarna to make her home there with the child.

GENTLEMAN (*to his* BROTHER): Mother and child to the country, in a home! Now it has straightened itself out!

LOUISE: And she asked me to go up to their apartment to put out their lights.

GENTLEMAN: Do it right away, Louise; and pull down the shades so we don't have to see it. (LOUISE *goes. The* CONFECTIONER *comes out again.*)

CONFECTIONER (*looks up*): I think the stormy weather's over.

GENTLEMAN: It really seems to have cleared up, and so we'll get moonlight.

CONFECTIONER: That was a blessed rain!

GENTLEMAN: Absolutely marvelous! Look, there comes the lamp-lighter, at last.

(*The* LAMPLIGHTER *comes in, lights the lamp.*)

GENTLEMAN: The first lamp! Now it's fall. That's our time, old men. It's beginning to turn dark, but then comes sanity and shines with its lamp so we don't go astray.

(LOUISE *can be seen upstairs through the windows; then it becomes dark up there.*)

GENTLEMAN (*to* LOUISE): Shut the windows and pull down the shades, so my memories may lie down to sleep in peace. The peace of old age! And this fall I'll move out of the silent house.

[CURTAIN]

Introduction to
'The House That Burned'

A FIRST READING may give the impression that Strindberg has failed to make the Stranger, the "character" with the most lines in *The House That Burned*, free of the dark flaws in human nature emphasized in Opus 2. Careful re-examination will show, however, that he is exceedingly human; among his frailties is his unfortunate but very human tendency to believe that he knows the truth about himself and others and not to hesitate about blurting out what he believes he knows as if it were the whole truth. Arvid Valström, a stranger literally and figuratively to others and to a great extent to himself, may be the one who carries the unifying motif in *The House That Burned*, but what he has to observe about the striking differences between appearance and reality, between reputation and fact, between memories of home and family and the truth about both is supplemented and varied, interpreted and reinterpreted, by the other "characters" in this second chamber play.

The plot is no more elaborate than the one in *Stormy Weather*. The Stranger returns to his neighborhood after years abroad, irresistibly drawn to his childhood home and intending to place a wreath as a token of affection and respect on the graves of his parents in the nearby cemetery. He finds that his home has just been destroyed by fire, perhaps deliberately set, with enough of the building remaining to provide evidence of crimes and sins long hidden from direct public view, none of them ever quite fully and openly labeled and classified, and all of them glossed over, covered up, or mislabeled within the family. Aided and abetted by the Stranger's habit of blurting out "truths," the neighbors and the police expose a neighborhood dominated by people in the funeral business and a house that had been anything but the model home its occupants had pretended it to be. The Stranger discovers that he cannot return home and has to wander on "until he is taken home" to a world that is the original, not a copy.

Houses do have their history, of course, and the house that burned and had been part of the block called the Morass did have an interesting and disturbing one, known completely by no one, deliberately distorted by its adult occupants, guessed at by the neighbors, suspected by the authorities, and deliberately colored for the children: "Oh, I've seen things; a lot, a whole lot has happened in this house, so much I thought it was time it got smoked out.—Ugh! What a house!" It is the web of its history that Strindberg unravels. In the process he exposes fact and fancy, the pleasant and the unpleasant, gaps between the generations, difficulties between siblings, neighborhood relations, and the like—in other words, fragments of all the material that makes up the web of living or, if you will, threads that, pulled from the cloth, suggest and to a degree state facts about discrepancies in family and neighborhood life.

The very name of the block—the Morass or Swamp—is a key to the whole neighborhood: "We all know each other, for there's something special about this street. The people who once move in here never get away from it; that's to say, the ones who move away always come back, sooner or later, until they're taken to the cemetery up at the end of the street . . . And all of us hate each other, are suspicious of each other, slander each other, torment each other . . ." Unlike the inhabitants of the silent house in *Stormy Weather,* the people in the Morass do not seek isolation, do not refrain from gossip, and do not attempt to practice resignation. Instead they are a gregarious lot who take a malicious delight in gossip and who cannot avoid active association with each other. In a broad sense, the neighborhood may be said to symbolize the community of man from which the individual yearns to escape but to which he is doomed to long to return. In that sense, Strindberg has here touched on the implications of human gregariousness, the human desire to belong, and, perhaps above all else, the essentially unbreakable isolation and loneliness of the individual. As the Stranger discovers, the native son may literally and physically return, but he cannot spiritually go home again.

The Stranger, who has a role in this chamber play parallel to that of the Gentleman in *Stormy Weather,* does have a special burden when he returns:

> But in death I had gained new skills . . . I saw right through people, read their thoughts, heard their intentions. When I was in a group, I saw them all naked . . . I've seen life from every point of the compass and all points of view, from above and from below, but always as if it had been staged especially for me; through that I've finally reconciled myself with part of the past, and have come to excuse other people's and my own so-called faults.

Even though he has long since at least figuratively awakened from the dead, he still remains a finite human being who is very much to be pitied: he is isolated and alone; he loses the comfort of tidied-up or false memories; he has a decidedly strong element of self-righteousness in his make-up; he is doomed to be a wanderer in search of a home; he goes on, only to a degree freed of illusions.

It is a curious neighborhood to which he returns. To be sure, all the buildings except his own "home"—the house that burned—are still there, among them the Last Nail, the inn where criminals used to receive their last drink on their way to Gallows Hill and where the hearse driver, the professional pallbearers, and funeral guests and survivors imbibe on their way to or from the cemetery at the end of the street. The big difference lies, of course, in the house that burned. Instead of the fine, prosperous, middle-class home, protected by exceptionally careful construction and by family myths, there are the exposed ruins, the contents revealed for what they really are, and the apple tree in the garden prematurely in bloom.

The neighbors are seen as neighbors, not as fully analyzed characters about whom one learns as much as possible. In other words, they are not examined as dynamic and complex "characterless characters" of the kind Strindberg had discussed in the Preface to *Lady Julie*. The neighbors know a great deal about each other and think they know even more, of course. Seen through the Stranger's eyes, they are a remarkably human lot: a dyer who has never learned very much about himself or others; a weary, uncertain old mason and his querulous old wife; a rehabilitated ex-convict whose rehabilitation no one has really accepted; a gardener who conceals his economic success behind pretended simple-mindedness; the hostess of the Last Nail, who believes her eyes are open to see the virtues and the frailties of others; a young couple "ready" for marriage and the repetition of a neighborhood pattern; a wife who finds comfort in the arms of a student financially unable to marry; and a silent painter observing the human comedy. In brief, they are a motley crowd of nominally Christian neighbors, none of whom practices the commandment to love one's neighbor as oneself.

Nor is what remains of the immediate family any better. The one remaining brother is in his second marriage; one wife has run off with another man, and the second has escaped him through faithlessness. Secretive, pretentious, cowardly, dishonest, pitiful, and insecure are perhaps the adjectives that best apply to a brother who is one in name but has never been one in spirit. The Stranger's family is like many another Strindbergian family and, for that matter, many actual families—anything but the ideal unit of communal living: "I had to revise my whole life. You know we lived in mutual admiration, we thought our family was the best, and we thought of our parents with almost religious reverence. I had to redo their faces, strip them, pull them down, and get them out of my mind. It was terrible! Afterward they began to haunt me. . . .

Do you see how little one knows about those nearest him, his home, his own life?"

Strindberg had the gift for using telling details that provide not only information but also suggestions that set the imagination going:

Sjöblom's painting while he listens to all the conversations, the name of a block (and many city blocks in Sweden do have names) that suggests a swamp of human pollution into which the people sink, the father's stock of "pornography" hidden behind other books in his locked bookcase, the parents' concealment of their precocious and unusual son's attempt at suicide, the uncertainty about the Student's paternity and the Stranger's fathering a child, and the clock that goes to pieces when it is examined. Each throws a great deal of light on the "web of lies, mistakes, and misunderstandings" which must be taken seriously.

Particularly interesting about *The House That Burned* are not so much the elements concerning the detective who investigates the fire as the commentary on life and the way in which that commentary is made: "Yes, of course, it's like that everywhere . . . When one's young, one sees the web set up: parents, relatives, friends, acquaintances, servants are the warp; later on in life one sees the weft; and the shuttle of fate carries the thread back and forth; sometimes it breaks but is tied together again, and then it goes on; the beam falls, the yarn's forced into twists and turns, and the web's done. In old age when one's eyes can really see, one discovers that all the twists and turns form a pattern, a cipher, an ornament, a hieroglyphic, which one can now interpret for the first time: That is life! The world weaver has woven it!" and the distressing corollary: "They could put a rope around everyone's neck if they wanted to be just, but they don't want to! Humanity's a terrible lot, ugly, sweaty, stinking; unclean underwear, dirty socks with holes in them, chilblains, corns, ugh! No, an apple tree in bloom is much prettier; look at the lilies of the field—it's as if they weren't at home here—and smell how fragrant they are!"

The House That Burned is undoubtedly one of the bluntest commentaries on the human condition ever recorded in literary form, but, sympathetically read in privacy or observed in the theater, the play can be a highly rewarding experience.

Opus 2

The House That Burned

Characters

RUDOLF VALSTRÖM, *the dyer*

ARVID VALSTRÖM, *the stranger* (*Rudolf's brother*), *sixty*

ANDERSSON, *the mason; the gardener's brother-in-law, seventy-five*

MELVINA, *the old woman, Andersson's wife*

GUSTAVSSON, *the gardener, Andersson's brother-in-law*

ALFRED, *the gardener's son*

ALBERT ERIKSSON, *the stonecutter, an ex-convict, the hearse driver's second cousin*

MATILDA, *the stonecutter's daughter*

THE HEARSE DRIVER, *the stonecutter's second cousin*

THE DETECTIVE, *a plainclothesman*

SJÖBLOM, *the painter*

MRS. VESTERLUND, *hostess of the inn "The Last Nail" and formerly a nursemaid in the dyer's home*

THE LADY OF THE HOUSE, *the dyer's wife*

THE STUDENT

The left half of the back consists of the walls of a one-story house that has burned down; one can see the wallpaper on the walls and the tile stoves.

Behind the walls can be seen a fruit orchard in bloom.

To the right an inn with a wreath on a pole; tables and benches outside the inn.

To the left in the foreground rescued pieces of furniture and household utensils heaped in a pile.

The PAINTER *is painting the window frames on the inn; he listens to all the conversations.*

The MASON *is digging in the ruins.*

DETECTIVE (*a* PLAINCLOTHESMAN, *enters*): Is the fire really out?

MASON: At least you can't see any smoke.

DETECTIVE: Then I want to put a few questions again. (*Pause. To the* MASON) You were born in this block?

MASON: Oh, yes! I've lived on this street for seventy-five years. This house was built before I was born. My father worked as a mason on it . . .

DETECTIVE: Then you know everybody in the neighborhood?

MASON: We all know each other, for there's something special about this street; the people who once move in here never get away; that's to say, the ones who move away always come back all the same, sooner or later, until they're taken to the cemetery up at the end of the street.

DETECTIVE: Do you have a special name for this block?

MASON: We call it the Morass; and all of us hate each other, are suspicious of each other, slander each other, torment each other . . . (*Pause*)

DETECTIVE: Listen, the fire broke out at ten-thirty in the evening. Was the front entrance closed then?

MASON: Well, I don't know about that—I live next door . . .

DETECTIVE: Where did the fire start?

MASON: Up in the attic room where the student lives.

DETECTIVE: Was he home?

MASON: No, he was at the theater.

DETECTIVE: Had he left his lamp burning?

MASON: Well, I don't know about that . . . (*Pause*)

DETECTIVE: Is the student related to the owner of the house?

MASON: No, I don't think so.—Are you a policeman?

DETECTIVE: How did it happen the inn didn't catch fire?

MASON: They threw fire screens over it and sprayed them.

DETECTIVE: Strange the heat didn't ruin the apple trees.

MASON: They were budding, and it had rained during the day, but the heat made them burst into bloom in the middle of the night, a little early, so to speak, for if there's frost, the gardener will lose out.

DETECTIVE: What sort of man is the gardener?

MASON: His name's Gustavsson . . .

DETECTIVE: But what sort of man is he?

MASON: Listen! I'm seventy-five . . . so I don't know anything bad about Gustavsson, and, if I did, I wouldn't stand here telling you! (*Pause*)

DETECTIVE: And the owner's name is Valström, a dyer, about sixty years old, married . . .

MASON: Keep going yourself! I won't be pumped any more.

DETECTIVE: Do they think it was arson?

MASON: They think that about all fires.

DETECTIVE: Whom do they suspect?

MASON: The interested party is always suspected by the fire insurance company: that's why I've never carried insurance.

DETECTIVE: Did you find anything when you were digging?

MASON: You usually find all the keys, for no one has time to take them out when the fire really gets going, except sometimes, by way of exception, when they're taken out . . .

DETECTIVE: The house didn't have electricity?

MASON: Not this old house, and that surely was a good thing, for now they can't blame it on a short circuit.

DETECTIVE: Blame? A good thing!—Listen . . .

MASON: Are you trying to trap me? Don't—then I'll deny everything.

DETECTIVE: Deny? You can't!

MASON: I can't?

DETECTIVE: No, indeed!

MASON: Yes, because there's no witness!

DETECTIVE: There isn't?

MASON: No! (*The* DETECTIVE *coughs. The* WITNESS *enters from the left.*)

DETECTIVE: Here's *one* witness!

MASON: Imagine—what a fox!

DETECTIVE: A person uses his mind even if he isn't seventy-five! (*To the* WITNESS) Now we'll take the gardener! (*They go out to the left.*)

MASON: Now I'm in a fine mess! That's what comes from talking! (*The* OLD WOMAN *comes in with food in a packet.*)

MASON: It's a good thing you came!

OLD WOMAN: Now we'll have breakfast and behave ourselves. You're probably hungry after all this to do; I wonder if brother-in-law Gustavsson will recover from this; he had started on hotbeds and was just going to dig the flower beds; go ahead, eat; Sjöblom the painter's already busy with the spatula. How in the world could Mrs. Vesterlund get off from the fire so nicely?—G'day, Sjöblom —now you have work. (MRS. VESTERLUND *comes out of the inn.*)

OLD WOMAN: G'day, g'day, Mrs. Vesterlund. You got out of that nicely, I do say, and say it's because . . .

MRS. VESTERLUND: I wonder who's going to pay me for what I'm losing today—there's a big funeral at the cemetery, and that's my best day; I had to carry both supplies and glasses out of the way . . .

OLD WOMAN: What funeral's on today? I see so many people going beyond the tollgate, and they'll be going to have a look at the fire, too . . .

MRS. VESTERLUND: I don't think it's a funeral, but they're going to put up a monument on the bishop's grave, I think—but the worst is the stonecutter's daughter was going to marry the gardener's son today, you know; he works in a store downtown, but now the gardener has lost everything he had. Isn't that his furniture over there?

OLD WOMAN: It's the dyer's, too, I think; it all came out in a hurry all mixed up. Where's the dyer now?

MRS. VESTERLUND: He's down at the police commissioner's giving his testimony.

OLD WOMAN: Oh yes! yes, yes! . . . See, there's my cousin, the hearse driver. He's always thirsty on his way home . . .

DRIVER: Hello, Melvina! So you set fire to the place last night, I hear! That looks pretty neat, but it would've been better if you'd got a new shack!

MRS. VESTERLUND: The Lord save us! Whom have you taken out there now?

DRIVER: I don't remember his name, and there was only *one* carriage, and no wreath on the coffin . . .

MRS. VESTERLUND: Then at least it wasn't anybody that'll be missed . . . If you want something to drink, you'll have to go out into the kitchen, for I haven't anything ready on this side yet; besides Gustavsson's coming over with his wreaths—something's going on at the cemetery today, you see . . .

DRIVER: Yes, they're putting up a monument for the bishop; I think he wrote books; and he collected insects; he was a bug expert, they tell me.

MRS. VESTERLUND: What does that mean?

DRIVER: He had cork slabs that he stuck needles in with flies on them . . . we don't understand that . . . but I guess it's so . . . May I go into the kitchen now?

MRS. VESTERLUND: Take the back entrance; then you'll get a drop . . .

DRIVER: But I want to talk with the dyer before I leave. I left the horses at the stonecutter's, he's my second cousin, you know; I don't like him—you know that, too, but we do have business dealings—that's to say I recommend him to survivors and that's why I put up my horses at his place sometimes. Tell me when the dyer comes; it's lucky he didn't have the dye works here . . .

(*Goes behind the inn;* MRS. VESTERLUND *out through the door*)

(MASON *has finished eating; begins to dig again.*)

OLD WOMAN: Are you finding anything?

MASON: Yes, nails and hinges; all the keys are hanging in a bunch there on the doorpost . . .

OLD WOMAN: Were they hanging there before, or have you collected them?

MASON: They were hanging there when I came.

OLD WOMAN: That's funny—then someone closed all the doors and took out the keys before it began to burn! That *is* funny!

MASON: Well, yes, it's a little funny—it made it harder to put out the fire and save things. Yes, yes! Yes, yes! (*Pause*)

OLD WOMAN: I worked for the dyer's father forty years ago, and I know them, both the dyer and his brother that went to America, though they do say he's come back; the father was a fine man, but the boys were just so-so.—Mrs. Vesterlund over there took care of this Rudolf; the brothers couldn't stand each other, were always fighting and squabbling.—Oh, I've seen things; a lot, a whole lot has happened in this house, so much I thought it was time it got smoked out.—Ugh! What a house! The one came, and the other left, but they came back, they died here, they were born here, they got married and were divorced here.— And for many years they thought their brother Arvid in America was dead—at least he never claimed his inheritance, but, as I said, they say now he's back, though no one's seen him—they certainly talk a lot!—There's the dyer back from the police station!

MASON: He doesn't look very happy, but you can't expect that . . . Well, who was the student up in the attic? Here they stick together like clay and straw.

OLD WOMAN: I don't know that, see! He had his meals with them and read with the children.

MASON: And with the lady of the house, too?

OLD WOMAN: No, they played what they call tennis and quarreled the rest of the time; they all quarrel and run each other down in this block—

MASON: Well, when they broke the student's door open, they found the floor full of hairpins; that came out, but there had to be a fire just . . .

OLD WOMAN: I don't think it was the dyer who came . . . but my brother-in-law Gustavsson . . .

MASON: Well, he's always mad, but today he's worse than ever; now he'll come and dun me for what I owe him since he has lost quite a bit in the fire . . .

OLD WOMAN: Sh-h!

GARDENER (enters with a large container of funeral wreaths and the like): I wonder—am I going to sell anything so we'll have enough to eat after this mess?

MASON: Didn't you carry insurance?

GARDENER: Yes, for the greenhouse panes, but this year I was going to save money and had only oiled paper. Imagine—that I could be such a damn fool (scratches his head)—and I won't be paid for that. I cut out six hundred paper panes, pasted, and oiled them! Yes, they always said I was the stupidest of seven children.

What a jackass, and what a dumbbell! And I went out drinking yesterday—why in hell did I have to go drinking just yesterday? When I need a clear head today. The stonecutter treated me, our kids are getting married tonight, but I should have said no.—I didn't want to! But I'm a weakling who can't say no. And that's how it is when they come and want to borrow money from me, too—I can't say no, poor fool that I am! And that detective was at me, asking questions and tripping me up; I should have kept my mouth shut like the painter over there, but I can't keep my mouth shut, so I said this and that, and he wrote it all down, and now I'm called to testify!

MASON: What did you tell him?

GARDENER: I said I thought—there was something wrong! and that someone had set fire to it!

MASON: Did you say that?

GARDENER: Go ahead—scold, I have it coming, for I'm a fool!

MASON: Who set it?—Don't let the painter embarrass you, and the old woman doesn't gossip.

GARDENER: Who set it? The student, naturally, since it started in his room . . .

MASON: No, *under* his room!

GARDENER: Was it under? Then I've really started something . . . I'll come to a bad end. Was it *under* his room? Underneath? In the kitchen?

MASON: No, it was a closet. See for yourself over there! It was the cook's closet.

GARDENER: Then it was she!

MASON: But don't say so, since you don't know!

GARDENER: The stonecutter wasn't friendly with the cook yesterday; he knew a lot, he did . . .

OLD WOMAN: You shouldn't repeat the stonecutter's words, for somebody who's served time can't be believed . . .

GARDENER: Huh, that was long ago; besides, the cook's a dragon— she always haggles about vegetables . . .

OLD WOMAN: Now the dyer's coming from the police commissioner
. . . quiet now!

(STRANGER *enters wearing a frock coat and a top hat with a mourning band and carrying a cane.*)

OLD WOMAN: It wasn't the dyer, but he's a lot like him!

STRANGER: How much does a wreath like this cost?

GARDENER: Half a crown.

STRANGER: That's not expensive.

GARDENER: Well, you see, I'm such a fool, I can't make you pay
through the nose.

STRANGER (*looks about*): Has there been . . . a fire . . . here?

GARDENER: Yes, the place burned down last night.

STRANGER: Good God! (*Pause*) Who owned the house?

GARDENER: Valström.

STRANGER: A dyer?

GARDENER: Yes, he's a dyer! (*Pause*)

STRANGER: Where is he?

GARDENER: He'll be back shortly.

STRANGER: Then I'll walk about a little—the wreath can lie there
until I get back—you see, I'm going to the cemetery afterward.

GARDENER: To see the bishop's monument?

STRANGER: What bishop?

GARDENER: Bishop Stecksén, who belonged to the academy, of
course.

STRANGER: Did he die?

GARDENER: Yes, a long time ago.

STRANGER: Oh!—I'll leave the wreath here for the time being. (*Goes
out to the left, looking very closely at the ruins*)

OLD WOMAN: Was he from the insurance company, maybe?

MASON: Nah, not that one! If he had been, he would have asked
other questions.

OLD WOMAN: But he's a lot like the dyer, all the same.

MASON: But he was taller.

GARDENER: Now I remember one thing—I have to have a wedding

bouquet for tonight, and I'm to go to my son's wedding, but I haven't any flowers and my black coat burned up. Why, it's absolutely . . . Mrs. Vesterlund was going to give the myrtle for the crown since she's the bride's godmother—she stole the shoot for that myrtle from the dyer's cook, who had got her start from his first wife, the one who ran away, but I was going to make a wreath out of it and I've forgotten to—I'm the biggest fool on God's green earth. (*Opens the door to the inn*)

Mrs. Vesterlund, may I have the myrtle now, and I'll make it? May I have the myrtle, I say!—Is there to be a wreath, too? . . . Is there enough?—No?—Then to hell with the wedding—that's all there's to it!—They'll have to go to the minister and have him marry them there, but the stonecutter will be furious.—What'll I do then?—I can't—haven't slept a wink all night!—It's too much for a human being.—Yes, I'm a poor stick, I know—just go ahead, scold.—There's the pot, well thank you, I should have a pair of scissors, too, I don't have one, and then I have to have steel wire, and packthread. Where'll I get them?—I don't want to run away from my work, not at all!—I'm just tired of everything; when you've slaved for fifty years, it burns up; I haven't the energy to start over; and it all comes at once, blow after blow; you know I'll just leave the whole mess . . . (*Goes*)

DYER (*enters, shaken, poorly dressed, his hands blue-black*): Is it out now, Andersson?

MASON: It's out.

DYER: Have they found out anything yet?

MASON: Have they! What one hides in snow appears in thaw.

DYER: What do you mean, Andersson?

MASON: He who digs, finds.

DYER: Have you found anything that can explain how the fire started?

MASON: Nah, nothing like that!

DYER: Then we're still suspected, all of us!

MASON: Not I, certainly?

DYER: Yes, indeed! You were seen in the attic at an unusual time, Andersson.

MASON: Why, I can't always go looking for tools I've forgotten at the usual time. When I fixed the tile stove in the student's room, I forgot my hammer.

DYER: And the stonecutter, the gardener, Mrs. Vesterlund, even the painter there, we're all suspected, the student, the cook, and I most of all. It was lucky though that I had paid the insurance the day before; otherwise, I'd have been in a hole.—Imagine: The stonecutter suspected of arson—the man who's afraid of doing the slightest wrong: he's so conscientious that if you ask him what time it is he'll answer you but won't swear to it because the clock *may* be off. We know about his two years in prison; he let himself be set straight; and now I'll swear he's the most decent and honest person in the block.

MASON: But the authorities suspect him just because he made a mistake . . . and lost his civil rights.

DYER: Yes, there are so many ways, so very many ways of looking at things, see.—You'll have to go now in any case; why, you're going to a wedding tonight!

MASON: Yes, that wedding . . . someone was looking for you a while ago, and he was coming right back.

DYER: Who was it?

MASON: He didn't say.

DYER: Was he a policeman?

MASON: I don't think so. There he comes! (*The* MASON *and the* OLD WOMAN *leave. The* STRANGER *enters.*)

DYER (*stares at him with curiosity, then with horror; wants to flee but cannot*): Arvid!

STRANGER: Rudolf!

DYER: You are Arvid?

STRANGER: Yes! (*Pause*)

DYER: So you're not dead?

STRANGER: Yes, in a way!—I'm back from America, after thirty years;

something kept drawing me back; I had to see my childhood home again—and it's in ruins. (*Pause*) Did it burn down last night?

DYER: Yes! You came at the right time! (*Pause*)

STRANGER (*slowly*): There's the place; how small it is when you think how much happened here!—There's the dining room with the painted walls: palms, cypress trees, temples under a rosy red sky; that's how I dreamed the world looked if one only got away from home!—And the tile stove with the pale flowers that grew out of seashells—the niche with zinc openings—I remember when we moved in when I was a child there was a name inscribed in the zinc—and Grandmother said the man with that name had taken his life in that room.—I soon forgot that; but later on when I married the suicide's niece, I thought my fate was sort of recorded in advance on that metal.—You don't believe in anything like that!—But you know how my marriage ended!

DYER: Yes, I've heard . . .

STRANGER: There's the nursery! Yes!

DYER: Let's not dig in the ruins!

STRANGER: Why not? When it has burned up, we can read in the ashes—as children we did that in the fire . . .

DYER: Sit down at this table.

STRANGER: What's this? The inn, The Last Nail, where the hearse drivers stopped in, and where criminals used to get their last drink before they were taken to Gallows Hill . . . who keeps it?

DYER: Mrs. Vesterlund, my nurse.

STRANGER: Mrs. Vesterlund! I remember her . . . It's as if the bench under me were sinking away and I were falling through time, sixty years, down into childhood—I smell the nursery air and feel the pressure on my heart—you older ones oppressed me, and you made such terrible noise that I was always frightened; I hid in the garden out of fear, was dragged out and beaten, always beaten, but couldn't understand why, and I don't know why yet!—But there was Mother . . .

DYER: Sh-h!

STRANGER: Yes, you were the favorite, and they always agreed with you . . . Then we got a stepmother.—Her father was a professional pallbearer, and we had seen him for many years riding by on the hearse . . . He finally got to know us, so he'd nod to us and grin as if he meant to say, "I'll certainly come and take you." And then he came into this house one day and was called Grandfather! When our father married his daughter!

DYER: That wasn't strange.

STRANGER: No, but how it all got woven together here, what happened to me and what happened to others . . .

DYER: I suspect it does everywhere . . .

STRANGER: Yes, of course, it's like that everywhere . . . When one's young, one sees the web set up: parents, relatives, friends, acquaintances, servants are the warp; later on in life one sees the weft; and the shuttle of fate carries the thread back and forth; and sometimes it breaks but is tied together again, and then it goes on; the beam falls, the yarn's forced into twists and turns, and the web's done. In old age when one's eyes can really see, one discovers that all the twists and turns form a pattern, a cipher, an ornament, a hieroglyphic, which one can now interpret for the first time: That is life! The world weaver has woven it! (*Pause. He gets up.*) I see the family photograph album on the scrap pile over there! (*He goes to the right and picks up an album.*) . . . It's the book of our lives! Father's mother and Mother's mother, Father and Mother, our brothers and sisters, the relatives, so-called friends and schoolmates, the maids, our godparents . . . And the strange thing is that I, who have been in America, Australia, the Congo, and Hong Kong, wherever I came, there was a fellow Swede, at least one, and however we poked about, that Swede knew either my family or at least a godfather or a maid, an acquaintance in common, in a word. On the island of Formosa I even ran into a relative . . .

DYER: Where did you get these notions?

STRANGER: Through this—whatever form life took—I've been rich and poor, high and low, have been in a shipwreck and in an earthquake, however life has presented itself, there has always been a connection and a repetition. In *that* situation I saw the result of something previous; when I met *that* particular person, I recalled something about *that* fellow from the past. There are even scenes in my life that have recurred several times, so that I've often said to myself: I've been in on this before. And things have happened that have seemed absolutely unavoidable or predestined.

DYER: What have you been all these years?

STRANGER: Everything! I've seen life from every point of the compass and all points of view, from above and from below, but always as if it had been staged especially for me; through that I've finally reconciled myself with part of the past, and have come to excuse other people's and my own so-called faults. You and I, for example, had several things to settle, didn't we . . . (*The* DYER *becomes more depressed and flinches.*) Well, don't be afraid!

DYER: I'm never afraid!

STRANGER: You certainly haven't changed.

DYER: Have you?

STRANGER: Have I? That's interesting!—Yes, you live in the notion you're very brave; and I remember when you got that false fixed idea; you had dived headfirst in the swimming class, and Mother said then: See, Rudolf really has courage! That was aimed at me, at me, whom you had robbed of courage and self-respect. But the day came when you had stolen apples and were weak enough not to admit it but blamed me.

DYER: Haven't you forgotten that?

STRANGER: I haven't forgotten it, but I've forgiven you.—I'm sitting looking at the apple tree, the very one, because I remember it so well. It's still over there, a pale yellow.—And if you look at it carefully, you'll find the mark of a large sawed-off branch.—It so happened I didn't get angry with you because of the unjust punishment, but got angry with the tree and cursed it.—Two years later that very branch had dried up and was sawed off. Then I happened to remember the fig tree that the Saviour cursed, but I didn't draw any arrogant conclusions.—But to this day I can list all the fruit trees by heart; and when I was down with yellow fever once in Jamaica, I counted them all! Most of them are still left, I see. There's the apple tree with the red-streaked fruit, and a chaffinch built her nest in that. I see the melon apples outside our attic window, where I prepared for my exam as a technician; there's the summer apple tree, there's the fall Astrachan; the cinnamon pear tree that looks like a little pyramid poplar; and there's the jam pear tree whose fruit never became ripe and which we despised, but Mother valued most; a cuckoo lived in the old tree; she turned and twisted her neck and had such a horrible cry . . . That's fifty years ago!

DYER (*angry*): What are you getting at?

STRANGER: Just as suspicious and evil-minded as ever! That's interesting.—I'm not getting at anything through my talk; the old memories are forcing their way out . . . I remember the orchard was rented out once, but we had the right to walk in it. It seemed to me then as if we had been expelled from Paradise—and the tempter was standing in back of every tree! In the fall when the apples were lying ripe on the ground, I yielded to the temptation; I couldn't resist . . .

DYER: So you stole, too?

STRANGER: Of course! But I didn't say I was innocent or accuse you! —Later on, when I was forty, I rented a lemon plantation in the southern states; well, I had thieves in the orchard every night; I couldn't sleep; I grew thin; I became sick . . . Then I thought of the poverty-stricken gardener Gustavsson . . . back here.

DYER: He's still alive.

STRANGER: Maybe he, too, stole apples when he was a child?

DYER: Most likely.

STRANGER: Why are your hands so black?

DYER: Because I handle the things I dye . . . Or did you mean something else?

STRANGER: What would that be?

DYER: That I don't have clean hands!

STRANGER: Nonsense!

DYER: You're probably thinking about the inheritance!

STRANGER: Just as small-minded as ever! You're exactly what you were when you were about eight.

DYER: And you're just as carefree, philosophical, and foolish!

STRANGER: It's strange.—How many times have we said what we're saying now? (*Pause*) I see here in your album . . . our brothers and sisters. Five are dead.

DYER: Yes.

STRANGER: And our schoolmates?

DYER: Some taken up, some left behind.

STRANGER: I ran into one in South Carolina—Axel Eriksson. Do you remember him?

DYER: Of course.

STRANGER: He told me one long night when we were on the train that our respected family, which enjoyed general admiration, was made up only of swindlers, that our wealth had been built up through smuggling here at the toll gate, and that this house was built with double walls to hide goods. Can you tell there were double walls?

DYER (*crushed*): That's why there were closets all over!

STRANGER: Eriksson's father had been a customs collector, knew our father, and told me things that turned my whole world upside down.

DYER: Didn't you beat him up?

STRANGER: Why should I?—But I got gray-haired that night; and I had to revise my whole life. You know we lived in mutual admiration, we thought our family was the best, and we thought of our parents with almost religious reverence. I had to redo their faces, strip them, pull them down, and get them out of my mind. It was terrible! Afterward they began to haunt me; pieces of the smashed figures would slip together but wouldn't fit, and it all became a waxworks museum of monsters. All the gray-haired men who visited our parents and were called uncles, who played cards and ate suppers, were smugglers, some of whom had stood in the pillory . . . Did you know that?

DYER (*completely crushed*): No!

STRANGER: The whole dye works was only a hiding place for smuggled yarn, which was redyed so it wouldn't be recognized.—I remember I always hated that smell of the dye bath, as something sickeningly sweet . . .

DYER: Why are you telling me all that?

STRANGER: Why should I keep still, and let you go about as a laughingstock when you brag about your respectable family? Haven't you noticed they laugh at you?

DYER: No! (*Pause*)

STRANGER: I see on the scrap pile over there our father's bookcase. You remember it was always locked. But one day when Father was away I found the key. I had seen the books in front through the glass panes—there were books of sermons, the works of great poets, books about orchards and gardening, collections of regulations about the customs and confiscation, the national laws, a book about foreign coins, a book about technology, which later determined my career; but I found out then that in back of these books there was room for other things, and I looked into it: first there was the cane—nowadays I know the bitter plant bears a fruit, which yields the essence of the color called dragon's blood—that's strange, of course.—Alongside it stood a jar with the label cyanide . . .

DYER: That was for the dye works, I suspect . . .

STRANGER: Perhaps for other things, too!—But here it comes: in bundles there were sections of a printed work with illustrated jackets, which aroused my interest . . . Well, without mincing

words, they were parts of a certain aristocrat's famous memoirs.—
I took them out and shut the bookcase. And under that big oak
over there I studied them. We called it the tree of knowledge, all
right. And with that I left the paradise of childhood and was
initiated, too early, into the secrets which . . . Well!

DYER: You, too?

STRANGER: Oh, you found them, too! (*Pause*) But—we'll talk about
something else, since all that's in ashes.—Did you have insurance?

DYER (*angry*): Didn't you ask that a while ago?

STRANGER: I can't remember. I often confuse what I've said with
what I had intended to say, mostly because I think so intensively
ever since the day I hanged myself in the closet.

DYER: What's that?

STRANGER: I hanged myself in the closet!

DYER (*slowly*): Was that what happened on that Maundy Thurs-
day evening that the rest of us children never found out about?
When you were taken to the hospital?

STRANGER (*slowly*): Yes!—Do you see how little one knows about
those nearest him, his home, his own life?

DYER: But why did you do it?

STRANGER: I was twelve, and I was tired of life! It was like going
into a great darkness . . . I didn't know what I was here for . . .
and I thought the world was a madhouse!—I discovered that one
day when all the school children were sent out with torches and
banners to celebrate "the destroyer of our country." I had just
finished reading a book that proved the worst of our country's
rulers [Charles XII] was its destroyer—and we were honoring
that fellow with songs and applause! (*Pause*)

DYER: What happened at the hospital?

STRANGER: I was put in the mortuary, you see, as someone dead. If
I was, I don't know—but when I woke up, I had forgotten most
of my past, and I began a new life, but in such a way the rest of
you considered me queer.—Have you remarried?

DYER: I have a wife and children. Somewhere.

STRANGER: When I became conscious, I thought I was in someone else's body; I took life calmly in a cynical way; I suppose that's how it was to be. And the worse it was, the more interesting it became . . . I considered myself someone else, and I observed, studied this other person and what happened to him, which made me insensitive to my own suffering. But in death I had gained new skills . . . I saw right through people, read their thoughts, heard their intentions. When I was in a group, I saw them all naked . . . Where did the fire start?

DYER: Why, they don't know.

STRANGER: But the paper says it started in a closet under the student's attic room. What student is that?

DYER (*shudders*): Is that in the paper? I haven't had time to read it today. What else does it say?

STRANGER: Everything!

DYER: Everything?

STRANGER: The double walls, the respected family of smugglers, the pillory, the hairpins . . .

DYER: What hairpins?

STRANGER: I don't know, but they're mentioned. Do you know?

DYER: No!

STRANGER: Everything came out, and they're expecting crowds of people to come to stare with open mouths at the exposed miserable mess.

DYER: Good God! And it pleases you that your family will be the object of scandal?

STRANGER: My family? I've never felt related to you, never have had any feelings for my fellow men or for myself; I just think it's interesting to look at people . . . What sort of person is your wife?

DYER: Does it say something about her, too?

STRANGER: Yes, about her and the student.

DYER: Nice! Then I was right! You'll see. Just wait!—There comes the stonecutter.

STRANGER: You know him?

DYER: So do you. A schoolmate. Albert Eriksson.

STRANGER: Whose father was a customs officer, and whose brother I
met on the train, the one who knew so much about our family.

DYER: Then it's that devil who's gossiped with the reporters.

(STONECUTTER *enters with a pickaxe, looks at the ruins.*)

STRANGER: That's . . . ghastly!

DYER: He has been in prison, too . . . two years . . . Do you know
what he did? He erased part of a contract I had with . . .

STRANGER: And you had him locked up; now he has revenged himself!

DYER: But the queer thing is he's now considered the most decent
man in the neighborhood; he has become a martyr and almost a
saint, so no one dares touch him.

STRANGER: That's very interesting!

DETECTIVE (*in plainclothes, enters, says to* STONECUTTER): Would you
tear down that wall?

STONECUTTER: The one by the closet?

DETECTIVE: Exactly!

STONECUTTER: That's where the fire started, and I'm sure there's a
candle or a lamp there. I know these people!

DETECTIVE: Go ahead, then.

STONECUTTER: The closet door did burn up, of course, but the double
floor collapsed; that's why we haven't found out about that, but
now we'll clear it up! (*Hacks away with his pickaxe*) See, there
it goes!—Now it's done!—There it went! Do you see anything?

DETECTIVE: Not yet!

STONECUTTER (*as before*): I see something now!—The lamp ex-
ploded, but its base is still there!—Who'd recognize this bit of
evidence?—I thought the dyer was sitting over there.

DETECTIVE: Yes, he's sitting there! (*Takes the base and shows it to
the* DYER) Do you recognize your lamp, sir?

DYER: It's not mine—it's the tutor's.

DETECTIVE: The student's? Where is he?

DYER: He's downtown, but will be back soon, I suppose, since his books are still here.

DETECTIVE: How did his lamp get into the cook's closet? Was he having an affair with her?

DYER: Presumably.

DETECTIVE: If he only admits the lamp is his, we'll arrest him. (*To the* DYER) What do you think about all this?

DYER: I? What's a person to think?

DETECTIVE: Well, what motive could he have had for setting fire to someone else's house?

DYER: I don't know. Spite . . . wanting to hurt . . . people can't be explained . . . maybe he wanted to hide something . . .

DETECTIVE: That was a poor method since all the nasty old facts were revealed.—Did he have a grudge against you?

DYER: Probably. I had helped him once when he needed it, and he hated me after that, of course!

DETECTIVE: Of course! (*Pause*) Who is the student?

DYER: A foundling, born to unknown parents.

DETECTIVE (*to the* DYER): Don't you have a grown daughter?

DYER (*angry*): Yes, of course, I do!

DETECTIVE: So you do. (*Pause. Then to the* STONECUTTER) Take your twelve men over here and tear the walls down in a hurry so we can see what else there is to find out. (*Leaves*)

STONECUTTER: It'll take only a minute! (*Goes out. Pause*)

STRANGER: Had you really paid your insurance premium?

DYER: Of course!

STRANGER: Personally?

DYER: No, I sent a messenger as usual.

STRANGER: You sent—someone else! That's like you.—Shall we go into the orchard for a while to look at the apple trees?

DYER: Yes, we can; then we'll get to see what happens afterward.

STRANGER: Now comes what's interesting!

DYER: Maybe not so interesting, if you get mixed up in it.

STRANGER: I?

DYER: Who knows?

STRANGER: What a web it is!

DYER: You did have a child in the orphanage, didn't you?

STRANGER: Bless you! . . . Let's go into the orchard.

[CURTAIN]

The same scenery, but with the walls torn down so that one can see the garden with all its spring flowers, daphnes, saxifrage, daffodils, narcissus, tulips, primroses, etc., and all the fruit trees in bloom.

The STONECUTTER, *the* MASON *with the* OLD WOMAN, *the* GARDENER, *the* HEARSE DRIVER, MRS. VESTERLUND, *the* PAINTER *stand lined up looking at the ruins.*

STRANGER (*enters*): There they stand rejoicing over the misfortune, waiting for the victim, who seems to be the main attraction. They consider it arson because they want it to be that!—And all these scoundrels were my friends and companions when I was young; I'm related to the hearse driver through my stepmother, whose father was a pallbearer—(*To those present*) Don't stand there, good people; there might be dynamite in the cellar—if there is, it could explode at any time. (*The crowd disperses and disappears.*)

STRANGER (*at the scrap pile; looking into various books*): They're the student's books!—The same nonsense as when I was young.— Livy's *Roman History,* in which every word is a lie, they say— but there's a book from my brother's collection!—*Columbus, or the Discovery of America!* That one's my book I got as a Christmas gift in 1857; my name has been erased; so somebody stole it from me, and I accused a maid, who was fired as a result! That's *nice;* maybe that led to her fall! Fifty years ago!—There's the frame of a family picture: my famous grandfather, the smuggler who was pilloried: *nice!* But what's this? Part of the mahogany bed—in which I was born!—Item: the leg of a dining table—passed down from generation to generation—Yes! They said it was ebony, it was admired because of that, and now it is exposed, after fifty years, by me, as ordinary stained maple—everything was stained in our house, so it wouldn't be recognized, and our childhood clothes were dyed, too, so our bodies were always stained! Ebony, humbug!—Here's the living-room clock, smuggled goods, too, which has measured out time for two generations; wound every Saturday when we got dried cod and ale soup for dinner—like an intelligent clock, it used to stop when anyone died, but, when I died, it kept on going.—Let me look at you, old friend; let me see what you look like inside. (*The clock goes to pieces when he touches it.*) Doesn't hold up so you can take hold of it. Nothing did, nothing! Vanity, mortality!—But there's the little globe that was on top of it, but should have been under it! Tiny, little world: the densest of all the planets, the heaviest, and therefore so heavy for you, so heavy to breathe, so heavy to bear: the cross is your symbol, but it could have been a fool's cap or a straitjacket—the world of illusion and fools!—Eternal God! Has your world gone astray in space? And how did it get to revolve so that your children got dizzy and lost their common sense so they can't see what is but only that which seems to be? Amen! There' the student!

(*The* STUDENT *enters; is looking for someone.*)

STRANGER: He's looking for the lady of the house! And telling everything he knows—with his eyes! Happy youth—whom are you looking for?

STUDENT (*embarrassed*): I'm looking for . . .

STRANGER: Speak up, young fellow, or be silent. I understand you very well anyway!

STUDENT: With whom do I have the honor of speaking?

STRANGER: It's no honor to speak with me, you know; I ran away to America once because of debt . . .

STUDENT: That wasn't the right thing to do . . .

STRANGER: Right or wrong, but it's a fact. You're looking for the lady of the house; she isn't here, but she'll soon be here like all the others; they're drawn to the scene of the fire like mosquitoes . . .

STUDENT: . . . to the light!

STRANGER: That's what *you* say, but I'd prefer to say the lamp, to choose a more significant expression.—But conceal your feelings, young man, if you can. I can conceal mine!—We were talking about the lamp. How was it with the lamp?

STUDENT: What lamp?

STRANGER: There you are! Denying and lying about the whole thing!—The lamp that stood in the cook's closet and set fire to the house.

STUDENT: I don't know anything about that.

STRANGER: Some blush when they lie; others get white about the nose.—This fellow has discovered a new way!

STUDENT: Are you talking to yourself, sir?

STRANGER: I have that bad habit!—Do you have living parents?

STUDENT: No, I don't.

STRANGER: Now you've lied again, but without knowing it!

STUDENT: I never lie!

STRANGER: Only three times just now! I know your father.

STUDENT: I don't believe it.

STRANGER: So much the better for me!—Do you see this tie pin? It's beautiful, yes! But I never get to see it, haven't any joy from wearing it, while everyone else gets pleasure out of it. At least that's not egotistic, and there are times when I'd like to see it on someone else's tie so I could admire it. Do you want it?

STUDENT: I don't understand . . . Maybe it's better not to have it, as you said.

STRANGER: Maybe!—Don't be impatient; she's coming right away! Is being young enviable?

STUDENT: No, I don't think so.

STRANGER: When one's young, one isn't one's own master, eats other people's bread, never has any money, may never speak in company, is treated like a fool, and when one can't marry, one has to look at other men's wives with all the dangerous consequences. Youth is humbug!

STUDENT: Yes, if the truth's to be told! When one's a child, one wants to become big, that's to say fifteen years old, study, get a top hat; later one wishes to become old, that's to say twenty-one! So no one wants to be young!

STRANGER: And when one gets really old, one wants to be dead. There's not much left that's desirable then!—Do you know you're to be arrested?

STUDENT: I am?

STRANGER: Yes, the detective said so a while ago.

STUDENT: I?

STRANGER: Does that amaze you? Don't you know that you have to be prepared for anything in this life?

STUDENT: What have I done?

STRANGER: You don't need to have done anything to be arrested; you're only suspected.

STUDENT: Then they could arrest everyone!

STRANGER: Absolutely right! They could put a rope around everyone's neck if they wanted to be just, but they don't want to! Humanity's a terrible lot, ugly, sweaty, stinking; unclean underwear, dirty socks with holes in them, chilblains, corns, ugh! No, a blooming apple tree's much prettier; look at the lilies of the field —it's as if they weren't at home here—and smell how fragrant they are!

STUDENT: Are you a philosopher, sir?

STRANGER: I'm a great philosopher!

STUDENT: You're only joking!

STRANGER: That's what you say to get away. Go on—go your way! Hurry up!

STUDENT: But I'm waiting for someone.

STRANGER: Yes, that's what I thought.—But you had better go meet her.

STUDENT: Did she tell you that?

STRANGER: She didn't need to.

STUDENT: Then I don't want to miss her . . . if what you say is so . . . (*Goes*)

STRANGER: Is he my child? But at the worst I, too, was a child once, and it wasn't wonderful or pleasant.—And I'm his . . . what else? Besides . . . who knows?—Now I'm going to call on Mrs. Vesterlund—she worked for my parents, was faithful and good-natured, and, when she had stolen for ten years, she was decorated as a faithful servant. (*Sits down at the table*) Here are Gustavsson's wreaths of wild cranberry—he sells them as genuine lingon —just as carelessly bound as forty years ago—everything he did was careless or stupid, and that's why it went badly for him. His knowing what he was like excused much of what he did. "Poor fool that I am," he used to say, and then he'd take off his cap and scratch his head.—There's a myrtle—(*He taps on the pot.*)— not watered, of course—he always forgot to water his plants, the fool . . . yet he wanted them to grow! (*The* PAINTER *appears.*) What painter's that? I suppose he belongs in the Morass and he probably has a thread in my web! (*The* PAINTER *stares at the* STRANGER, *who stares at him.*) Well, do you recognize me?

PAINTER: Is—it—Mr. Arvid?

STRANGER: Has been and is, if being perceived is being! (*Pause*)

PAINTER: I should really be angry with you.

STRANGER: Go ahead—be angry! But let me know why! Then things generally straighten out.

PAINTER: Do you remember . . .

STRANGER: Unfortunately I have an excellent memory!

PAINTER: Do you remember a boy called Robert?

STRANGER: Yes, indeed! He was a big rascal who really could draw!

PAINTER (*slowly*): And who was to enter the academy to become a painter, an artist. But that was back in those days—when color blindness was fashionable. You were a technician then, Mr. Arvid, and were to examine my eyes before your father, my patron, would keep me in art school . . . So you took two skeins of yarn from the dye works, the one red, the other green; and you asked me. I answered by calling the red one green, and vice versa. With that my career was ruined . . .

STRANGER: Well, that's how it should be!

PAINTER: No!—For the truth is that I could tell the colors, but couldn't tell their *names* apart. I found that out first when I was thirty-seven . . .

STRANGER: That's a painful story, but I didn't know better, so you'll have to forgive me.

PAINTER: How can I?

STRANGER: Not knowing better is forgivable!—Listen to me now! I was going to join the navy; test sailed as an extra cadet, became sort of seasick; was rejected. But I could take the sea—my seasickness came from having imbibed too much. So my career was ruined, and I chose another . . .

PAINTER: What do I have to do with the navy? I dreamt about Rome and Paris . . .

STRANGER: Well-l! One dreams about so much when one's young, and when one's old, too! besides, all that was long ago. What's that to talk about?

PAINTER: How can you say that? Maybe you can give me the life I should have had . . .

STRANGER: No, I can't. But I don't owe you that either! That trick with the yarn I learned at school, and you should have known the names of the colors.—Be off with you as far as you can get—one bungler less can only be a blessing for humanity!—There's Mrs. Vesterlund!

PAINTER: How can he talk like that? But he's going to get his!

(MRS. VESTERLUND *comes on stage*.)

STRANGER: How do you do, Mrs. Vesterlund! It's I, Mr. Arvid, so don't be afraid! I've been in America! How are you? I'm fine! And there has been a fire here; your husband's dead, he was a policeman, a very decent fellow; I liked him because of his good nature and friendly manner; he was a harmless wit who never hurt anyone—I remember once . . .

MRS. VESTERLUND: Good Lord! Is it my Arvid, the one I took care of . . .

STRANGER: Well, that wasn't I; that was my brother, but that doesn't matter—just as pleasant—I was talking about your husband who died, thirty-five years ago; he was a kind man, my especially good friend . . .

MRS. VESTERLUND: Yes, he died—(*pause*)—but I don't know anything special about that.—Mr. Arvid, you're maybe confusing . . .

STRANGER: I don't confuse . . . I remember old man Vesterlund well, and I liked him very much . . .

MRS. VESTERLUND (*slowly*): It's a shame to say it, of course, but he certainly didn't have such a good nature.

STRANGER: He didn't?

MRS. VESTERLUND: Well . . . he had a sort of way of getting in good with people, but he didn't mean what he said . . . or he said it backward . . .

STRANGER: What's that? Didn't he mean what he said? Maybe he was a hypocrite?

MRS. VESTERLUND: It's a shame to say it, but I think . . .

STRANGER: Maybe he wasn't quite honest?

MRS. VESTERLUND: Well-l! He—was—a little—well, he didn't mean what he said! But, Mr. Arvid, how have you been?

STRANGER: Now I understand!—What a scoundrel! And I've been saying good things about him for thirty-five years, missed him, almost mourned his passing away; I bought a wreath for his coffin out of my tobacco allowance . . .

MRS. VESTERLUND: What? What was that?

STRANGER: What a rascal! (*Pause*) Well! He fooled me one Tuesday in Lent and said if I'd remove every third egg from the chickens, they'd lay more. I did, got a beating, and almost ended up in court . . . But I never suspected he was the informer . . . He'd be in the kitchen sponging—the maids could do what they wanted with things—now I see him in his true colors!—And now I'm getting angry at someone who has been in his grave for thirty-five years!—So he was sarcastic, and I didn't understand that then. Though I do now!

MRS. VESTERLUND: Yes, he was a little sarcastic—I know that!

STRANGER: Now I remember still more . . . And I've said good things about that scoundrel for thirty-five years! And I attended his funeral—that's when I got my first toddy—he used to flatter me, called me professor, the heir to the estate . . . Ugh!—There we have the stonecutter! Go in now, ma'am, or we'll have a squabble when that fellow comes with his bills; go on, ma'am; we'll meet again!

MRS. VESTERLUND (*going in*): No, we won't meet again; people should never meet again—it's never the same as it was, and people always rip things to pieces for one. Why did you have to say all that when it wasn't bothering me before? . . . (*Goes in*)

    (*The* STONECUTTER *enters.*)

STRANGER: Come on!

STONECUTTER: What's that?

STRANGER: Come on! (*The* STONECUTTER *stares.*) Are you looking at my tie pin?—I bought it at Charing Cross in London.

STONECUTTER: I'm no thief!

STRANGER: No, but you practice the noble art of forgery! You erase!

STONECUTTER: That's true, but it was a dishonest contract that was about to kill me.

STRANGER: Why did you sign it?

STONECUTTER: Because I was in financial trouble!

STRANGER: That is a motive!

STONECUTTER: But now I have my revenge!

STRANGER: Why, that's nice!

STONECUTTER: And now they'll go to jail!

STRANGER: Didn't we ever fight when we were boys?

STONECUTTER: No, I was too young!

STRANGER: Haven't we lied about each other, or stolen something, or ruined each other's careers, or seduced each other's sisters?

STONECUTTER: No, but my father was a customs official, and yours was a smuggler . . .

STRANGER: There you are! Always something!

STONECUTTER: And when my father couldn't prove it, he was fired.

STRANGER: And you're going to take it out on me because your father was a fool?

STONECUTTER: Why did you say there was dynamite in the cellar?

STRANGER: Now you're lying again! I said there could be dynamite there—why, everything's possible.

STONECUTTER: However—the student has been arrested! Do you know him?

STRANGER: Very little, but his mother was a maid in your house. She was both good and beautiful; I courted her; during that time she bore a child.

STONECUTTER: Aren't you its father then?

STRANGER: No-o! But since paternity may not be denied, I suppose I'm sort of a stepfather!

STONECUTTER: So they lied about you?

STRANGER: Of course! But then that's common enough . . .

STONECUTTER: And I testified against you . . . on oath!

STRANGER: I can believe that. But what's the difference? Nothing matters!—Now we'll quit repeating all that—otherwise we'll be back to the butcher's rope and the brush on the fire!

STONECUTTER: But consider me—I've perjured myself . . .

STRANGER: Yes, that's not pleasant, but things like that do happen . . .

STONECUTTER: That's terrible! Isn't it terrible to be alive?

STRANGER (*his hand over his eyes*): Yes! It . . . is . . . beyond . . . all . . . description . . . terrible!

STONECUTTER: I don't want to live any longer . . .

STRANGER: You have to! (*Pause*) Have to! Listen, the student has been arrested. Can't he be released?

STONECUTTER: Hardly!—I'll say one thing since we're talking nicely: he's innocent but can't clear himself; for the only witness who could prove his innocence would by so doing prove his guilt—in something else.

STRANGER: The woman with the hairpins?

STONECUTTER: Yes!

STRANGER: Is it the old one or the young one?

STONECUTTER: You'll have to figure that out for yourself, but it wasn't the cook.

STRANGER: What a web!—But who put the lamp there?

STONECUTTER: His worst enemy.

STRANGER: Did his worst enemy set the fire?

STONECUTTER: Well, I don't know that.—Only the mason knows!

STRANGER: Who is the mason?

STONECUTTER: He's the oldest one in the place, is sort of related to Mrs. Vesterlund, knows the secrets of the whole house, shares some secret with the dyer so that fellow won't testify.

STRANGER: Who's the lady of the house, my sister-in-law?

STONECUTTER: Well!—She was the governess in the house when his first wife ran away!

STRANGER: What sort of person is she?

STONECUTTER: Hm. Sort of person? Well, I don't know what you mean. Do you mean professionally? The name and the profession are recorded on the census list, but that doesn't have to do with her character, only with her job.

STRANGER: I mean her temperament.

STONECUTTER: Oh—well, one's temper varies. Mine depends on whom I'm talking with. With a decent person, I'm decent, and with a mean one I get like a wild animal.

STRANGER: But we were talking about her everyday temperament.

STONECUTTER: Well-l, nothing much to say: like people in general;

gets angry if anyone irritates her; good-tempered again. One can't always be in the same frame of mind.

STRANGER: I mean—is she cheerful or gloomy?

STONECUTTER: When everything's going well, she's cheerful; when everything goes wrong, she's sad or angry—like the rest of us.

STRANGER: Yes, but what's her manner?

STONECUTTER: Well, isn't that the same thing really? As an educated woman she has a refined manner, although, that's to say, she can get coarse, she, too, when she gets angry.

STRANGER: All that didn't tell me much about her!

STONECUTTER (*pats him on the shoulder*): No, you don't find out much about people, sir!

STRANGER: He's superb!—Well, what do you think of my brother, the dyer? (*Pause*)

STONECUTTER: Well, he has a good manner. I don't know anything else, because I can't find out what he conceals, of course.

STRANGER: Excellent!—Still! His hands are always black, but we know they're white underneath.

STONECUTTER: But then they have to be scraped first, and he doesn't let anyone do that.

STRANGER: Fine!—But who are those young people coming over there?

STONECUTTER: The gardener's son and my daughter, who were to have been married tonight but have had to postpone it because of the fire.—I'll go now; I don't want to embarrass them.—You understand, a father-in-law like me.—Good-bye! (*Goes. The* STRANGER *withdraws behind the inn but can be seen by the audience.* ALFRED *and* MATILDA *come in, hand in hand.*)

ALFRED: I had to come to look at where the fire had been—I had to—

MATILDA: What's that to look at?

ALFRED: I've had such a bad time in this house I often wished it would catch fire . . .

MATILDA: Well, I knew it shaded the garden and orchard too much;

things should grow better now; just so they don't build a new and bigger house . . .

ALFRED: It's lovely and open, airy and sunny here, of course, and I've heard they're going to make a street of it . . .

MATILDA: Probably you're going to move, then?

ALFRED: Yes, we're all going to move, and I like that; I like what's new; I'd like to emigrate . . .

MATILDA: Heavens, no! Do you know our doves had their nests on the roof here, and when it burned down last night, they flew around at first, but when the roof collapsed, they flew right into the fire . . . They couldn't part from their old home!

ALFRED: But we have to get away from here—away! Father says the soil here's worn out . . .

MATILDA: I heard what's left from the fire is to be hauled out into the country to build up the soil . . .

ALFRED: You mean the ashes . . .

MATILDA: Yes, they say it's good to sow in ashes . .

ALFRED: New soil is better . . .

MATILDA: But your father, the gardener, is ruined . . .

ALFRED: Not at all—he has money in the bank!—Yes, he complains, but they all do . . .

MATILDA: Has he . . . Hasn't he been ruined by the fire?

ALFRED: Not in the least! But he's a wise old scamp, even though he calls himself a fool . . .

MATILDA: What am I going to believe?

ALFRED: He has lent money to the mason . . . and to several others.

MATILDA: I don't know what's what. Am I dreaming?—We've been weeping all morning about your father's misfortune and about the postponement of our wedding . . .

ALFRED: Poor girl! But the wedding's tonight!

MATILDA: Hasn't it been postponed?

ALFRED: It's been set back two hours so Father will have time to get his new coat.

MATILDA: And we who have wept . . .

ALFRED: Wasted tears! So many tears!

MATILDA: It annoys me that they were wasted, even though . . Imagine that my father-in-law can be such a scamp . . .

ALFRED: Yes, he's a big joker, to put it mildly.—He always says he's tired, but that's only laziness; he's very, very lazy . . .

MATILDA: Don't say anything else bad about Father-in-law—but let's go—I have to get dressed, and put up my hair.—Think of it: Father-in-law isn't what I thought he was—going about acting and fooling people like that!—Maybe you're like that, too—so that one doesn't know who you are!

ALFRED: You'll find that out afterward!

MATILDA: When it's too late!

ALFRED: Never too late . . .

MATILDA: You're so wicked in this place . . . Now I'm afraid of all of you . . .

ALFRED: Surely not of me?

MATILDA: I don't know what I'm to believe . . . Why haven't you told me before that Father-in-law is well off? . . .

ALFRED: I wanted to test you and find out if you loved me when I was poor.

MATILDA: They say afterward that they wanted to test, but that's why I'll never be able to believe in anyone any more . . .

ALFRED: Go and change your clothes! I have to order carriages

MATILDA: Will we get carriages?

ALFRED: Of course!—Closed carriages!

MATILDA: Closed carriages? Tonight? That will be fun! Come, come quickly! We're getting closed carriages!

ALFRED (*takes her hand, and they skip out*): Here you have me!— Hi!

STRANGER: Bravo!

(*The* DETECTIVE *enters, speaks softly to the* STRANGER, *who answers in the same way, in the course of about half a minute, whereupon the* DETECTIVE *leaves.*)

LADY OF THE HOUSE (*enters, dressed in black; stares for a long time at the* STRANGER): Aren't you my brother-in-law?

STRANGER: Yes, I am. (*Pause*) Do I correspond to the descriptions or accounts you've heard?

LADY: Frankly speaking: no!

STRANGER: People usually don't, and I'll admit the description I got of you a while ago isn't much like you either.

LADY: Yes, people are very unfair to each other, and they depict each other according to their own image . . .

STRANGER: And they're like theater directors assigning roles to each other; some accept the role; others hand it back and prefer to improvise . . .

LADY: What role have you been playing?

STRANGER: The seducer's!—Not because I've been one; I have never seduced anyone, neither a single girl nor a married woman, but once when I was young I was seduced, and that's why I got the role. It's strange that it was forced on me so I took it: and I've gone about for twenty years with the bad conscience of a seducer . . .

LADY: So you were innocent?

STRANGER: Yes indeed!

LADY: How strange! My husband to this day talks about the Nemesis that has pursued you because you seduced another man's wife.

STRANGER: I can well believe that.—But your husband's a still more interesting case: he has lied together a whole character for himself. Isn't it true that he's cowardly when he's up against it in life?

LADY: Yes, of course, he's cowardly.

STRANGER: And brags about his courage, which is only brutality.

LADY: *You* really know him!

STRANGER: Yes, and no!—And you've been living in the belief you married into a respected family that has always been respectable?

LADY: I thought so until this morning . . .

STRANGER: Then it collapsed!—What a web of lies, mistakes, misunderstandings! And one is to take it seriously!

LADY: Do you?

STRANGER: Sometimes! Very seldom nowadays. I go about like a sleepwalker on a housetop—I know I'm sleeping, but I am awake —and I'm only waiting to be awakened.

LADY: They say you've been on the other side . . .

STRANGER: I've been across the river, but I don't remember anything, but—that everything there *was* what it seemed to be! That's the difference!

LADY: When nothing bears being touched, what can one hold onto?

STRANGER: Don't you know?

LADY: Tell me! Tell me!

STRANGER: Sorrow makes patience; patience makes experience; experience makes hope; but hope doesn't permit frustration.

LADY: Hope, yes!

STRANGER: Yes, hope!

LADY: Don't you ever think it's fun to be alive?

STRANGER: Of course; but even that's an illusion. I tell you, when one's born without a film over one's eyes, one sees life and people as they are . . . and one has to be a pig to thrive here in the filth.—When one has seen enough of the blue mists, one turns one's eyes inward to look into one's own soul. There's really something to look at there . . .

LADY: What?

STRANGER: Oneself! But when one has seen oneself, one dies!

LADY (*covers her eyes with her hands. Pause*): Will you help me?

STRANGER: If I can!

LADY: Try!

STRANGER: Wait!—No, I can't do that!—He has been innocently arrested! You alone can get him released, but you can't do that! It's a net that has not been woven by human beings . .

LADY: But he isn't guilty.

STRANGER: Who is guilty? (*Pause*)

LADY: No one!—It was an accidental fire!

STRANGER: I know!

LADY: What am I going to do?

STRANGER: Suffer! It will pass. Even this is vanity.

LADY: Suffer?

STRANGER: Suffer! But hope!

LADY (*extends her hand to him*): Thank you!

STRANGER: And have for comfort—

LADY: What?

STRANGER: That you're not suffering innocently!

(*The* LADY *bows her head and goes. The* STRANGER *goes up onto the ruins. The* DYER *enters, happy.*)

DYER: Are you haunting the ruins?

STRANGER: Ghosts thrive on ruins.—Now you're happy?

DYER: Now I'm happy.

STRANGER: And brave?

DYER: Whom should I fear? And what?

STRANGER: Your happiness tells me you don't know an important fact . . . Have you the courage to hear a misfortune?

DYER: What?

STRANGER: Are you turning pale?

DYER: I?

STRANGER: A great misfortune!

DYER: Speak up!

STRANGER: The detective was just here . . . and told me . . . confidentially . . .

DYER: What?

STRANGER: That the insurance premium was paid two hours too late . . .

DYER: Good heavens . . . what are you saying?—I sent my wife with the money!

STRANGER: But she sent the bookkeeper . . . and he got there too late!

DYER: Then I'm ruined! (*Pause*)

STRANGER: Are you weeping?

DYER: I'm ruined!

STRANGER: Yes! Can't you bear it?

DYER: What am I going to live on? What am I going to do?

STRANGER: Work!

DYER: I'm too old, have no friends . . .

STRANGER: You'll probably get some now! People always sympathize with an unfortunate person—I had my best moments in misfortune.

DYER (*wild*): I'm ruined!

STRANGER: But in the days of prosperity and good fortune I had to walk alone; envy couldn't conceal itself under friendship . . .

DYER: I'll sue the bookkeeper!

STRANGER: Don't!

DYER: He's going to pay . . .

STRANGER: You never change! What's the point of living when you never learn anything?

DYER: I'll sue him; he's a scoundrel; he hated me because I slapped him once . . .

STRANGER: Forgive him—as I forgave you, when I refrained from collecting my inheritance.

DYER: What inheritance?

STRANGER: Incorrigible! Unmerciful! Cowardly! Untruthful!—Go in peace, Brother!

DYER: What inheritance are you talking about?

STRANGER: Listen, Brother, Rudolf, my mother's son at any rate, you had the stonecutter locked up because he erased . . . fine . . . but you erased in my *Christopher Columbus, or, The Discovery of America.*

DYER (*hit*): Wha—wha—wha—? Columbus?

STRANGER: Yes, *my* book that became yours! (*The* DYER *is silent.*) Yes! And I understand that you carried the student's lamp into the closet; I understand *that;* I understand everything, but do you know that the dining-room table wasn't of ebony?

DYER: Wasn't it?

STRANGER: It was maple!

DYER: Maple?

STRANGER: The pride of the house, valued at two thousand!

DYER: That, too? Humbug, that, too!

STRANGER: Yes!

DYER: Ugh!

STRANGER: The debt is written off! The case is canceled, the matter can't be cleared up, the parties give up . . .

DYER (*rushes out*): I'm ruined!

STRANGER (*takes his wreath from the table*): I thought I'd go out to the graveyard with this wreath—to my parents' grave, but I'll lay it here on the ruins of my family home! My childhood home! (*Prays silently*) And so: out into the wide, wide world again, Wanderer!

[CURTAIN]

Introduction to

'The Ghost Sonata'

OPUS 3, a chamber play designed originally for his own Intimate Theater and certainly for little theaters in general, is a major result of Strindberg's scrutiny of man and his homes.

While *Stormy Weather* and *The House That Burned* undoubtedly stemmed from experiences in and about homes of his own, *The Ghost Sonata* concerns what he had seen and heard and what he had guessed at about the homes of neighbors. The two first chamber plays do have timeless and universal application in terms of the discrepancy between appearance and reality; aging people can understand the Gentleman's desire to withdraw into isolation from the storms of life and can appreciate what it would be like to return to a childhood home only to have one's illusions about family and home completely shattered. It is obviously just as timeless and universal to wonder and to speculate about what has gone on and is going on behind the attractive façades of neighboring houses. Such matters have engaged human beings since the earliest times, but no other writer has probed the possibilities implicit in the differences between the lives of neighbors as they seem to be and as they are in as arresting a way as Strindberg did.

In *The Ghost Sonata* Strindberg has obviously borrowed certain techniques from the sonata form, specifically the division into three parts and the statement, development, and recapitulation of two contrasting themes. While it is possible to analyze in detail the probable influence of Beethoven's Piano Sonata in D Minor (Op. 31, No. 2) on Strindberg's play, there is a danger of distorting the nature and the extent of that influence. It is certain, however, that

183

The Ghost Sonata breaks into three parts: what might be called
(a) the vision of the home and the people in it as they seem to be;
(b) their unmasking; and (c) the presentation of the doctrine that
they and, by implication, all other human beings need to accept if
life is to be bearable. It is certain, too, that the play has two contrasting themes: *perfectionism* or, if you will, *idealism,* represented
by Arkenholz; and *vampirism,* represented by Hummel. What
Strindberg has done is to convert musical techniques into the speech
and the action of the stage, into the idiom of the theater. This is an
example of a broad adaptation of the techniques of one art form
into those of another, rather than a highly detailed and subtly intricate one.

What is intricate in this chamber play are the ideational implications of Strindberg's use of the techniques suggested by the sonata
form, his use of one form of the dream-related experience, his
probing of human motives and behavior in depth, his use of symbols
to convey what he considered basic truths, and his clear restatement
of the conclusions he had reached about man and the world in
which he lives.

The Ghost Sonata is not an analysis of specific people as is, for
example, *Creditors.* The latter play makes full use of the evidence
the senses have to offer the observer, and of the power to sort out,
classify, and use that evidence rationally to come to conclusions the
thinking individual can find logical. *The Ghost Sonata* is based
primarily on another way of getting at the truth about human
beings: synthesis rather than analysis, insight rather than reasoning, sudden illumination rather than patient mental effort. It is the
way of the poet, not that of the scientist; it is the result of inspiration, not of patient work in the laboratory.

It is as if Strindberg has deliberately set his imagination free to
remove the protective camouflage, the masks that people assume to
make life either more bearable or seemingly more pleasant than it
actually is. In that sense, *The Ghost Sonata* is a dream play, although, unlike *A Dream Play,* it is not structurally based on the

form of a typical dream. It is, rather, distortion through the imagination, a caricaturing of life, a restructuring according to a pattern of blunt and essentially cruel revelation of truth. The total effect, it seems to me, is that of a nightmare. It seems to me, too, that Strindberg in *The Ghost Sonata* is again emphasizing the central motif of *A Dream Play:* human beings are to be pitied.

Surely the human beings exposed in *The Ghost Sonata* to the demands of perfectionism or idealism, on one hand, and to the manipulations of vampirism, on the other, are to be pitied. Arkenholz, the young student and the Sunday child, may approach being a model of integrity as Strindberg suggests in telling his story, but his effect on poor suffering humanity is pretty much like that of the vampire Hummel—destructive. To clarify what Strindberg has to say about both and about the contrasting themes they represent, one need only consider what each of them is, wants, and does. Doing so will reveal what Strindberg is saying about people, the life that they might dream of leading, and the life that they all must lead, given variations in degree and in quality.

Young Arkenholz sees the apartment in the aristocratic house as the home of culture, refinement, and beauty. For him, the idealistic outsider, looking in, it is a paradise on earth: "I walked by here yesterday when the sun shone on the windows, and, imagining all the beauty and luxury there must be in there, I said to my companion: How lucky it would be to have an apartment there, four flights up, a beautiful young wife, two handsome little children, and an income of 20,000 . . ." It is an idealist's dream, from Strindberg's point of view. Like other Strindbergian idealists, Arkenholz is dedicated to perfectionism; implicit in this are the highest standards of behavior, no compromising with the truth once one believes one has attained it, the pursuit of the ideal no matter what the cost to himself or others, and the absolute rejection of masks designed to conceal flaws of any kind. Strindberg does not make the mistake of making his idealist omniscient; Arkenholz is decidedly finite, as a close examination of the information supplied about him will show. Arkenholz is no Gregers Werle, to be sure, but much of what he does is as unfortunate in its results as Gregers Werle's presentation of the claims of the ideal. The Arkenholz who can work at helping those injured in the collapse of a building cannot refrain from blurting out the whole bitter truth that destroys the girl he loves. What Strindberg is saying is that perfectionism, in spite of its essential value and worth, is—carried to its ultimate conclusions—destructive.

At first glance Arkenholz and Hummel are contrasts in white and black. Hummel is, along with Edgar in *The Dance of Death,* a superb example of the Strindbergian vampire as defined in that play:

> KURT: . . . Just now when he felt his life slipping away, he clung to mine, began to settle my affairs as if he wanted to creep into me and live my life.
>
> ALICE: That's his vampire nature exactly . . . to seize hold of other people's lives, to suck interest out of other people's lives, to arrange and direct for others when his own life has become absolutely without interest for him. And remember, Kurt, don't ever let him get hold of your family affairs, don't ever let him meet your friends, for he'll take them away from you and make them his own . . . He's a magician at doing that! . . . If he meets your children, you'd soon see them on intimate terms with him; he'd advise them and bring them up according to his own whims, and, above all, against your wishes.

Hummel is that sort of person, figuratively one of the living dead who go to work to retain life through feeding on others. In the opening scene, he obviously enlists the aid of Arkenholz. In the second, he indulges in what may well be the finest example of Strindbergian unmasking of human beings, stripping them of their material and spiritual props, and depriving them of the illusions that permit them to go on living. In the process of showing the old vampire at work, Strindberg demonstrates that evil destroys when it exposes others to the full glare of truth, when it blocks and frustrates them in their attempts at continuing to live, and steals them, their things, and their ideas.

In *The Ghost Sonata* the threads in the web of life are difficult to untangle. Strindberg probably made the pattern of human relationships in the "aristocratic" apartment house almost inextricable deliberately. As he emphasizes in every autobiographical volume from *The Son of a Servant* (1887) on, such patterns are not only complex but ultimately impossible to unravel completely, either by those directly involved or by interested observers.

In keeping with his concept of the chamber play, every last "character" contributes to the formulation of what may be called the doctrine in *The Ghost Sonata*. While Hummel and Arkenholz have the most lines and are constantly present in body and spirit, even Lady Beate von Holsteinkrona, who has no lines, reinforces an important segment of the idea Strindberg expresses in this play: human beings are to be pitied. But it is the Colonel's wife, who is Hummel's ex-fiancée, the mother of Adèle, and both Mummy and Parrot, who makes the core of Strindberg's thinking even clearer: "But I can stop time in its course—I can reduce the past to nothing, undo what has been done; but not with bribes, not with threats—but through suffering and repentance—(*Goes up to Hummel*) We are poor human beings, we know that; we have sinned; we have done wrong, we like everyone else. We are not what we seem for we are essentially better than we ourselves when we condemn our sins and faults." The poor miserable human beings need cushions to keep going, and the cushioning will take the form of illusions, of life lies. Adèle needs her faith in beauty, truth, and goodness; robbed of these, she dies. Even Hummel cannot bear a full measure of absolute truth; he, too, dies behind the death screen.

The essential doctrine is humanity and resignation; that is, people must accept themselves and their fellows for what they are—pitiable finite creatures; must not inquire too closely into the validity of appearances; and must resign themselves to the facts of the human condition. In other words, the doctrine is that of accepting this world as a bad copy, from which release comes only with death and escape into the original. *A Ghost Sonata* is, then, a curiously ironic application of, "Know the truth, and the truth shall set you free."

Among the ensemble of "characters," no one seems to annoy readers and commentators more than the Cook. Scholars who examine Strindberg's play largely from a biographical point of view trace her origin to Strindberg's extreme fastidiousnes about food and drink and his consequent difficulties with various women who prepared meals for him in his declining years. Be that as it may, the vampire cook nevertheless serves fantastically well as a symbol of one life-crippling element in an environment in which a ghost tea or a ghost supper is a standard fact of life. The horror of the Cook's appearance and her shocking behavior in the presence of two young people, the idealistic Arkenholz and the lovely but delicate Adèle, are excellent confirmations of a set of distressing situations in a neighboring "home."

Perhaps as distressing as anything is the monotonous repetition:

> BENGTSSON: It's the usual ghost supper, as we call it. They'll drink tea, not say a word, or the Colonel alone will speak; and then they'll crunch away at small cakes, all at the same time, so it sounds like rats in an attic.
>
> JOHANSSON: Why is it called a ghost supper?
>
> BENGTSSON: They look like ghosts . . . And they've kept this up for twenty years, always the same people, who say the same thing, or keep still so they won't have to be ashamed.

Nor are these ghostlike "characters" and their regularly recurring ghost suppers the only illustrations of the Strindbergian notion that everything repeats itself. There are, for example, such striking and distressing matters as Adèle's daily struggles to keep the dirt of life at a distance.

It is perhaps primarily because of the inclusion of living dead who go through the motions of the mechanics of living, the implicit commentary on complacent automatons who do not begin to understand the human condition, the lack of clear indication of any genuine purpose in human living, and the seemingly obsessive concern with food that many people have found in *The Ghost Sonata* major sources of inspiration for the drama of the absurd. Surely Strindberg's emphasis on man's isolation and loneliness and his suggestion of human anguish in a nightmarish world are others. Consider the beautiful woman who has grown old and wasted and is spoken of as a mummy, who then looks and becomes immobile, and who, labeled a parrot, "speaks" like one and "parrots" what she is told to.

Strindberg has not failed, however, to note that there is beauty and goodness in the world, too. The Hyacinth Room with its beautiful flowers and its two beautiful young people is as attractive as the young outsider had thought it was—from the outside—until he and Adèle indulge in an orgy of denigration that approaches analysis and by so doing destroy every prospect of happiness for them as a couple. It is this unwillingness to accept life as it is and the tendency to probe it until everything has been stripped of beauty and poetic meaning that makes the Hyacinth Room the room of ordeals. Strindberg more than implies that the acceptance of people and the human condition as well as suffering and repentance are extremely important. That is the gist of what he says in his difficult lyric:

> I saw the sun, so I seemed
> to have seen the Hidden One;
> everyman enjoys his deeds;
> happy the one who does good.
> For deeds done in the heat of your anger
> do not do penance with evil;
> comfort the one you have distressed
> with your goodness; that will help you.
> No one fears the one who does no evil.
> Good it is to be innocent.

In the full glare of the truth, one may think one has seen the One who has *not* been revealed, the One who can explain who needs explanation. The ironic use of "enjoys" (*njuter* in the original) should be noted.

The Ghost Sonata is the chamber play that has never failed to arouse interest from the time it first appeared in print until our own day. It has been labeled Strindberg's most pessimistic statement of his idea of human nature. It has been criticized for including what some people consider irrelevant and absurd matter. It has been included quite regularly on the required study lists for courses in modern drama. It has been interpreted and reinterpreted. But it has never failed to arouse interest. That fact accounts for its presentation in amazingly numerous productions in Sweden and abroad. Probably not a little of the interest stems from the common enough human curiosity about what is going on in "the strange house" next door, speculation about this in terms of personal experience, and reaching rather distressing conclusions about man and what he has made of his world.

Opus 3

The Ghost Sonata

Characters

DIRECTOR HUMMEL, *the old man*

ARKENHOLZ, *the student*

THE MILKMAID, *an apparition*

THE CARETAKER'S WIFE

THE CARETAKER

THE DEAD MAN, *a consul*

THE DARK LADY, *daughter of the Dead Man and the Caretaker's Wife*

THE COLONEL

ADÈLE, *the young lady*

AMALIA, *the Mummy, the Colonel's wife, Adèle's mother*

THE ARISTOCRAT, *called Baron Skanskorg, betrothed to the Dark Lady (the Caretaker's daughter)*

JOHANSSON, *Hummel's servant*

BENGTSSON, *the Colonel's servant*

LADY BEATE VON HOLSTEINKRONA, *Hummel's ex-fiancée, now a white-haired old lady*

THE COOK

BEGGARS

Scene 1

Setting

The corner of the first two floors of a modern apartment building; on the first floor a round living room; on the second story above it a balcony and a flagpole can be seen.

Through the Round Room's open windows can be seen when the shades are raised a white marble statue of a young woman, surrounded by palms and brightly lighted by sunlight. In the window to the left pots of hyacinths (blue, white, pink).

On the balcony rail in the corner one floor up can be seen a blue silk quilt and two white pillows. The windows to the left are hung with white sheets. It is a bright Sunday morning.

In the foreground in front of the façade is a green bench.

To the right in the foreground is a street drinking fountain, to the left a bulletin board (an advertising column).

To the left at the back is the entrance, which reveals the staircase, the stairs of white marble and the banister of mahogany and brass; on both sides of the entrance on the sidewalk are laurel bushes in tubs.

The corner with the Round Room faces also a cross street.

To the left of the entrance on the first floor is a window with a gossip mirror.

193

When the curtain rises the bells of several churches at a distance are ringing.

The entrance is open; a WOMAN IN BLACK *is standing motionless on the stairs.*

The CARETAKER'S WIFE *sweeps the entry way; then she polishes the brass in the entrance; then she waters the laurels.*

The OLD MAN *is sitting in a wheelchair by the advertisement column reading a newspaper; he has white hair and beard and wears glasses.*

The MILKMAID *comes in from the corner with milk bottles in a wire basket; she is wearing summer clothes, including brown shoes, black stockings, and a white beret; she takes off the beret and hangs it on the fountain; she wipes the sweat from her forehead; she takes a drink out of the dipper; she washes her hands; straightens her hair, using the water as a mirror.*

A steamboat bell can be heard ringing, and now and then the deep notes of an organ in a nearby church breaks the silence.

After a couple of minutes of silence, when the GIRL *has finished her toilet, the* STUDENT *comes in from the left, unshaven and showing he has not slept. He goes right up to the fountain. Pause.*[1]

STUDENT: May I use the dipper? (*The* GIRL *pulls the dipper toward herself.*) Haven't you finished soon? (*The* GIRL *looks at him with horror.*)

HUMMEL (*to himself*): Who's he talking to?—I don't see anyone!— Is he crazy? (*Continues to watch with amazement*)

STUDENT: What are you staring at? Do I look so terrible?—Well, I didn't get any sleep last night—I suppose you think I was out living it up . . . (*The* GIRL *as before*) Drinking punch, eh?— Do I smell of punch? (*The* GIRL *as before*) I haven't shaved, I know . . . Give me a drink of water, girl; I deserve it! (*Pause*) Well! Then I'll have to tell you—I bandaged up injured people and kept watch over the sick all night; you see, I was there when that house collapsed last night . . . now you know.

(GIRL *rinses the dipper; then gives him a drink.*)

STUDENT: Thanks! (*The* GIRL *does not move.*)

STUDENT (*slowly*): Will you do me a big favor? (*Pause*) The thing is my eyes are inflamed, as you see, and my hands have touched both the injured and the dead; so I can't safely touch my eyes . . . Would you take my clean handkerchief, dampen it in fresh water, and bathe my poor eyes?—Would you?—Would you be a good Samaritan? [2]

(GIRL *hesitates but does as he has requested.*)

STUDENT: Thank you! (*He takes up his purse. The* GIRL *makes a gesture indicating refusal.*) Forgive me for being thoughtless, but I'm not quite awake . . .

HUMMEL (*to the* STUDENT): Excuse me, but I heard you were in on the accident, last night . . . I was just reading about it, in the paper . . .

STUDENT: Is it in already?

HUMMEL: Yes, the whole thing; your picture, too, but they're sorry they didn't find out the name of the fine student . . .

STUDENT (*looks at the article*): Really? Yes, that's me! Well!

HUMMEL: Whom were you talking to just now?

STUDENT: Didn't you see? (*Pause.*)

HUMMEL: Is it impertinent to ask—to find out—what your name is?

STUDENT: What's the point? I don't like publicity—if you're praised, they find fault with you, too—the art of belittling has been developed to the nth degree—besides, I don't want any reward . . .

HUMMEL: Perhaps you're wealthy?

STUDENT: Not at all . . . the very opposite! I'm extremely poor.

HUMMEL: Listen . . . I think I've heard that voice of yours before . . . I had a friend when I was young who spoke like you—he's the only other person with the same pronunciation . . . Are you possibly related to Mr. Arkenholz, the merchant? [3]

STUDENT: He was my father.

HUMMEL: The ways of fate are strange . . . I saw you as a child, under particularly difficult circumstances . . .

STUDENT: Yes, they say I was born in the midst of a bankruptcy . . .

HUMMEL: Yes, exactly!

STUDENT: May I ask what your name is?

HUMMEL: I'm Director Hummel . . .

STUDENT: Are you . . . ? Then I do remember . . .

HUMMEL: You've often heard my name mentioned in your family, have you?

STUDENT: Yes!

HUMMEL: And perhaps mentioned with a certain disapproval?

   (STUDENT *remains silent.*)

HUMMEL: Yes, I can imagine!—I suppose they said I was the one who ruined your father?—Everyone who brings on his ruin by stupid speculation believes he was ruined by the one he couldn't fool. (*Pause*) The fact is your father made me lose 17,000 crowns, my total savings at the time.

STUDENT: It's strange how stories can be told in two such contrary ways.

HUMMEL: You surely don't think I'm lying?

STUDENT: What shall I think? My father didn't lie!

HUMMEL: That's very true—a father never lies . . . but I'm a father, too, so . . .

STUDENT: What are you trying to get at?

HUMMEL: I saved your father from disaster, and he repaid me with all the terrible hatred gratitude causes . . . He taught his family to slander me.

STUDENT: Perhaps you made him ungrateful by poisoning your help with unnecessary humiliation.

HUMMEL: All help is humiliating, sir.

STUDENT: What do you want of me?

HUMMEL: I don't demand the money, but, if you'll do me some small favors, I'll be well repaid. You see I'm a cripple; some say it's my own fault; others blame my parents; I prefer to blame life itself with its snares, for if one avoids one snare, one falls right into the next. But I can't run up stairs or ring doorbells, so I say to you: Help me!

STUDENT: What can I do?

HUMMEL: First of all, push my chair so I can read the playbills. I want to see what they're putting on tonight . . .

STUDENT (*pushes the wheelchair*): Don't you have a man with you?

HUMMEL: Yes, but he has gone on an errand. He'll soon be back . . . Are you a medical student?

STUDENT: No, I'm studying languages, but as far as that goes, I don't know what I'm going to be . . .

HUMMEL: Well, well!—Do you know mathematics?

STUDENT: Yes, pretty well.

HUMMEL: That's good!—Would you want a job perhaps?

STUDENT: Yes, why not?

HUMMEL: Fine! (*Reads a playbill*) They're giving *The Valkyrie*[4] this afternoon . . . Then the colonel and his daughter will be there, and, since he always sits at the end of the sixth row, I'll put you next to him . . . Would you call from the telephone kiosk over there and order a ticket for the sixth row, seat number 82?

STUDENT: Am I to go to the opera during the day?

HUMMEL: Yes! And you're to obey me; then it will go well for you! I want you to be happy, rich, and honored; your début yesterday as a brave rescuer will make you famous tomorrow—then your name will be worth a lot.

STUDENT (*going to the telephone kiosk*): What a strange adventure . . .

HUMMEL: Are you a gambler?

STUDENT: Yes, that's my misfortune . . .

HUMMEL: We'll make it your fortune!—Telephone now! (*He reads the paper.*)

(*The* LADY IN BLACK *has come out on the sidewalk and talks to the* CARETAKER'S WIFE; *the* OLD MAN *listens, but the audience does not hear anything.*)

(*The* STUDENT *comes in again.*)

HUMMEL: Did you get it?

STUDENT: Yes!

HUMMEL: Do you see that house?

STUDENT: I've certainly looked at it . . . I walked by here yesterday when the sun shone on the windows, and, imagining all the beauty and luxury there must be in there, I said to my companion: How lucky it would be to have an apartment there, four flights up, a beautiful young wife, two handsome children, and an income of 20,000 . . .

HUMMEL: Did you say that? Did you! There you are! I love that house, too . . .

STUDENT: Do you speculate in houses?

HUMMEL: Well-l, yes! But not in the way you mean . . .

STUDENT: Do you know the people who live there?

HUMMEL: All of them. At my age, one knows everybody, their fathers and forefathers, and one's always related to them in some way—I turned eighty recently—but no one knows me, not really— I am interested in the destinies of other people . .

(*The shade in the Round Room is raised; the* COLONEL—*dressed in civilian clothes—can be seen; after looking at the thermometer he goes back into the room, stopping in front of the marble statue.*)

HUMMEL: See, there's the colonel whom you'll be sitting next to this afternoon . . .

STUDENT: Is that the colonel? I don't understand any of this, but it's like a fairy tale . . .

HUMMEL: My whole life has been like a book of fairy tales, sir; but though the tales are different, they all hang together on a thread, and the theme recurs regularly.

STUDENT: And the marble statue in there?

HUMMEL: It's a statue of his wife, naturally . . .

STUDENT: Was she that wonderful?

HUMMEL: Wel-l-l! Yes!

STUDENT: Well, was she?

HUMMEL: We can't really judge a human being, can we?—And if I tell you that she left him, that he beat her, that she came back, that she remarried him, and that *she*'s sitting in there like a mummy and worships her own statue, you'd think *I*'m crazy.

STUDENT: I don't understand!

HUMMEL: I imagine not!—Then there's the hyacinth window. That's where his daughter lives . . . she's out riding now, but she'll be back soon . . .

STUDENT: Who's the dark lady talking with the caretaker's wife?

HUMMEL: Well, that's a little complicated, but it has to do with the dead man, up there where the white sheets [5] can be seen . . .

STUDENT: Who was he?

HUMMEL: He was a human being, like the rest of us, but what was most obvious was his vanity . . . If you were a Sunday child, you'd soon see him come out to look at the consulate's flag at half mast—he was a consul, you see, and liked crowns, lions, frills, and colored ribbons.

STUDENT: You mentioned Sunday child [6]—they say I was born on a Sunday . . .

HUMMEL: Really! Are you . . . ? I can believe that . . . I saw it in the color of your eyes . . . But then you can see what others can't. Have you noticed that?

STUDENT: I don't know what others see, but sometimes . . . well, one doesn't talk about that, of course . . .

HUMMEL: I was almost sure! But you can tell me . . . because I . . . understand things like that . . .

STUDENT: Yesterday, for example . . . I was drawn to the ordinary street where the house later collapsed . . . I got there and stopped in front of the building, which I had never seen before . . . Then I noticed a crack in the wall, heard the floors splitting; I jumped up and grabbed a child who was walking right below the wall . . . The next second the house collapsed . . . I was safe, but in my arms, where I thought I had the child, was nothing . . .

HUMMEL: Well, I must say . . . Though I did believe . . . Explain one thing: why did you gesture just now at the fountain? Why did you talk to yourself?

STUDENT: Didn't you see the milkmaid I was talking to?

HUMMEL (*shudders*): Milkmaid?

STUDENT: Yes, of course—the one who gave me the dipper.

HUMMEL: Really? That's how it was? . . . Well, I can't see, but I can do other things . . . (*A* WHITE-HAIRED WOMAN *sits down by the gossip mirror beside the window.*) Look at the old woman by the window! Do you see her?—Fine! She was my fiancée, once sixty years ago . . . I was twenty.—Don't be afraid—she doesn't recognize me! We see each other every day, but that doesn't affect me in the slightest, even though we vowed eternal faithfulness to each other then—eternal!

STUDENT: How foolish you were! We never say anything like that to our girls nowadays.

HUMMEL: Forgive us, young man, we didn't know any better!— But can you see that that woman once was young and beautiful?

STUDENT: No, I can't. Yes-s, there's something attractive about her face, but I can't see her eyes!

(*The* CARETAKER'S WIFE *comes out with a basket and spreads fir twigs.*[7])

HUMMEL: The caretaker's wife!—Well, the dark lady over there is her daughter by the dead man, and that's why her husband got his job as caretaker . . . but the dark lady has a lover, who's aristocratic and expects to get rich; he's in the midst of getting a divorce from his wife, who's giving him a stone house to get rid of him, you see. The aristocratic lover is the son-in-law of the dead man, and you can see his bed clothes being aired out on the balcony [8] up there . . . That is complicated, I think!

STUDENT: That's terribly complicated!

HUMMEL: Yes, it is, any way you look at it, though it seems simple.

STUDENT: But who was the dead man, then?

HUMMEL: You asked just now, and I answered; if you could look around the corner to the service entrance, you'd see a gang of beggars that he helped . . . when he felt like it . . .

STUDENT: So he was a charitable man?

HUMMEL: Yes . . . sometimes.

STUDENT: Not always?

HUMMEL: No! . . . People are like that! Now if you'll push my chair a little so I'm in the sun—I get terribly cold; when you can never be up and about, your blood congeals—I suppose I'm going to die soon—I know that, but before I do I have a few things to arrange—take my hand; feel how cold I am.

STUDENT: Like ice! (*Shrinks back*)

HUMMEL: Don't leave me; I'm tired; I'm alone; but I haven't always been like this, you understand; I have an unbelievably long life behind me—unbelievably—I have made people unhappy, and people have made me unhappy; the one will have to cancel out the other—but before I die, I want to see you happy . . . Our destinies are linked through your father—and other things . . .

STUDENT: But let go my hand; you're taking my strength; you're freezing me. What do you want?

HUMMEL: Patience, and you'll see . . . and understand . . . There comes the young lady . . .

STUDENT: The colonel's daughter?

HUMMEL: Yes! Daughter! Look at her!—Have you ever seen such a masterpiece?

STUDENT: She's like the marble statue in there . . .

HUMMEL: Well, that's her mother!

STUDENT: You're right—I've never seen such a woman born of woman.—Happy the man who'll lead her to the altar and home!

HUMMEL: You can see that!—Not everyone sees her beauty . . . Fine, that's how it's to be!

*

The YOUNG LADY *enters from the left dressed in the modern English Amazon* [9] *fashion; walks slowly, without looking at anyone, up to the entrance where she stops to say a few words to the* CARETAKER'S WIFE; *then she goes in. The* STUDENT *covers his eyes with his hand.*

HUMMEL: Are you weeping?

STUDENT: Before what's hopeless there's only despair!

HUMMEL: I can open doors and hearts just so I have an arm to do my will . . . Serve me, and you'll have the power . . .

STUDENT: Am I to make a pact? Am I to sell my soul?

HUMMEL: Sell nothing!—You see, I have *taken,* all my life; now I have a longing to give, give! But no one wants to receive . . . I am rich, very rich, but have no heirs—yes, one rascal who torments the life out of me . . . be like a son to me; inherit while I'm alive; enjoy life so I see it—at least from a distance.

STUDENT: What shall I do?

HUMMEL: Go and hear *The Valkyrie* first!

STUDENT: That *is* settled—what else?

HUMMEL: Tonight you'll be sitting in there in the round room!

STUDENT: How am I going to get in?

HUMMEL: Through *The Valkyrie!*

STUDENT: Why have you chosen me as your medium? Did you know me before this?

HUMMEL: Yes, of course! I've had my eyes on you for a long time . . . But look . . . up there on the balcony how the maid's raising the flag to half mast in honor of the consul . . . and she's turning the bed clothes . . . Do you see that blue quilt?—That was made for two to sleep under, but now it's for one . . .

(*The* YOUNG LADY *appears—she has changed her clothes—and waters the hyacinths in the window.*)

HUMMEL: There's my little girl! Look at her!—She's talking to the flowers. Isn't she like the blue hyacinth? . . . She gives them a drink, only pure water, and they transform the water into colors and fragrance . . . now the colonel's coming with the paper!— He's showing her the collapsed house . . . now he's pointing to your picture! She isn't indifferent . . . she's reading about your achievement . . . I think it's getting cloudy. What if it should rain? Then I'd be in a nice mess if Johansson doesn't get back soon . . .

(*It becomes cloudy and darkens; the* OLD WOMAN *by the gossip mirror closes her window.*)

HUMMEL: Now my fiancée's closing her window . . . Seventy-nine years old . . . The gossip mirror's the only mirror she uses, because in that she doesn't see herself, only the outside world, and from two directions, but the world can see her; she hasn't thought of that . . . A good-looking old woman, as far as that goes . . .

(*Now the* DEAD MAN *in his winding sheets comes out of the entrance.*)

STUDENT: Good God, what am I seeing?

HUMMEL: What do you see?

STUDENT: Don't you see the dead man, in the entrance?

HUMMEL: I see nothing, but I expected precisely this! Tell me . . .

STUDENT: He's going out on the street . . . (*Pause*) Now he's turning his head and looking at the flag.

HUMMEL: What did I say? I suspect he'll count the wreaths, too, and read the calling cards . . . woe to the one who's missing!

STUDENT: Now he's round the corner . . .

HUMMEL: He's going to count the beggars at the service entrance . . . the poor are very decorative: "followed by the blessings of many," yes, but he won't get my blessing!—Just between you and me, he was a big scoundrel . . .

STUDENT: But charitable . . .

HUMMEL: A charitable scoundrel, who was always thinking of a beautiful funeral . . . when he knew the end was near, he cheated the government out of 50,000 . . . now his daughter in another man's marriage is wondering about inheriting . . . the scoundrel . . . he hears everything we say, and let him!—There comes Johansson!

(JOHANSSON *enters from the left.*)

HUMMEL: Report (JOHANSSON *does so softly the audience cannot hear him.*) So he's not at home? You're a fool!—And the telegraph office?—Nothing! . . . Go on! . . . Six o'clock tonight?

That's fine!—Special edition?—His whole name! Student . . .
Arkenholz, born . . . parents . . . splendid . . . I think it's beginning to rain . . . What did he say? . . . Really! . . . Oh!—
He didn't want to?—Then he has to!—There comes the aristocrat!
—Push me around the corner, Johansson, so I can hear what the
poor people are saying . . . And, Arkenholz, wait for me
here . . . Do you understand?—Hurry, hurry!

(JOHANSSON *pushes the wheelchair around the corner.*)

(*The* STUDENT *stands looking at the* YOUNG LADY, *who is now
loosening the soil in the flowerpots. The* ARISTOCRAT *comes in
dressed in mourning, addresses the* DARK LADY *who has come out
onto the sidewalk.*)

ARISTOCRAT: Well, what can we do about that?—We'll have to wait!

LADY: But I can't wait!

ARISTOCRAT: Really? Then go to the country!

LADY: I don't want to.

ARISTOCRAT: Come this way; otherwise, they'll hear what we're saying. (*They go toward the bulletin board and continue their con-
versation so no one else hears them.* JOHANSSON *comes in from the
right. Goes up to the* STUDENT)

JOHANSSON: My master asked you not to forget that other matter!

STUDENT (*slowly*): Listen—tell me first: who is your master?

JOHANSSON: Well! He's a lot, and has been everything.

STUDENT: Is he sane?

JOHANSSON: Well, what's that?—All his life he has been looking for
a Sunday child, he says, but that need not be true . . .

STUDENT: What does he want? Is he greedy?

JOHANSSON: He wants power . . . All day long he rides about in his
chariot like the god Thor [10] . . . he looks at houses, tears them
down, opens streets, settles squares: but he breaks into houses, too,
creeps in through windows, plays havoc with people's lives, kills
his enemies, and never forgives.—Can you imagine, sir, that little
cripple has been a Don Juan, even though he has always lost his
women?

STUDENT: How do you explain that?

JOHANSSON: Well, he's so sly he gets the women to leave when he's tired of them . . . But now he's a sort of horse thief in the human market; he steals people, in many ways . . . He has stolen me literally out of the hands of justice . . . You see, I had made a mistake, but one which only he knew about; instead of having me locked up, he made me his slave; I slave for my food, which isn't the best . . .

STUDENT: What does he want to do in this house?

JOHANSSON: Well, I don't want to say! It's pretty complicated.

STUDENT: I think I'll walk away from all this . . .

JOHANSSON: Look, the young lady dropped her bracelet through the window . . . (*The* YOUNG LADY *has dropped her bracelet through the open window.*)

　(*The* STUDENT *goes up slowly, picks up the bracelet, and hands it to the* YOUNG LADY, *who thanks him stiffly. The* STUDENT *then goes back to* JOHANSSON.)

JOHANSSON: So you're thinking of leaving . . . That isn't as easy as you think once he has his net over your head . . . And he's afraid of nothing between heaven and earth . . . Yes, one thing, or, more accurately, one person . . .

STUDENT: Wait . . . maybe I know!

JOHANSSON: How can you?

STUDENT: I'll guess!—Is it . . . a little milkmaid he's afraid of?

JOHANSSON: He always turns away when he meets a milk cart . . and he talks in his sleep: he must have been in Hamburg once . . .

STUDENT: Can you believe this man?

JOHANSSON: You can believe everything and anything—about him!

STUDENT: What is he doing around the corner?

JOHANSSON: He's listening to the poor people . . . Sows a little word, picks out one stone at a time until the house collapses . . . figuratively speaking . . . you see, I'm an educated man and have been a bookdealer . . . Shall we go?

STUDENT: I have a hard time being ungrateful . . . This man rescued my father once, and now he's asking only a slight favor in return . . .

JOHANSSON: What?

STUDENT: I'm to see *The Valkyrie*.

JOHANSSON: I don't understand that . . . But he always has new ideas . . . See, now he's talking to the policeman . . . he always keeps in good with policemen and makes use of them, gets them involved, binds them with false promises and prospects, all the while he's pumping them.—You'll see he'll be received in the round room before nightfall! [11]

STUDENT: What does he want there? What does he have to do with the colonel?

JOHANSSON: Well . . . I can guess, but I don't know! You'll no doubt find out when you get there!

STUDENT: I'll never be received there . . .

JOHANSSON: That depends on you!—Go to *The Valkyrie* . . .

STUDENT: Is that the way?

JOHANSSON: Yes, since he said so!—Look, look at him, in his battle chariot, drawn in triumph by the beggars, who won't get one penny by way of reward, only a hint there'll be something at his funeral!

HUMMEL (*comes in, standing up in his wheelchair, pulled by a* BEGGAR, *followed by others*): Hail the noble young man, who in spite of danger to his own life saved many during yesterday's accident! Hail, Arkenholz! (*The* BEGGARS *uncover their heads but do not shout "hurrah." The* YOUNG LADY, *at the window, waves her handkerchief. The* COLONEL *stares out through his window. The* OLD WOMAN *stands up at her window. The* MAID *on the balcony raises the flag all the way.* HUMMEL *continues.*) Applaud him, fellow citizens. It's Sunday, of course, but the ass in the well and the grain on the field absolve us,[12] and though I'm no Sunday child, I have the gifts of prophecy and of healing, for I recalled a drowned person to life once . . . yes, but it was in Hamburg one Sunday forenoon like this . . .

(*The* MILKMAID *enters, seen only by the* STUDENT *and the old man* HUMMEL; *she stretches up her arms like a drowning person and fixes the glance of the old man.*)

HUMMEL (*sits down; collapses with horror*): Johansson! Take me away! Quickly!—Arkenholz, don't forget *The Valkyrie!*

STUDENT: What is all this?

JOHANSSON: We'll see! We'll certainly see!

[CURTAIN]

SCENE 2

The interior of the Round Room: at the back a white tile stove with a mirror, a clock, and candelabras; to the right the hall with a perspective of a green room with mahogany furniture; to the left is the statue, shadowed by palms, and can be concealed by curtains; to the left at the back a door to the Hyacinth Room, in which the YOUNG LADY *is sitting reading. The audience can see the back of the* COLONEL; *he is writing in the Green Room.*

BENGTSSON, *the servant, in livery, comes in from the hall with* JOHANSSON *in full dress and white tie.*

BENGTSSON: You're to serve while I take their coats. Have you ever done this before?

JOHANSSON: Well, I push a battle chariot days as you know, but in the evenings I serve as a waiter at parties, and it has always been my dream to get into this house . . . These people are queer, aren't they?

BENGTSSON: Yes-s, a little unusual, one might say.

JOHANSSON: Is it going to be a musical evening, or what?

BENGTSSON: It's the usual ghost supper, as we call it. They'll drink tea, not say a word, or the Colonel alone will speak; and then they'll crunch away at small cakes, all at the same time, so it sounds like rats in an attic.

JOHANSSON: Why is it called a ghost supper?

BENGTSSON: They look like ghosts . . . And they've kept this up for twenty years, always the same people, who say the same thing, or keep still so they won't have to be ashamed.

JOHANSSON: Isn't there a lady of the house, too?

BENGTSSON: Oh yes, but she's crazy; she sits in a closet because her eyes can't stand the light . . . She is sitting in here . . . (*Points at a wallpapered door in the wall*)

JOHANSSON: In there?

BENGTSSON: Yes indeed—I told you they're a little unusual . . .

JOHANSSON: What does she look like?

BENGTSSON: Like a mummy . . . Do you want to see her? (*Opens the wallpapered door*) See, there she is!

JOHANSSON: Good Heav–

MUMMY (*babbles*): Why do you open the door? Haven't I said it's to be closed? . . .

BENGTSSON (*coaxingly*): Ta, ta, ta, ta! Polly, be good now; then Polly'll get something good!—Pretty Polly!

MUMMY (*like a parrot*): Pretty Polly! Is Jacob there? Gr-r-r!

BENGTSSON: She thinks she's a parrot, and maybe she is . . . (*To the* MUMMY) Polly, whistle for us! (*The* MUMMY *whistles.*)

JOHANSSON: Well, I've seen a lot, but nothing to match this!

BENGTSSON: You see, when a house gets old, it gets moldy, and when people are together tormenting each other for a long time, they go crazy. This lady of the house—quiet, Polly!—this mummy has been sitting here for forty years—the same husband, the same furniture, the same relatives, the same friends . . . (*Closes the closet door*) And what has happened in this house—I hardly know . . . Look at that statue . . . it's the lady as a young woman!

JOHANSSON: Good Lord!—Is that the mummy?

BENGTSSON: Yes!—Why, it's enough to make one weep! But through the power of imagination or something else, this lady has acquired certain of the talkative bird's peculiarities— So she can't stand cripples and sick people . . . She can't stand her own daughter, because she's sick . . .

JOHANSSON: Is the young lady sick?

BENGTSSON: Didn't you know?

JOHANSSON: No! . . . And the colonel—who is he?

BENGTSSON: You'll find out, I suspect!

JOHANSSON (*observing the statue*): It's terrible to imagine . . . How old is the lady now?

BENGTSSON: No one knows . . . but they say that when she was thirty-five, she looked as if she were nineteen and she convinced the colonel that's what she was . . . In this house . . . Do you know what that black Japanese screen next to the couch is for?— It's called the death screen and is put up when someone's dying, exactly as in hospitals . . .

JOHANSSON: It's a terrible house . . . And the student wishes to get into it because he thinks it's Paradise . . .

BENGTSSON: What student? Oh, that one! The one who's coming here tonight . . . The colonel and the young lady met him at the opera, both of them found him charming . . . Hm! . . . But now it's my turn to ask: who's your master? The director in the wheelchair . . . ?

JOHANSSON: Well-l!—Is he coming, too?

BENGTSSON: He hasn't been invited.

JOHANSSON: That fellow comes uninvited! if necessary! . . .

(HUMMEL, *the old man, appears in the hall on crutches, wearing a frock coat and a top hat, steals forward, listening.*)

BENGTSSON: He's a regular rascal, eh?

JOHANSSON: Absolutely!

BENGTSSON: He looks like the devil himself!

JOHANSSON: And he's a magician, too, I think!—he goes through locked doors . . .

HUMMEL (*enters, takes* JOHANSSON *by the ear*): Scoundrel!—Watch out! (*To* BENGTSSON) Announce me to the colonel!

BENGTSSON: But we're expecting company . . .

HUMMEL: I know! But my visit's almost expected, if not exactly looked forward to . . .

BENGTSSON: Oh! What was the name? Director Hummel!

HUMMEL: Exactly!

(BENGTSSON *goes through the hall to the Green Room; he shuts the door to that room behind him.*)

HUMMEL (*to* JOHANSSON): Get out! (JOHANSSON *hesitates.*) Get out! (JOHANSSON *disappears into the hall. The* OLD MAN *inspects the room; stops in front of the statue with great amazement.*) Amalia! . . . It's she! . . . She! (*He wanders about the room, touching things; arranges his wig in front of the mirror; returns to the statue.*)

MUMMY (*from the closet*): Pretty Polly!

HUMMEL (*extremely startled*): What was that? Is there a parrot in the room? But I don't see any!

MUMMY: Is Jacob there?

HUMMEL: The place is haunted!

MUMMY: Jacob!

HUMMEL: I'm frightened! . . . So that's the kind of secrets they have in this house! (*He looks at a painting, his back to the closet.*) There he is! . . . He!

MUMMY (*comes out of closet, in back of* HUMMEL, *and jerks at his wig*): Gr-r? Is it you?

HUMMEL (*jumps*): Good God in heaven!—Who is it?

MUMMY (*speaking in her normal voice*): Is it you, Jacob?

HUMMEL: My name is Jacob, really . . .

MUMMY (*with emotion*): And mine is Amalia!

HUMMEL: No, oh no . . . Oh, good heav–

MUMMY: This is how I look! Yes!—And *have* looked like that! We learn a lot through living, don't we?—I live mostly in the closet, both to get out of seeing and to get out of being seen . . . But, Jacob, what are you looking for here?

HUMMEL: My child! Our child . . .

MUMMY: She's sitting there!

HUMMEL: Where?

MUMMY: There, in the Hyacinth Room!

HUMMEL (*looks at the young lady*): Yes, it's she! (*Pause*) What does her father—I mean the colonel—say? Your husband?

MUMMY: I was angry with him once; then I told him everything . . .

HUMMEL: Wel-l?

MUMMY: He didn't believe me but answered: "That's what all wives say when they want to kill their husbands."—That was a terrible crime—why, his whole life has been falsified, his family tree, too; I sometimes read in the book of peerage, and then I think: she has a false identification card like an ordinary maid, and that's punishable in the reformatory.

HUMMEL: Many do—it seems to me I remember yours had a false year of birth . . .

MUMMY: My mother taught me to do that . . . it wasn't my fault . . . But you had the biggest blame in our crime, though . . .

HUMMEL: No, your husband caused our crime when he took my fiancée from me! My nature's such I can't forgive before I have punished—I took that as an imperative duty . . . I still do!

MUMMY: What are you after in this house? What do you want? How did you get in?—Is it my daughter? If you touch her, you'll have to die!

HUMMEL: I want to do her anything but harm!

MUMMY: But you'll have to spare her father!

HUMMEL: No!

MUMMY: Then you'll have to die—in this room—behind this screen . . .

HUMMEL: Maybe . . . but I can't let go once I have my teeth in something . . .

MUMMY: You want her to marry the student. Why? Why, he's nothing and has nothing.

HUMMEL: He'll get rich, through me!

MUMMY: Were you invited to come here tonight?

HUMMEL: No, but I intend to have myself invited to the ghost supper!

MUMMY: Do you know who is coming?

HUMMEL: Not really.

MUMMY: The baron . . . who lives upstairs, and whose father-in-law was buried today . . .

HUMMEL: The one who's getting divorced to marry the caretaker's daughter . . . The one who once was your—lover!

MUMMY: And then your former fiancée, who was seduced by my husband, is coming . . .

HUMMEL: A fine collection . . .

MUMMY: God, if we could die! *If* we could only die!

HUMMEL: Why do you get together?

MUMMY: Crimes and secrets and guilt bind us together!—We have broken up and left each other infinitely many times, but then we're drawn together again . . .

HUMMEL: I think the colonel's coming . . .

MUMMY: Then I'll go in to Adèle . . . (*Pause*) Jacob, consider what you're doing! Spare him . . . (*Pause. She goes.*)

COLONEL (*enters, cold, reserved*): Please be seated! (*The* OLD MAN *sits down slowly. Pause. The* COLONEL *stares at* HUMMEL.) You're the one who wrote this letter, sir?

HUMMEL: Yes!

COLONEL: Your name is Hummel?

HUMMEL: Yes! (*Pause*)

COLONEL: Since I know you've bought up all my outstanding notes, it follows that I'm at your mercy. What do you want?

HUMMEL: I want to be paid, in one way or another.

COLONEL: How?

HUMMEL: Very simply—let's not talk about the money—only put up with me in your house—as a guest!

COLONEL: If you'll be satisfied with that little . . .

HUMMEL: Thank you!

COLONEL: And then?

HUMMEL: Fire Bengtsson!

COLONEL: Why should I? My faithful servant, who has been with me for a generation—who has the national medal [13] for faithful service—why should I fire him?

HUMMEL: He's all that—only in your imagination—He's not what he seems to be!

COLONEL: Who is really?

HUMMEL (*flinches*): True! But Bengtsson has to go!

COLONEL: Do you want to run my house?

HUMMEL: Yes! Since I own everything here—furniture, curtains, dishes, linens . . . and the rest!

COLONEL: What rest?

HUMMEL: Everything! I own everything—it's mine!

COLONEL: All right, it's yours! But my coat of arms and my good name will still be mine!

HUMMEL: No, not even that! (*Pause*) You're not a nobleman!

COLONEL: What? Have you no shame?

HUMMEL (*takes up a paper*): If you'll read this excerpt from the book of peerage, you'll see that the family whose name you bear has been extinct for a hundred years!

COLONEL (*reads*): I've heard rumors like that, but I inherited my name from my father . . . (*Reads*) That's right! You're right . . . I'm not a nobleman!—Not even that!—Then I'll take off my signet ring.—It's true—it belongs to you . . . Here you are!

HUMMEL (*puts the ring in his pocket*): Now we'll continue!—You aren't a colonel, either!

COLONEL: I'm not?

HUMMEL: No! You were an acting colonel in the American voluntary service, but after the war in Cuba [14] and the reorganization of the army all earlier titles were abolished . . .

COLONEL: Is that true?

HUMMEL (*touching a pocket*): Do you want to read?

COLONEL: No, that's not necessary! . . . Who are you that have the right to strip me like this?

HUMMEL: You'll see, I suspect! But as far as the stripping goes . . . do you know who you are?

COLONEL: Have you no shame?

HUMMEL: Take off your wig and look in the mirror, but take out your teeth and shave off your moustache, let Bengtsson untie your corset, and we'll see if the servant *x y z* doesn't recognize himself; the one who sponged food in a certain kitchen . . .

(*The* COLONEL *reaches for the handbell on the table.*)

HUMMEL (*stopping him*): Don't touch the bell; don't call Bengtsson —if you do, I'll have him arrested . . . The guests are coming— Keep calm; we'll keep on playing our old roles.

COLONEL: Who are you? I recognize your look and your voice . . .

HUMMEL: Don't ask, just keep still, and do as you're told!

STUDENT (*enters; bows to the* COLONEL): Colonel!

COLONEL: Welcome to my house, young man! Your noble behavior at the great disaster has put your name on everyone's lips, and I consider it an honor to have you in my house . . .

STUDENT: Colonel, my humble origins . . . your brilliant name and noble birth . . .

COLONEL: May I present Mr. Arkenholz, Director Hummel . . . Would you join the ladies?—I must finish a talk with the director . . .

(*The* STUDENT *is shown into the Hyacinth Room, where he can be seen talking shyly with the* YOUNG LADY.)

COLONEL: A superb young man, musical, sings, writes poetry . . . If he were a nobleman and an equal, I'd have nothing against . . . well . . .

HUMMEL: What?

COLONEL: My daughter . . .

HUMMEL: *Your* daughter!—Apropos her, why is she always sitting in there?

COLONEL: She has to sit in the Hyacinth Room when she's not out! It's a peculiarity of hers . . . There we have Lady Beate von Holsteinkrona . . . a charming woman . . . a secular canoness [15] with an income just big enough for her rank and circumstances . . .

HUMMEL (*to himself*): My fiancée! (*She enters; white-haired; looks crazy.*)

COLONEL: Lady von Holsteinkrona, Director Hummel! (*She curtseys; sits down.*)

(*The* ARISTOCRAT *comes in, looks secretive, dressed in mourning; sits down.*)

COLONEL: Baron Skanskorg . . .

HUMMEL (*in an aside, without getting up*): It's the jewel thief, I think . . . (*To the* COLONEL) Bring in the mummy, and the collection's complete . . .

COLONEL (*in the door to the Hyacinth Room*): Polly!

MUMMY (*enters*): Gr-r!

COLONEL: Shall we have the young people come in, too?

HUMMEL: No! Not the young people! They're to be spared . . .

(*All of them sit in a circle, silent.*)

COLONEL: May we have the tea served now?

HUMMEL: What would be the point? No one likes tea, and that's why we're not going to play the hypocrite. (*Pause*)

COLONEL: Shall we converse then?

HUMMEL (*slowly and with pauses*): Talk about the weather, which we know; ask how we are, which we know; I prefer silence; then one hears thoughts and sees the past; silence can conceal nothing . . . which words can; I read the other day that the differences between languages really arose among primitive peoples in order to conceal the secrets of the tribe from the rest; so languages are symbols, and the one who finds the key understands all the languages of the world; but that does not prevent secrets from being revealed without a key, and especially if paternity has to be proved, but proof in court is something else; two false witnesses are enough if they're in full agreement, but on such issues as I'm referring to, one does not take any witnesses along; nature itself has provided man with a sense of shame, which tries to conceal what should be concealed; still, we glide into situations without wanting to, and opportunities sometimes present themselves, when the most secret of secrets must be revealed, when the mask is torn from the deceiver, when the villain is exposed . . .

(*Pause; all observe each other in silence.*)

How quiet it has become!

(*Long silence*)

For example: here in this respectable house, in this beautiful home, in which beauty, culture, and wealth have been united . . .

(*Long silence*)

All of us sitting here, we know who we are . . . don't we? . . . I don't need to say . . . and you know me, even though you pretend you don't . . . In there my daughter, *mine,* is sitting—you know that, too . . . She has lost the desire to live without knowing why . . . but she withered in this air which breathed crimes, deception, and all kinds of falseness . . . that's why I sought a friend for her, in whose presence she could experience light and warmth from a noble act . . .

(*Long silence*)

That was my mission in this house: to get rid of the weeds, expose the crime, bring the accounts to a conclusion, so that the young people may have a fresh start in this home, which I have given them!

(*Long silence*)

Now I grant you safe conduct, each and every one in turn and order—the one who stays I'll have arrested!

(*Long silence*)

Hear how the clock ticks away, like the deathwatch beetle in the

wall! Can you hear what it says? "Time! Time! Time! Time!"
When it strikes, in a little while, then your time is up; then you
may go, but not before. But it threatens first, before it strikes!—
Listen! Now it's warning you, "The clock can strike." I, too, can
strike.

(*He strikes the table with his crutch.*)

Did you hear that?

(*Silence*)

MUMMY (*goes up to the clock and stops it; then speaks lucidly and
seriously*): But I can stop time in its course—I can reduce the past
to nothing, undo what has been done; but not with bribes, not
with threats—but through suffering and repentance—(*Goes up to
HUMMEL*) We are poor human beings, we know that; we have
sinned; we have done wrong, we like everyone else. We are not
what we seem, for we are essentially better than ourselves when
we condemn our sins and faults; but that you, Jacob Hummel,
with your false name, insist on being our judge shows that you
are worse than we miserable creatures! Nor are you the one you
seem to be!—You are a thief of human beings, for you stole me
once with false promises; you murdered the consul who was
buried here today; you killed him with his promissory notes—you
have stolen the student by binding him with an imaginary debt
of his father's, who never owed you a penny . . .

(HUMMEL *has tried to stand up to speak, but has fallen back in
his chair and shrinks more and more during the following
speeches.*)

MUMMY: But there is a dark spot in your life I don't quite know,
but I suspect . . . I think Bengtsson knows about it! (*Rings the
table bell*)

HUMMEL: No, not Bengtsson! Not that fellow!

MUMMY: Oh ho, so he does know! (*Rings again*)

(*The little* MILKMAID *appears in the hall doorway, unseen by
everyone but* HUMMEL, *who flinches; the* MILKMAID *disappears
when* BENGTSSON *comes in.*)

MUMMY: Do you know this man, Bengtsson?

BENGTSSON: Yes, I know him, and he knows me. Life has its ups and downs, as you know, and I have worked for him, and he has worked for me. He was, for example, a sponger as the cook's boy friend in my kitchen for two whole years—since he had to leave at three o'clock, dinner was ready at two, and the family had to eat food warmed up after that ox—but he drank up the meat juices, too, so that what was left had to be eked out with water—he sat out there like a vampire sucking all the nutritive value out of the house so that we became like skeletons—and he tried to get us into prison when we called the cook a thief.

Later on I ran across this man in Hamburg under another name. He was a loan shark or bloodsucker; but he was also accused of luring a girl out on to the ice to drown her, because she had witnessed a crime he was afraid would be discovered . . .

MUMMY (*brushes her hand across* HUMMEL's *face*): That's you! Hand over the promissory notes and your last will and testament!

(JOHANSSON *appears in the hall door and watches the scene with great interest since he is about to be set free from slavery.*)

HUMMEL *takes out a bundle of papers and throws it on the table.*)

MUMMY (*strikes* HUMMEL's *back*): Polly! Is Jacob there?

HUMMEL (*like a parrot*): Jacob is there!—Pretty Polly! G-r-r-r!

MUMMY: Can the clock strike?

HUMMEL (*clucks*): The clock can strike! (*Imitates the cuckoo clock*) Cuck-oo, cuckoo! . . .

MUMMY (*opens the closet door*): The clock has struck!—Get up; go into the closet where I have been sitting for twenty years weeping over our sin.—There's a cord hanging in there that can represent the one you strangled the consul with up there, and with which you intended to strangle your benefactor . . . Go! (HUMMEL *goes into the closet. The* MUMMY *shuts the door.*) Bengtsson, put the screen in front of it! The death screen!

(BENGTSSON *puts the screen in front of the door.*)

MUMMY: It is done!—God be merciful to his soul!

ALL: Amen!

  (*Long silence*)

  (*In the Hyacinth Room the* YOUNG LADY *accompanies the* STU-
DENT *by playing a harp as he recites the following song after a
prelude.*)

I saw the sun, so I seemed
to have seen the Hidden One;
everyman enjoys his deeds;
happy the one who does good.
For deeds done in the heat of your anger
do not do penance with evil;
comfort the one you have distressed
with your goodness; that will help you.
No one fears the one who does no evil;
Good is it to be innocent.[16]

[CURTAIN]

SCENE 3

  *A room in a somewhat bizarre style, oriental motifs. Hyacinths
of all colors everywhere. On the tile stove is a large seated Buddha
with a bulb in his lap, and out of it the stalk of a shallot has shot
up, bearing a globe-shaped cluster of white starlike flowers.*

  (*To the right at the back, a door out to the Round Room: the
COLONEL and the MUMMY are sitting there silent, doing nothing;
even a part of the death screen can be seen. To the left: a door to
the dining area and kitchen.*

  The STUDENT *and the* YOUNG LADY (ADÈLE) *by the table; she sits
at her harp; he is standing.*

YOUNG LADY: Sing for my flowers!

STUDENT: Is this the flower of your soul?

YOUNG LADY: My only one! Do you love the hyacinth?

STUDENT: I love it above all others—its virginal form, which rises slim and straight from the bulb, rests on the water and sinks its pure white roots into the colorless water; I love its colors: the innocent pure snow white, the lovely honey yellow, the youthful pink, the mature red, but above all the blue, the dewy, deep-eyed, faithful blue [17] . . . I love them all, more than gold and pearls, have loved them since I was a child . . . they have all the splendid qualities I lack . . . But! . . .

YOUNG LADY: What?

STUDENT: My love is not returned, for these beautiful flowers hate me . . .

YOUNG LADY: What do you mean?

STUDENT: Their fragrance, strong and pure from the first winds of spring which have passed over melting snow, confuses my senses, deafens me, blinds me, crowds me out of the room, bombards me with poisonous arrows that make my heart sad and my head hot! Don't you know the story of this flower?

YOUNG LADY: Tell it!

STUDENT: But first the interpretation. The bulb is the earth, which rests in the water or lies in the dust; now the stalk shoots up, straight as the earth's axis, and at the top sit six-pointed starflowers.

YOUNG LADY: And above the earth the stars! That's wonderful. Where did you learn that? How did you see that?

STUDENT: Let me think!—In your eyes!—So it's a copy of the cosmos . . . That's why Buddha sits with the bulb, the earth, brooding over its growing outward and upward, transforming itself into a heaven.—Poor earth's to become a heaven! Buddha's waiting for that.

YOUNG LADY: Now I see—isn't the snowflake six-pointed like the hyacinth?

STUDENT: You're right!—Then the snowflakes are falling stars . . .

YOUNG LADY: And the snowdrop is a snowstar . . . grown out of snow.

STUDENT: But yellow and red Sirius, the largest and the most beautiful of the stars in the firmament, is the narcissus with its yellow and red chalice and six white rays . . .

YOUNG LADY: Have you seen the shallot in bloom?

STUDENT: Yes, of course I have.—It bears its flowers in a ball, a globe like the heavenly dome strewn with white stars . . .

YOUNG LADY: Wonderful! Whose thought was that?

STUDENT: Yours!

YOUNG LADY: Yours!

STUDENT: Ours!—We have given birth to something together—we are married . . .

YOUNG LADY: Not yet . . .

STUDENT: What remains?

YOUNG LADY: Waiting, trials, patience!

STUDENT: Fine! Try me! (*Pause*) Tell me! Why are your parents sitting so silent in there, without saying a single word?

YOUNG LADY: Because they haven't anything to say to each other, because the one doesn't believe what the other says. My father put it like this: What's the point of talking—we can't fool each other anyway.

STUDENT: That's terrible . . .

YOUNG LADY: There comes the cook . . . Look at her, how big and fat she is . . .

STUDENT: What does she want?

YOUNG LADY: She wants to ask me about dinner—you see, I keep house while Mother's ill . . .

STUDENT: Do we have to worry about the kitchen?

YOUNG LADY: Well, we have to eat . . . Look at the cook—I can't bear to look at her . . .

STUDENT: Who is that huge woman?

YOUNG LADY: She belongs to the Hummel family of vampires; she eats us up . . .

STUDENT: Why don't you fire her?

YOUNG LADY: She won't go! We can't manage her—we have her for our sins . . . Don't you see we're wasting away . . .

STUDENT: Don't you get food?

YOUNG LADY: Yes, we get many dishes, but all the strength is gone . . . She boils the meat until we get only fibers and water while she drinks up the stock herself; and when it's a roast, she cooks it until it's drained of juices and drinks the stock herself; everything she touches loses its juice—it's as if she sucked with her eyes; we get the warmed-over leavings when she has drunk the coffee; she drinks wine out of the bottles and fills them with water . . .

STUDENT: Send her away!

YOUNG LADY: We can't!

STUDENT: Why not?

YOUNG LADY: We don't know! She won't go! No one can manage her—she has robbed us of our strength!

STUDENT: May I get rid of her for you?

YOUNG LADY: No! I think it's supposed to be the way it is!—Now she's here. She'll ask what we're to have for dinner. I'll say this and that . . . she'll object, and it will be as she wants.

STUDENT: Let her decide by herself, then.

YOUNG LADY: She doesn't want to.

STUDENT: It's a strange house! It's bewitched!

YOUNG LADY: Yes!—But now she turned back when she saw you!

COOK (*in the doorway*): No, that wasn't why! (*Grins so her teeth show*)

STUDENT (*to the cook*): Get out!

COOK: When I want to! (*Pause*) Now I want to! (*Disappears*)

YOUNG LADY: Don't get excited!—Practice patience! She's one of the ordeals we're undergoing in this home. But we have a maid, too. We have to tidy up and clean after she's through!

STUDENT: Now I'm sinking! *Cor in æthere!* A song!

YOUNG LADY: Wait!

STUDENT: A song!

YOUNG LADY: Patience!—This room is called the room of ordeals—
it's beautiful to look at but consists of nothing but pure flaws . . .

STUDENT: Unbelievable; but one must look into that. It's beautiful
but a little cold. Why don't you have a fire going?

YOUNG LADY: It smokes . . .

STUDENT: Can't the chimney be cleaned?

YOUNG LADY: That doesn't help . . . Do you see the writing. desk
over there?

STUDENT: An exceptionally beautiful one!

YOUNG LADY: But one leg's too short. Every day I put a piece of cork
under the leg, but the maid takes it away when she sweeps, and I
have to cut a new one. The penholder's inky every morning, and
the writing utensils, too; I have to wash them when she's through
every blessed day. (*Pause*) What's the worst job you know?

STUDENT: Counting laundry! Ugh!

YOUNG LADY: That's my job! Ugh!

STUDENT: What else?

YOUNG LADY: To be awakened at night when I have to get up to put
the upper hook on the window . . . the one the maid has forgotten.

STUDENT: What else?

YOUNG LADY: To get up on a ladder and repair the damper cord
after the maid has torn it off.

STUDENT: What else?

YOUNG LADY: To sweep after her, to dust after her, to make a fire in
the tile stove after her—she just puts in the wood! To watch the
dampers, to dry the glasses, to set the table over again, to open
the bottles, to open the windows and air out, to make my bed
over again, to rinse the water decanter when it gets green with
algae, to buy matches and soap that we're always out of, to wipe
chimneys and trim the wicks, so the lamps won't smoke, and so
the lamps won't go out when we have company, I have to fill
them myself . . .

STUDENT: A song!

YOUNG LADY: Wait!—First the drudgery, the drudgery of keeping the dirt of life at a distance.

STUDENT: But you're wealthy, have two servants!

YOUNG LADY: That doesn't help! It wouldn't even if we had three! It's hard to live, and I'm tired sometimes . . . Imagine having a nursery, too!

STUDENT: The greatest joy of all . . .

YOUNG LADY: And the most expensive . . . Is life worth that much trouble?

STUDENT: I suppose it depends on the reward one expects for all that trouble . . . I wouldn't shrink from anything if I could win your hand.

YOUNG LADY: Don't talk like that!—You can never win me.

STUDENT: Why not?

YOUNG LADY: You may not ask that question. (*Pause*)

STUDENT: You dropped the bracelet from the window . . .

YOUNG LADY: Because my hand has become so thin . . . (*Pause*)
    (COOK *appears with a Japanese bottle in her hand.*)

YOUNG LADY: There's the one who's devouring me and all of us.

STUDENT: What's that in her hand?

YOUNG LADY: It's a coloring bottle with scorpion letters on it! It's soya, which changes water to bouillon, which replaces the juices, in which one cooks cabbage, and of which one makes turtle soup.

STUDENT (*to the* COOK): Get out!

COOK: You suck the strength out of us, and we out of you; we take the blood, and you get the water in return—colored water. It is coloring!—Now I'll go, but I'll stay anyway as long as I want to! (*Goes*)

STUDENT: Why did Bengtsson get a medal?

YOUNG LADY: Because of his great merits.

STUDENT: Hasn't he any flaws?

YOUNG LADY: Yes, very great ones, but one doesn't get a medal for those. (*They smile.*)

STUDENT: You have a lot of secrets in this house . . .

YOUNG LADY: Like all others . . . Let us keep ours! (*Pause*)

STUDENT: Do you like frankness?

YOUNG LADY: Yes, within reason!

STUDENT: Sometimes I get a mad urge to say everything I think, but I know the world would collapse if one were really frank. (*Pause*) I was at a funeral the other day . . in church—it was very solemn and beautiful.

YOUNG LADY: That was Director Hummel's?

STUDENT: My false benefactor's, yes!—At the head of the coffin stood an older friend of the dead man, and he held the mace; the minister impressed me because of his dignified manner and his moving words.—I wept, all of us wept.—Afterward we went to an inn . . . There I learned that the mace bearer had loved the dead man's son . . .

  (*The* YOUNG LADY *stares fixedly at him trying to understand what he means.*)

STUDENT: And that the dead man had borrowed money from his son's admirer . . . (*Pause*) The next day the minister was arrested—he had embezzled the church funds!—That *was* nice, wasn't it?

YOUNG LADY: Ugh! (*Pause*)

STUDENT: Do you know what I'm thinking about you now?

YOUNG LADY: Don't tell me—then I'll die!

STUDENT: I have to; otherwise I'll die! . . .

YOUNG LADY: In the insane asylum they say everything they think . . .

STUDENT: Exactly!—My father ended up in an insane asylum . . .

YOUNG LADY: Was he sick?

STUDENT: No, he was well, but he was crazy! Well, it broke out once—under these circumstances . . . Like all the rest of us he had a circle of acquaintances that for the sake of brevity he called friends; they were a crowd of mean wretches like people in general. But he had to have some companionship since he couldn't be absolutely isolated. Well, one doesn't tell people what one thinks of them ordinarily, and he didn't, either. Of course he knew how false they were; he knew their treachery thoroughly . . . but he was a wise man and well brought up, so he was always polite. But one day he gave a big party—it was in the evening; he was tired after the day's work, and from the effort partly to keep still, partly to talk nonsense with his guests . . .

(*The* YOUNG LADY *shudders.*)

STUDENT: Well, at the table he tapped for silence, took his glass to give his speech . . . Then the brakes let go, and in a long speech he stripped the whole company, one after the other, told them all their falseness. And weary he sat down right on the table and told them to go to hell!

YOUNG LADY: Ugh!

STUDENT: I was there, and I'll never forget what happened afterward! . . . Father and Mother came to blows, the guests rushed to the door . . . and Father was taken to the insane asylum where he died! (*Pause*) Keeping still too long, quiet waters turn rotten, and that's how it is in this house, too. There's something more that's rotten here! And I thought it was Paradise when I saw you go in the first time . . . Then I stood there on a Sunday morning looking in; I saw a colonel who was not a colonel; I had a noble benefactor who was a bandit and had to hang himself; I saw a mummy who was not a mummy, and a virgin— talking about that: where is virginity? where is beauty? In nature and in my mind when it's in its Sunday clothes! Where is honor and faith? In fairy tales and children's plays! where is anything that keeps what it promises? . . . In my imagination!—Now your flowers have poisoned me, and I have given the poison to you—I asked that you would be my wife in a home with poetry, song, and music; and then the cook came in . . . *Sursum corda!* Try once more to strike fire and glory out of the golden harp . . . Try, I beg you; I ask it on my knees . . . Well, then I'll do it myself! (*Takes the harp, but the strings make no sound.*) It's deaf and silent! Imagine the most beautiful flowers are so poisonous, are the most poisonous—why, the curse rests on all creation and on life . . . Why didn't you want to be my bride? Because you're sick at the very source of life . . . now I feel the vampire in the kitchen beginning to suck me dry; it's a lamia [18] that nurses the children—it's always in the kitchen that the family's children are nipped in the bud, if they haven't already been in the bedroom . . . there are poisons that take away sight, and poisons that open eyes—I seem to be born with the latter kind, for I can't see the ugly as beautiful, or call evil good—I can't! Jesus Christ descended into hell—that was his journey on earth, this madhouse, this reformatory, this charnel house the earth; and the madmen killed him, when he wanted to set them free, but the robber was released, the robber always gets people's sympathy!—Alas for all of us. Savior of the world, save us; we perish!

(*The* YOUNG LADY *has collapsed, seems to be dying, rings the bell, and* BENGTSSON *comes in.*)

YOUNG LADY: Bring the screen! Quickly—I'm dying!

(BENGTSSON *fetches the screen, opens it, and places it in front of the* YOUNG LADY.)

STUDENT: The liberator is coming! Welcome, pale and gentle one!— Sleep, beautiful, unhappy, innocent girl, without blame for your suffering, sleep without dreams, and, when you reawaken . . . may you be greeted by a sun that does not burn, in a home without dust, by kinsmen without shame, by a love without flaw . . . Wise, gentle Buddha, sitting there waiting for a heaven to grow out of the earth, grant me patience in my trials, purity of will, that hope may not come to nought!

(*The strings of the harp sigh; the room is filled with a white light.*)

I saw the sun, so I seemed
to have seen the Hidden One;
everyman enjoys his deeds;
happy the one who does good.
For deeds done in the heat of your anger

do not do penance with evil;
comfort the one you have distressed
with your goodness; that will help you.
No one fears the one who does no evil;
Good it is to be innocent.

  (*Moaning can be heard behind the screen.*)
Poor little child, child of this world of illusions, guilt, suffering,
and death, the world of everlasting change, disappointments, and
pain! May the Lord of Heaven be merciful to you on your
journey . . .

  (*The room disappears; Böcklin's* Island of the Dead [19] *becomes the backdrop; soft, quiet, pleasantly sad music can be
heard from outside.*

[CURTAIN]

Notes on

'The Ghost Sonata'

1. The setting is what Strindberg could see from his apartment windows and the street below his Stockholm home shortly after the turn of the century. The sounds (the church bells, the sweeping of the entry, the gushing fountain, the ringing of the steamboat bell, the deep notes from the church organ); the plants (potted palms, laurels, and hyacinths); the dress of the people, including that of the white-capped student; and various items such as the bulletin board and the gossip mirror (which was supposed to permit one to see without being seen) were typical of the time.

2. See Stephen C. Bandy's "Strindberg's Biblical Sources for *The Ghost Sonata*," *Scandinavian Studies* 40 (August 1968): 200–9. The pertinent passage occurs in John 4:7–14.

3. A closer translation of the original, *"som inte kunde säga fönster, utan alltid sa funster,"* would be, "who couldn't say window, but always said wendow." Incidentally, the name Arkenholz has impressed many as German in origin and perhaps in implication. I have, however, seen no evidence indicating that Strindberg meant anything particular by the name (*Ark,* ark; *holz,* wood). Noah's Ark was, of course, reserved for the elect.

4. Richard Wagner's opera *Die Walküre (The Valkyrie),* 1854, reflects Schopenhauer's pessimistic views of man and life. *The Valkyrie,* which is part of *The Ring of the Nibelung,* certainly conveys the conclusion that the world is evil and that life is not worth the living.

5. Covering windows with white sheets during mourning is a Swedish tradition, just as flying the flag at half mast in honor of someone dead is a common western practice.

6. The old notion was that a child born on Sunday has an especially

229

powerful sixth sense, as the following lines suggest. Arkenholz, for example, sees the dead as well as the living.

7. A Swedish funeral custom.

8. Even to this day one can see bed clothes aired daily on balconies of Swedish apartment houses.

9. In riding costume or habit.

10. The old Scandinavian god of thunder. For details about him and his chariot, see Peter A. Munch's *Norse Mythology: Legends of Gods and Heroes,* trans. Sigurd B. Hustvedt (New York: American-Scandinavian Foundation, 1970).

11. Strindberg's biographers and others assume his model was one Isaac Hirsch, a wealthy philanthropist, whose actions Strindberg observed and whose motives he suspected. The preceding and following lines about Hummel are a reflection then of Strindberg's use of the people about him as sources for material for his creative writing. An all-too-obvious do-gooder outside a fine apartment house could be wondered at and was.

12. See Luke 14:5: "Which of you shall have an ass or an ox fallen into a pit, and will not straightway pull him out on the sabbath day?"

13. A common Swedish practice: honoring servants for long and faithful service.

14. The Spanish-American War (1898). Swedes have participated in American wars from the Revolution on, as Strindberg notes in various places in his works.

15. *Stiftsfröken* is difficult to translate. The woman who is so classified is an unmarried noblewoman who belongs to an order providing her with an income designed to cover the bare necessities of food, shelter, clothing, and keeping up appearances.

16. Literally: "I saw the sun, so it seemed to me as if I had seen the Hidden One [the One who is veiled, concealed]; every human being "enjoys" his deeds; happy the one who practices good. For the deed of your wrath which you have done do not make up for it with evil; comfort the one you have distressed with your goodness; you will have comfort [from that]. No one fears [the one] who did no evil; it is good to be innocent."

17. See any encyclopedia for an explanation of the symbolic signifi-

cance of colors and flowers. Strindberg, incidentally, like most Swedes of his time had botanized in the tradition of Carl von Linné, the great eighteenth-century Swedish botanist.

18. A lamia is a vampire and a man-eater with the head and breasts of a woman and the body of a serpent.

19. The famous Swiss artist Arnold Böcklin. A copy of this painting was hung on either side of the proscenium in the Intimate Theater.

Introduction to
'The Pelican'

THE OLD NOTION that the pelican feeds its young with its own life blood has long since been rejected by those who know birds, but the notion that the pelican may serve as a symbol of motherly self-sacrifice has at least an ideational survival in the generally accepted notion that mothers are sacred and therefore above criticism. That Strindberg had long before 1907 rejected the validity of that notion is obvious to anyone who remembers such mothers as Laura in *The Father* (1887), Tekla in *Creditors* (1888), and Alice in *The Dance of Death* (1900). In none of his earlier plays had he concentrated his attention on a mother and motherhood as intensely as he did in his fourth chamber play. Practically everything anyone in the ensemble of characters says or does in *The Pelican* concerns one mother—what she is, what she has done, and what her family has become as a result. Strindberg does not, of course, present the mother in this play as typical.

The Swedes who regard *The Pelican* as a sort of sequel to the companion plays *The Dance of Death* I and II are undoubtedly right within certain limits. The same husband and wife probably served as primary models for the two couples. Elise and her late husband did celebrate their silver anniversary after twenty-five years of marital hell. It is as Martin Lamm and others have pointed out, as if Strindberg, having heaped the major share of the blame on Edgar, the husband, in *The Dance of Death,* was now inclined to take a closer look at the wife's role in the creation of the marital hell. But, while such matters may link the earlier plays with Opus 4, the latter remains a thoroughly independent work of art which can be read or staged without consideration of the earlier plays.

In keeping with his concept of the chamber play, Strindberg allows all the characters to contribute to the development of the motifs and themes without letting any character dominate either the substance or the form. The fates of the late father, the son, the daughter, and even the son-in-law and the servant are as important as that of the mother. Only in the sense of being the major key in getting at what has poisoned human life within the four walls of a very strange "home" can Elise be said to be the central character. In other words, just as Laura must be given every bit as much attention as Captain Adolf in *The Father,* the rest of the inhabitants of the strange home demand attention equal to that given Elise, the mother.

But "the one single great distortion of nature" that Elise is needs initial examination if one is to appreciate what Strindberg is saying in *The Pelican.* He does give flashes of revealing insight into her as an egotist-vampire, as "a big thief," as a wife, as the mistress of a household, as a mother, and as a mother-in-law. Basic to and overlapping all these roles is the theme of sleepwalking.

Strindberg has made it clear what he meant by the term:

> SON: You went about like a sleepwalker and couldn't be awakened; that's why you couldn't change, either. Father said "that if they put you on the rack and tortured you, you couldn't be made to admit a fault or admit you had lied . . ."

and a little later:

> SON: Are you waking up?
> MOTHER: Yes, I'm waking up as if from a long, long sleep! It's terrible! Why couldn't anyone wake me up before?

Elise is perhaps the most striking of that large group of human beings whom Strindberg observed, studied, and then, through the miracle of the creative process, made unforgettable in his dramas or his prose fiction: the sleepwalkers. They are essentially unaware of the significance of what they do; they do not examine and evaluate and judge their actions; they seem to operate on some instinctively egotistic plane which permits them to look after what on one level are their own interests but what are, from a Strindbergian and humane point of view, the very things that rob them of the all important rewards of happy relations with other human beings. A further implication is, it seems to me, that a sleepwalker such as Elise may even lull others into sleepwalking or into a state closely resembling it.

It is a curiously selfish pattern of living that the sleepwalker Elise has worked out for herself within a marriage lasting well over twenty-five years. If it were not for the very real possibility that such a pattern has been worked out and followed by actual people, according to one's own observations and the testimony of psychiatrists, the story Strindberg tells would strike many a rational person as ridiculous. It isn't a pattern that illustrates the Emersonian "Eat it up; wear it out; make it do." What Elise has done is to skimp and save on such basic matters as adequate lighting, adequate heating, and adequate food for her family in order to provide satisfaction for herself. Note that the horrifying "Turn on a couple of lights! But only a couple!" and "We can't afford to burn up our money . . ." are followed by the telling

> son: We've heard that for twenty years, though we've been able to afford silly trips abroad that we could brag about . . . and eaten dinner at a restaurant for a hundred crowns—the price of four cords of birchwood—four cords for one dinner!

Take just one comment on the food Elise has placed on her family's table:

> son: She stole from the household money, she made up imaginary bills, she bought the poorest food at the highest prices, she ate in the kitchen in the forenoon and gave us watered-down food; that's why we children have turned out badly, always sick and hungry; she stole from the money for wood—we had to freeze. When Father discovered that, he warned her; she promised to improve but kept on and made discoveries—soybean sauce and cayenne pepper!

It is an indictment implicit in the revealing testimony of the servant Margret, the daughter, the son, the dead husband, and the man who was both Elise's boy friend and her son-in-law. Elise is something quite different from a frugal Yankee.

Those who find the attention to food, lighting, and heating overemphasized in this play, as many have found the vampire cook in *The Ghost Sonata* absurd and ridiculous, should remember that *The Pelican* is in its fashion a dream play; and Strindberg had pointed out in his explanatory note to *A Dream Play* that absurdities may very well be part of the dream experience and that, as he pointed out in his letter to Emil Schering (page 3), there is a definite logic in the conglomeration that makes up the dream—even in seeming absurdities. Food can be ruined, the most nutritional juices can be consumed by the cook or others and never reach the table, a house or apartment may be inadequately lighted and heated, and there may be foolish expenditures for travel and eating out. But the housekeeper and "homemaker" in a house where the breadwinner had an income of over twenty thousand back in Strindberg's day must have been quite an inefficient person even for an egotistic sleepwalker. But although one may not appreciate major emphasis on the details of housekeeping in a play, it must be admitted that the details Strindberg presents are anything but absurd in themselves.

At least one murder has been committed in that strange house or, more accurately, that strange apartment. To be sure, it was a psychic murder, one for which the murderer and her accomplices cannot be held accountable under the civil law. As every student of Strindberg knows, he had not only devoted an essay to defining and explaining psychic murder and suicide in "Själamord. Apropos Rosmersholm" back in 1887 * but had proceeded to illustrate the crimes in one literary work after the other, from *The Father* (1887) on.

* See my translation, "Psychic Murder. (Apropos 'Rosmersholm')," *Drama Review,* 13 (Winter 1968): 113–18.

Elise has been guilty of at least one major psychic murder, which she does not really deny:

> MOTHER: Imagine, all the same: he writes to his son that he was murdered.
>
> SON-IN-LAW: There are many ways of committing murder . . . and your way had the advantage that it doesn't come under the criminal code!
>
> MOTHER: Say "our way"! For you were along helping, when you irritated him into fury and brought him to despair . . .
>
> SON-IN-LAW: He stood in my way and didn't want to step aside! So I had to give him a shove . . .
>
> MOTHER: The only thing I blame you for is that you lured me away from home . . . and I won't forget that evening, the first in your home, when we were sitting at the festive table and we heard from the garden those horrible cries that we thought came from the prison or the insane asylum . . . Do you remember? It was he walking down in the garden in the dark and rain, crying out because he missed his wife and children . . .

Nevertheless a little earlier, in speaking to this particular accomplice, she had said: "Imagine: he's rising up from the grave and talking—he's not dead. I can never live here—he writes that I murdered him . . . I didn't! Why, he died of a stroke; the doctor certified that . . . but he says something else, too; it's a lie, all of it! that I ruined him!"

Nevertheless, the wife of whom it can justly be said, "She's so wicked, she's to be pitied," has intimations of guilt: she is afraid of her memories, and the portrait of her late husband, the movement of his rocking chair, the postfuneral and deathroom smells of fir twigs and carbolic acid, and the bloody butcher's bench (the red chaise longue) on which he died torture and terrify her.

In a thoroughly depressing way she has enlisted as accomplices not only the son-in-law, the daughter, and the servant, but what Strindberg calls the whole secret gang of women who have come to and quickly gone from the strange home. The full horror of what she has done in enlisting accomplices become particularly clear in the testimony given by those extremely effective witnesses in the ensemble—the son and the daughter. By weakening and training her son (and her husband's potential ally), and by not only weakening and training her daughter but also marrying her off to the man she "loves," she has, apparently instinctively, seen to it that they have become tools that she can easily manipulate.

The telling details about training a daughter to pretend, to lie, and to connive in order to deceive her father; arranging to have her marry the man who has an understanding with her mother; and bringing her up to be sterile and incomplete are there, as are the revealing bits of information about what made the son a weakling:

> SON: But do you know why I'm weak like this? You never nursed me, but had a wet nurse and a bottle; and when I got older, I was allowed to go with her to visit her sister, who was a prostitute; and there I got to see secret scenes, which otherwise only dog owners offer the children in spring and fall on the open street! When I told you—I was four—what I had seen in that den of iniquity, you said it was a lie, and you spanked me for telling a lie though I spoke the truth. That maid, encouraged by your approval, initiated me at the age of five into all the secrets . . . I was only five . . . And then I had to starve and freeze, like Father and the rest. Now I learn for the first time you stole from the household money and the money for wood . . . Look at me, Pelican; look at Gerda who hasn't any real bosom!—How you murdered my father you know, when you drove him to despair that can't be punished by the law; how you murdered my sister you know best, but now she knows, too!

What the son, the awakened sleepwalker, has said is, of course, that Elise is guilty of at least three psychic murders, one fully accomplished and two complete except in a nominal sense.

In keeping with what he said about his concept of the chamber play, Strindberg has made use of the intimate form, has treated the motif of the destructive vampire who pretends to be a pelican in the mythical sense, has limited the number of characters to five, and has set his imagination free to create on the bases of experience and observation. The play is simply but not too simply constructed with no elaborate apparatus. What seems particularly significant—from the point of view of a Strindbergian chamber play—is how effectively he has each instrument or voice or, if you will, character in the ensemble take over in turn the exposé of a family home that may justly be labeled an antihome.

While the ending of the play may seem melodramatic at first reading, it is particularly appropriate to the logic of an ugly dream with few if any redeeming elements. The three awakened sleepwalkers should have, according to Strindberg's way of looking at it, no other recourse: Elise knows what she has done and can no longer take refuge in sleepwalking; both her son and her daughter are so crippled that life can never become meaningful for them; and the strange "house" had better go up in flames. If there is any hope for such people, it lies, Strindberg believed, in a life beyond this.

Opus 4

The Pelican

Characters

THE MOTHER, *Elise, a widow*
HER SON, *Fredrik, a law student*
HER DAUGHTER, *Gerda*
HER SON-IN-LAW, *Axel, Gerda's husband*
MARGRET, *a servant, the cook*

A living room; at the back a door to the dining room; to the right a balcony door in pan coupé.

A chiffonier, a desk, a chaise longue with a purplish-red plush cover; a rocking chair.

The MOTHER, *dressed in mourning, comes in, sits down in an easy chair; dawdles; listens, uneasy, now and then.*

Off stage Chopin's Fantaisie Impromptu œuvre posthume, *Op. 66 is being played.* MARGRET, *the cook, enters from the back.*

MOTHER: Please shut the door.

MARGRET: Are you alone, ma'am?

MOTHER: Shut the door, please.—Who's playing?

MARGRET: Ghastly weather tonight, blowing and raining . . .

MOTHER: Please shut the door—I can't stand this smell of carbolic acid and fir twigs . . .

MARGRET: I knew that, ma'am; that's why I said the master should have been taken to his tomb right away . . .

MOTHER: The children were the ones who wanted the funeral at home . . .

MARGRET: Why do you stay here, ma'am? Why don't you move?

MOTHER: Our landlord won't let us move, and we can't . . . (*Pause*) Why did you take the cover off the red chaise longue?

MARGRET: I had to send it to the cleaners. (*Pause*) Why, ma'am, the master drew his last breath on that sofa, you know. But get rid of the sofa . . .

MOTHER: I'm not allowed to disturb anything until everything in the estate has been listed . . . that's why I'm imprisoned here . . . and I can't stand being in the other rooms . . .

MARGRET: Why not?

MOTHER: My memories . . . everything unpleasant, and that terrible smell . . . Is it my son who's playing?

MARGRET: Yes. He's not happy in here; he's uneasy; and he's always hungry; he says he has never had enough to eat . . .

MOTHER: He has always been delicate—ever since he was born . . .

MARGRET: A bottle baby should have rich food after he has been weaned . . .

MOTHER (*sharply*): Well? Has he lacked anything?

MARGRET: Not exactly, but all the same, ma'am, you shouldn't have bought the cheapest and the worst; and to send children to school when they've had only a cup of chicory coffee and a roll isn't right.

MOTHER: My children have never complained about the food . . .

MARGRET: Really? Not to you, ma'am; they haven't dared, but when they grew up, they came out to me in the kitchen . . .

MOTHER: We have always been in limited circumstances . . .

MARGRET: Oh no! I read in the paper that the master paid taxes on twenty thousand some years . . .

MOTHER: There wasn't any left!

MARGRET: Well, well! But the children are delicate. Miss Gerda, the young lady, I mean, isn't fully developed though she's over twenty . . .

MOTHER: What are you saying?

MARGRET: Well, well! (*Pause*) Shouldn't I start a fire, ma'am? It's cold in here.

MOTHER: No, thank you—we can't afford to burn up our money . . .

MARGARET: But Mr. Fredrik freezes all day long so that he has to take a walk or keep warm at the piano . . .

MOTHER: He has always been cold . . .

MARGRET: How come?

MOTHER: Take care, Margret . . . (*Pause*) Is someone walking out there?

MARGRET: No, no one's walking out there . . .

MOTHER: Do you think I'm afraid of ghosts?

MARGRET: I, I don't know . . . But I won't stay here very long . . . I came here as if I were condemned to watch over the children . . . I wanted to leave when I saw how the servants were mistreated, but I couldn't or I wasn't allowed to . . . Now that Miss Gerda is married, I feel I've done my duty and my hour of release will soon come, though not quite yet . . .

MOTHER: I don't understand a word of what you're saying—the whole world knows how I've sacrificed myself for my children, how I've looked after my house and my duties . . . you're the only one who accuses me, but I don't pay any attention to that. You may leave when you want to; I don't intend to have any servant any more when the young people move into this apartment . . .

MARGRET: May it go well for you, ma'am . . . Children aren't grateful by nature, and mothers-in-law aren't very welcome, unless they bring a lot of money along . . .

MOTHER: Don't worry . . . I'll pay for myself, and still help out about the house . . . besides my son-in-law is unlike all other sons-in-law . . .

MARGRET: Is he?

MOTHER: Yes, he is! He doesn't treat me like a mother-in-law but like a sister, not to say woman friend . . .

(MARGRET *grimaces*.)

MOTHER: I know what you're thinking. But I like my son-in-law— I've a right to, and he deserves it . . . my husband didn't like him; he was envious, not to say jealous . . . yes, indeed, he honored me with his jealousy though I'm not so young any more . . . Did you say something?

MARGRET: No, I didn't!—But I thought someone came in . . . It's Mr. Fredrik, for he's coughing. Shall I light the fire?

MOTHER: That's unnecessary!

MARGRET: Ma'am!—I've frozen, I've starved in this house . . . that doesn't matter, but give me a bed, a decent bed—I'm old and tired . . .

MOTHER: No point in doing that now when you're going to leave . . .

MARGRET: True! I forgot! But for the sake of the reputation of the house, burn up my bedclothes that people have died on so you won't have to be ashamed before the next servant comes—if any will!

MOTHER: No one will!

MARGRET: But if someone does, she won't stay . . . I've seen fifty housemaids come and go . . .

MOTHER: Because they were immoral people; all of you are . . .

MARGRET: Thank you very much!—Well! Now your time's coming! Everyone has her time . . . has her turn . . .

MOTHER: Haven't you said enough to me soon?

MARGRET: Yes, soon! Very soon! Sooner than you think! (*Goes*)

(*The* SON *enters, carrying a book, coughing. He stammers slightly.*)

MOTHER: Please shut the door.

SON: Why?

MOTHER: Is that how you should answer me?—What do you want?

SON: May I read in here? It's very cold in my room.

MOTHER: You're always cold.

SON: When I sit still, I feel it more if it's cold! (*Pause. At first pretends to read*) Is the inventory ready yet?

MOTHER: Why do you ask? Can't we wait until we're through mourning? Don't you mourn for your father?

SON: Yes . . . but . . . he's well off, I think . . . and I don't begrudge him rest, the peace he has at last. But that doesn't prevent me from finding out what my situation is . . . if I'm going to finish my studies without borrowing . . .

MOTHER: Why, Father didn't leave anything; you know that; debts perhaps . . .

SON: But his business is surely worth something?

MOTHER: But it's not a business, where there's no stock, no goods, you see!

SON (*thinking that over first*): But the firm, the name, the customers . . .

MOTHER: You can't sell customers . . . (*Pause*)

SON: Yes, they say you can!

MOTHER: Have you been seeing a lawyer? (*Pause*) So that's how you're mourning your father!

SON: No, no, no!—But one thing at a time.—Where are Gerda and her husband?

MOTHER: They got home this morning from their wedding trip and are staying at a boarding house.

SON: Then they'll at least get enough to eat!

MOTHER: You're always talking about food. Have you had anything to complain about?

SON: No, not at all!

MOTHER: But tell me one thing. A while back when I had to live away from home for a time, you were here alone with your father. —Didn't he ever say anything about his financial situation?

SON (*engrossed in his book*): No, nothing special.

MOTHER: Can you explain that he didn't leave anything when he earned twenty thousand a year?

SON: I don't know anything about his affairs, but he said the house was very expensive; and, then, he bought all this new furniture lately.

MOTHER: So that's what he said! Do you suppose he had debts?

SON: I don't know. He had had, but he had paid them.

MOTHER: Where did the money go? Did he leave a will? He hated me and threatened several times to leave me penniless. Could he possibly have hidden his savings somewhere? (*Pause*) Is someone walking out there?

SON: No, I don't hear anyone.

MOTHER: I'm a little nervous because of the funeral and his business affairs.—But your sister and her husband are going to take over this apartment, you know—you'll have to look for a room in town for yourself!

SON: Yes, I know.

MOTHER: You don't like your brother-in-law, do you?

SON: No, we don't have anything in common.

MOTHER: But he's a good boy and a fine one.—You should like him; he deserves it!

SON: He doesn't like me—besides he was mean to Father.

MOTHER: Whose fault was that?

SON: Father wasn't mean . . .

MOTHER: Oh no?

SON: Someone *is* walking out there, I think!

MOTHER: Turn on a couple of lights. But only a couple! (*The* SON *lights electric lights; pause*)

MOTHER: Won't you put Father's portrait in your room? The one on that wall.

SON: Why should I?

MOTHER: I don't like it; his eyes look mean.

SON: I don't think so!

MOTHER: Then take it away! Since you like it, you may have it!

SON (*takes down the portrait*): Yes! Then I will! (*Pause*)

MOTHER: I'm expecting Axel and Gerda . . . Do you want to see them?

SON: No! I'm not anxious to . . . I can go into my room, I suppose . . . If I may only have a little fire in my stove.

MOTHER: We can't afford to burn up our money . . .

SON: We've heard that for twenty years, though we've been able to afford silly trips abroad that we could brag about . . . and eaten dinner at a restaurant for a hundred crowns—the price of four cords of birchwood—four cords for one dinner!

MOTHER: You talk!

SON: Yes, there was something wrong here, but it'll be over now, I hope . . . when the accounts are settled . . .

MOTHER: What do you mean?

SON: I mean the inventory of the estate and those other things . . .

MOTHER: What other things?

SON: Debts and things that haven't been settled . . .

MOTHER: Oh!

SON: But may I buy some warm clothes?

MOTHER: How can you ask for that now? You should certainly be thinking of earning something yourself soon . . .

SON: When I have my degree.

MOTHER: You'll have to borrow like everyone else, I suppose.

SON: Who would lend me money?

MOTHER: Your father's friends.

SON: He didn't have any friends! An independent man can't have any friends since friendship is nothing but indulging in mutual admiration . . .

MOTHER: You're wise, aren't you? You've learned that from your father!

SON: Yes, he was a wise man—who behaved foolishly now and then.

MOTHER: Listen!—Are you thinking of getting married?

SON: No, thanks! Keeping a lady companion for young bachelors, serving as a legal front for a coquette, equipping one's best friend, that is, one's worst enemy, for a campaign against oneself . . . Oh, no, I'll steer clear of that!

MOTHER: What! What's that?—Go to your room. I've had enough for today. You've been drinking!

SON: I always have to drink a little, partly for my cough, partly to make myself feel I've had enough to eat.

MOTHER: So there's something wrong with the food again?

SON: Nothing wrong, but it's so light it tastes of air!

MOTHER (*taken aback*): Now you may go!

SON: Or the food's so spiced with pepper and salt one gets hungry from eating it! It's what one might call spiced air!

MOTHER: You're drunk, I think! Go on—get out!

SON: Yes . . . I'll go! I was going to say something, but this can be enough for today!—Yes! (*Goes*)

    (MOTHER *uneasy, walks about, pulls out bureau drawers. The* SON-IN-LAW *enters hastily.*)

MOTHER (*greets him enthusiastically*): At last! There you are, Axel! I've been longing for you, but where's Gerda?

SON-IN-LAW: She's coming later. How are you? How's everything?

MOTHER: Sit down and let me ask first—why, we haven't seen each other since the wedding.—Why did you come back so soon? Why, you were going to be away eight days and you've been gone only three.

SON-IN-LAW: Well, it got boring, you know, when we had talked ourselves out—we felt disturbingly alone, and we were so used to your company we missed you.

MOTHER: Really! Oh, well, we three have stuck together through good times and bad, and I've been of some use to you two, I think.

SON-IN-LAW: Gerda's a child who doesn't understand the art of living; she has her prejudices; she's a little stubborn, unbelievably so about some things . . .

MOTHER: Well, how did you like the wedding?

SON-IN-LAW: Absolutely perfect! Absolutely! And the verses—how did you like them?

MOTHER: The verses to me, you mean? Well, I suppose no other mother-in-law has received verses like that at her daughter's wedding . . . Do you remember what they said about the pelican, who gives its lifeblood to its young? I wept, I really did . . .

SON-IN-LAW: At first, yes, but then you danced every dance. Gerda was almost jealous of you.

MOTHER: That wasn't the first time—she wanted me to come dressed in black—in mourning, as she said, but I didn't pay any attention to that. Am I to obey my children?

SON-IN-LAW: Of course not. Why, Gerda gets crazy if I so much as look at a woman . . .

MOTHER: What? Aren't you happy?

SON-IN-LAW: Happy? Well, what does that mean?

MOTHER: So! You've already quarreled?

SON-IN-LAW: Already? Why, we never did anything else after we got engaged . . . And now there's this, too: I have to leave her for a while—I'm a lieutenant in the reserves . . . It's really funny, but it seems she likes me less when I'm out of uniform . . .

MOTHER: Why don't you wear your uniform, then? I'll have to admit I hardly recognize you in civilian clothes. You're really another person . . .

SON-IN-LAW: I'm not permitted to wear my uniform except when I'm on duty and on parade days . . .

MOTHER: Not permitted?

SON-IN-LAW: Yes, it's a regulation . . .

MOTHER: I'm sorry for Gerda all the same; she got engaged to a lieutenant, but she's married to a bookkeeper!

SON-IN-LAW: What can I do about that? We do have to live! Apropos living: how's the financial situation?

MOTHER: Frankly speaking, I don't know! But I'm beginning to be suspicious of Fredrik.

SON-IN-LAW: Why?

MOTHER: He talked very strangely here tonight . . .

SON-IN-LAW: That blockhead . . .

MOTHER: They're generally sly, and I'm not sure there isn't a will or savings . . .

SON-IN-LAW: Have you searched?

MOTHER: I've looked in all his drawers . . .

SON-IN-LAW: In the boy's?

MOTHER: Of course, and I always look through everything in his wastebasket, for he writes letters, which he tears to pieces . . .

SON-IN-LAW: That's nothing, but have you searched the old man's chest of drawers?

MOTHER: Yes—of course . . .

SON-IN-LAW: Thoroughly? All the drawers?

MOTHER: All of them!

SON-IN-LAW: But there are usually secret drawers in every chest.

MOTHER: I hadn't thought of that!

SON-IN-LAW: Then we'll have to search it!

MOTHER: No, don't touch it; it has been sealed by the executor.

SON-IN-LAW: Can't we avoid the seal?

MOTHER: No! No!

SON-IN-LAW: Yes, if we loosen the boards in back—all secret drawers are toward the back . . .

MOTHER: We'd have to have tools . . .

SON-IN-LAW: Oh, no. We could do it anyway . . .

MOTHER: But Gerda mustn't know anything about it.

SON-IN-LAW: No, of course not . . . she'd blab it to her brother right away . . .

MOTHER (*shuts the doors*): I'll shut the doors to be safe . . .

SON-IN-LAW (*examines the back of the chest of drawers*): Imagine: someone's been at it . . . The back's loose . . . I can put in my hand . . .

MOTHER: The boy has done that . . . you see why I was suspicious . . . Hurry up; someone's coming!

SON-IN-LAW: There are papers here . . .

MOTHER: Hurry up; someone's coming . . .

SON-IN-LAW: An envelope . . .

MOTHER: Gerda's coming! Give me the papers . . . quickly!

SON-IN-LAW (*hands her a large envelope, which she hides*): Look here! Hide it!

  (*Someone pulls at the doors, then knocks loudly.*)

SON-IN-LAW: Why did you lock them? . . . We're lost!

MOTHER: Be quiet!

SON-IN-LAW: You are a fool!—Open them!—Or I will!—Step aside! (*He opens the doors.*)

GERDA (*enters, depressed*): Why did you lock yourselves in?

MOTHER: Aren't you going to say hello first, dear? Why, I haven't

seen you since the wedding. Did you have fun on your trip? Tell
me all about it and don't look so sad!

GERDA (*sits down on a chair, depressed*): Why had you shut the
door?

MOTHER: Because it opens by itself, and I'm tired of nagging about
it every time someone comes in. Shall we think about furnishing
your apartment now? You're going to live here, aren't you?

GERDA: We have to, I suppose . . . it makes no difference to me—
what do you say, Axel?

SON-IN-LAW: Well, this will be fine, I think, and your mother won't
have a bad time of it . . . When we get along so well . . .

GERDA: Where is Mother going to live then?

MOTHER: Here, darling—I'll only put in a bed!

SON-IN-LAW: Are you going to put a bed in the living room, Elise?

GERDA (*snaps to attention when she hears "Elise"*): Do you
mean . . .

SON-IN-LAW: I mean your mother . . . but it will work out . . .
we'll help each other, and on what your mother pays we can
live . . .

GERDA (*brightens*): And I'll get a little help with the housekeeping . . .

MOTHER: Of course, dear . . . but I don't want to do the dishes!

GERDA: Do you think I'd let you? Besides, it'll all be fine just so I
may have my husband to myself! They may not look at him . . .
They did, of course, over there in the boarding house, and that's
why our trip was so short . . . but anyone who tries to take him
from me is going to die! I'll kill her!

MOTHER: Now we'll go out and begin to move the furniture . . .

SON-IN-LAW (*catches his MOTHER-IN-LAW's eyes*): Fine! But Gerda
can start here . . .

GERDA: Why? I don't like to be in here alone . . . when we have
moved in, I can be calm about being in here . . .

SON-IN-LAW: Since you're afraid of the dark, we'll all three go . . .
(*All three go out.*)

(*The stage is empty; the wind is blowing at the windows and howling in the tile stove; the back door begins to bang, paper from the desk flies about the room, a palm on the console is shaken violently, a photograph falls down from the wall. Now can be heard the* SON'S *voice:* "Mama!" *Immediately thereafter:* "Shut the window!" *Pause. The rocking chair moves.*)

MOTHER (*enters, beside herself, with a paper in her hand; she is reading it*): What's that? The rocking chair's moving!

SON-IN-LAW (*follows*): What was that? What's happening? May I read it? Is it the will?

MOTHER: Shut the door! Why, we're blowing away. I have to open a window because of the smell. It wasn't a will—it was a letter to the boy in which he lies about me and—you!

SON-IN-LAW: Let me read it!

MOTHER: No, you'll only be poisoned. I'll tear it to pieces; how lucky it didn't fall into his hands . . . (*She tears the paper to pieces and throws them into the tile stove.*) Imagine: he's rising up from the grave and talking—he's not dead! I can never live here—he writes that I murdered him . . . I didn't! Why, he died of a stroke; the doctor certified that . . . but he says something else, too; it's a lie, all of it! that I ruined him! . . . Listen, Axel, see to it we get out of this apartment soon! I can't stand it here! Promise me!—Look at the rocking chair!

SON-IN-LAW: It's the draft!

MOTHER: Let's get away from here! Promise me!

SON-IN-LAW: I can't . . . I counted on an inheritance since you hinted at that; otherwise I wouldn't have got married; now we'll have to take it as it is, and you may consider me a deceived son-in-law—and a ruined one! We have to stick together to be able to live; we have to save, and you'll have to help us!

MOTHER: You mean I'm to be a servant in my own home?

SON-IN-LAW: Necessity forces . . .

MOTHER: You are a scoundrel!

SON-IN-LAW: Mind your manners, old woman!

MOTHER: A servant to you!

SON-IN-LAW: Find out how your maids who have had to starve and freeze have had it. You won't have to!

MOTHER: I have my life annuity . . .

SON-IN-LAW: It isn't enough for an attic room, but here it will do for the rent, if we're careful . . . and if you aren't, I'll leave!

MOTHER: Leave Gerda? You've never loved her . . .

SON-IN-LAW: You know that better than I . . . You rooted her out of my mind, forced her aside, except in the bedroom, you let her keep that . . . and if she should have a child, you'll take it away from her, too . . . She doesn't know anything yet, understands nothing, but she's waking up from her sleepwalking. Watch out when she opens her eyes.

MOTHER: Axel! We must stick together . . . We mustn't part . . . I can't live alone; I'll agree to everything—but not the chaise longue . . .

SON-IN-LAW: Yes! I don't want to ruin the apartment by making a bedroom here—now you know!

MOTHER: But let me get another . . .

SON-IN-LAW: No, we can't afford to, and this one is attractive.

MOTHER: Ugh! Why, it's a bloody butcher's bench!

SON-IN-LAW: Nonsense! . . . But if you don't want to, you have the attic room and the loneliness, the meeting house, and the poorhouse.

MOTHER: I give up!

SON-IN-LAW: You're doing the right thing . . . (Pause)

MOTHER: Imagine all the same: he writes to his son that he was murdered.

SON-IN-LAW: There are many ways of committing murder . . . and your way had the advantage that it doesn't come under the criminal code!

MOTHER: Say "our way"! For you were along helping, when you

irritated him into fury and brought him to despair . . .

SON-IN-LAW: He stood in my way and didn't want to step aside! So I had to give him a shove . . .

MOTHER: The only thing I blame you for is that you lured me away from home . . . and I won't forget that evening, the first in your home, when we were sitting at the festive table, and we heard from the garden those horrible cries, that we thought came from the prison or the insane asylum . . . Do you remember? It was he walking down in the garden in the dark and rain, crying out because he missed his wife and children . . .

SON-IN-LAW: Why talk about that now? And how do you know it was he?

MOTHER: He said so in the letter!

SON-IN-LAW: Well, what's that to us? He was no angel . . .

MOTHER: No, he wasn't, but he had human feelings sometimes—yes, somewhat more than you . . .

SON-IN-LAW: You're beginning to change sides . . .

MOTHER: Don't get angry! Why, we have to get along!

SON-IN-LAW: We have to; we are doomed . . .

    (*Hoarse cries from within*)

MOTHER: What's that? Listen! It is he . . .

SON-IN-LAW (*coarsely*): Which he?

    (MOTHER *listens.*)

SON-IN-LAW: Who is it?—The boy! I suppose he has been drinking again!

MOTHER: Was it Fredrik? It was so like *him*—I thought—I'll never bear it! What's wrong with him?

SON-IN-LAW: Go and see. The rascal is drunk, I suppose!

MOTHER: Don't talk like that! Why, he's my son, in any case!

SON-IN-LAW: In any case yours! (*Takes out his watch*)

MOTHER: Why are you looking at your watch? Don't you want to stay for supper?

SON-IN-LAW: No, thanks! I never drink tea water and never eat rancid anchovies . . . or porridge . . . besides I have to go to a meeting . . .

MOTHER: What meeting?

SON-IN-LAW: Business that doesn't concern you! Do you intend to act like a mother-in-law?

MOTHER: Are you going to leave your wife the first evening you're in your home?

SON-IN-LAW: That doesn't concern you either!

MOTHER: Now I know what lies ahead for me—and my children! Now comes the unmasking—

SON-IN-LAW: Now it comes!

[CURTAIN]

The same set. Someone is playing Godard's "Berceuse" from Jocelyn *off stage.* GERDA *is sitting at the desk. Long pause.*

SON (*enters*): Are you alone?

GERDA: Yes. Mother's in the kitchen.

SON: Where's Axel?

GERDA: He's at a meeting . . . Sit down and talk, Fredrik; keep me company!

SON (*sits down*): Yes, we've never talked before. We avoided each other, we weren't particularly close . . .

GERDA: You were always on Father's side, and I on Mother's.

SON: Perhaps that will change now!—Did you really know Father?

GERDA: What a strange question! But I saw him only through Mother's eyes . . .

SON: But you did see that he liked you?

GERDA: Why did he want to break and prevent my engagement?

SON: Because he didn't consider Axel the support you needed!

GERDA: And he was punished for that, too, when Mother left him.

SON: Was it your husband who lured her into leaving?

GERDA: Both he and I! I wanted Father to know how it feels to be separated—he wanted to separate me from my fiancé.

SON: That cut his life short, though . . . And take my word for it: he wanted only what was good for you!

GERDA: You stayed with him. What did he say? How did he take it?

SON: I can't describe his agony . . .

GERDA: What did he say about Mother?

SON: Nothing! . . . But, after all I've seen, I'll never get married! (*Pause*) Are *you* happy, Gerda?

GERDA: Yes, indeed! When you've got the one you wanted, you're happy!

SON: Why did your husband leave you the first evening?

GERDA: He had business—a meeting.

SON: At a restaurant?

GERDA: What are you saying? Are you sure?

SON: I thought you knew!

GERDA (*weeps, her face in her hands*): Oh God, my God!

SON: Forgive me—I've hurt you!

GERDA: Yes, very, very much! I want to die!

SON: Why didn't you stay on your trip longer?

GERDA: He was anxious about his business; he longed to see Mother; why, he can't be away from her . . .

    (*They fix each other's glance.*)

SON: Really? (*Pause*) Was the trip pleasant aside from that?

GERDA: Yes!

SON: Poor Gerda!

GERDA: What are you saying?

SON: Well, you know, of course, Mother is curious, and she can really use the telephone!

GERDA: What's that? Has she been spying?

SON: She always does . . . most likely she's listening to us right now—behind some door . . .

GERDA: You're always thinking the worst about Mother.

SON: And you always the best! I wonder why? Why, you know how she is . . .

GERDA: No! And I don't want to know . . .

SON: That's something else you don't want; you have some reason for it . . .

GERDA: Sh-h! I'm sleepwalking, I know, but I don't want to be awakened! Then I wouldn't be able to live!

SON: Don't you think we're all sleepwalking?—I'm studying law, court proceedings. Well, I read about great criminals, who can't explain how it happened . . . they thought they were doing the right thing, until they were caught and woke up! If that isn't a dream, it must be sleep!

GERDA: Let me sleep! I know I'll wake up, but I hope I won't for a long time! Ugh! All this that I don't know, but sense! Do you remember as a child? . . . People called us mean if we said the truth . . . you're very mean, they always said to me, when I declared something bad was bad . . . so I learned to keep still . . . then I was liked because of my good disposition; so I learned not to say what I thought, and then I was ready to step out into life!

SON: One is supposed to overlook his neighbor's faults and weaknesses, it's true . . . but the steps beyond that are evasion and flattery . . . It's hard knowing how one should be . . . sometimes it's a duty to speak out . . .

GERDA: Sh-h!

SON: I'll keep still. (Pause)

GERDA: No, speak out, but not about that! I hear your thoughts in your silence! When people get together, they talk, they talk endlessly just to conceal their thoughts . . . to forget, to deafen themselves . . . They want to hear new things about others, but they conceal their own troubles.

SON: Poor Gerda!

GERDA: Do you know what the greatest affliction is? (Pause) It's finding out happiness amounts to nothing!

SON: Now you said it!

GERDA: I'm freezing; give us a little fire!

SON: Are you frozen, too?

GERDA: I've always been cold and hungry!

SON: You, too! It's strange in this house.—But if I go out after wood, there'll be trouble—she won't get over it for eight days!

GERDA: Maybe a fire has been laid; Mother used to put in wood to fool us . . .

SON (*goes to the tile stove and opens the doors*): There really are a few sticks! . . . (*Pause*) But what's this?—A letter! torn to pieces. I can light it with that . . .

GERDA: Fredrik, don't light it—we'll get a nagging that will never end. Come and sit down again so we can talk . . .

   (SON *goes; sits down; puts the letter on the table beside him. Pause*)

GERDA: Do you know why Father hated my husband?

SON: Yes! Your Axel came and took his daughter and his wife from him so that he was left alone; and the old man noticed someone else got better food than he did; you used to lock yourselves in the living room, enjoying music and reading, but always what Father did not like; he was forced out, eaten out of his own home; and that's why he finally turned to the tavern.

GERDA: We didn't think about what we were doing . . . poor Father!—It's good to have parents with blameless names and reputations, and we can be thankful . . . Do you remember our parents' silver wedding? What talks and verses they got in their honor!

SON: I remember, but I thought it was a joke to celebrate a marriage as happy when it had been a hell . . .

GERDA: Fredrik!

SON: I can't help it, but you know how they lived . . . Don't you remember when Mother wanted to jump out the window, and we had to hold her back?

GERDA: Sh-h!

SON: There were reasons we don't know . . . and during their separation, when I was looking after the old man, he seemed to want to talk, several times, but the words never crossed his lips . . . I sometimes dream about him . . .

GERDA: I do, too!—When I see him in my dreams, he's thirty years old . . . he looks at me in a friendly way, as if he wanted to tell me something, but I don't understand what he wants . . . sometimes Mother's along; he isn't angry with her, because he loved her in spite of everything up to the very end . . . you remember how beautifully he spoke of her at the silver wedding, thanking her, *in spite of everything* . . .

SON: In spite of everything! That was saying a lot, and yet too little!

GERDA: But it was beautiful! She did have one great virtue, though . . . she took care of her house!

SON: Well, that's the big question!

GERDA: What's that?

SON: How you stick together! The minute one touches the housekeeping, you're on her side . . . it's like freemasonry or a secret gang . . . I've even asked old Margret, who's my friend, about the economy of the house. I've asked her why we never got enough to eat here at home . . . then that talkative soul kept her mouth shut . . . kept her mouth shut and got angry . . . Can you explain it?

GERDA (*sharply*): No!

SON: I hear you're a freemason, too!

GERDA: I don't understand what you mean!

SON: Sometimes I wonder if Father was a victim of that secret gang that he must have uncovered.

GERDA: Sometimes you talk like a fool . . .

SON: I remember Father used the word *gang* occasionally, in a joking way, but at the end he kept still . . .

GERDA: It's terribly cold in here, cold like the grave . . .

SON: Then I'll light the fire no matter what happens! (*He takes the torn letter, first without paying attention to it, then his eyes catch what it is about and he begins to read*.) What's this? (*Pause*) "To my son!" . . . In his handwriting! (*Pause*) It's for me! (*He reads, falls down into a chair and continues silently*.)

GERDA: What are you reading? What is it?

SON: It's terrible! (*Pause*) It's absolutely horrible!

GERDA: Tell me what it is! (*Pause*)

SON: It's too much . . . (*To* GERDA) It's a letter from my dead father . . . to me! (*He reads on*.) Now I'm waking up out of my sleep! (*He throws himself on the chaise longue and cries out with pain, but stuffs the letter into his pocket*.)

GERDA (*on her knees beside him*): What is it, Fredrik? Tell me what's wrong!—Are you sick? Tell me!

SON (*raises his head*): I can't go on living!

GERDA: Tell me, then!

SON: It's too unbelievable! (*Controls himself; gets up*)

GERDA: It may be untrue!

SON (*irritated*): No, he doesn't lie from the grave . . .

GERDA: He could have had a sick imagination . . .

SON: The secret gang! Back to that again! Then I will tell you! —Just listen!

GERDA: I think I already know it all, but I don't believe it anyway!

SON: You don't want to!—But this is how it is. The woman who gave us life was a big thief!

GERDA: No!

SON: She stole from the household money, she made up imaginary bills, she bought the poorest food at the highest prices, she ate in the kitchen in the forenoon and gave us the watered-down, warmed-over food; she skimmed the cream off the milk; that's why we children have turned out badly, always sick and hungry; she stole from the money for wood—we had to freeze. When Father discovered that, he warned her; she promised to improve but kept on and made discoveries—soybean sauce and cayenne pepper!

GERDA: I don't believe a word!

SON: The secret gang!—But here's the worst: that tramp who's your husband, Gerda, has never loved you, but he loves your mother!

GERDA: Ugh!

SON: When Father found that out, and when your husband borrowed money from your mother, our mother, the scoundrel concealed the game by proposing to you! These are the major lines—you can imagine the details!

GERDA (*weeping into her handkerchief, then*): I already knew this, but didn't know it . . . it didn't quite get to my consciousness—it was too much!

SON: What can be done to save you from your degradation?

GERDA: Go away!

SON: Where?

GERDA: I don't know.

SON: So we'll wait to see how things develop!

GERDA: One's so defenseless against one's mother; why, a mother is sacred . . .

SON: The hell she is!

GERDA: Don't say that!

SON: She's as sly as an animal, but her self-love often blinds her . . .

GERDA: Let's run away!

SON: Where? No, stay, until the scoundrel drives her out of the house!—Sh-h! The scoundrel's coming home!—Sh-h!—Gerda, we two will be freemasons now. I'll give you the word. The password. "He struck you on your wedding night!"

GERDA: Remind me of that often. Otherwise I'll forget. I'd be so glad to forget!

SON: Our lives have been ruined . . . nothing to respect, to look up to . . . one can't forget . . . let's live to restore ourselves and our father's reputation!

GERDA: And administer justice!

SON: Say vengeance! (*The* SON-IN-LAW *enters.*)

GERDA (*pretending*): Hello!—Did you have fun at the meeting? Did you get anything good to eat?

SON-IN-LAW: It was canceled.

GERDA: Did you say it was closed?

SON-IN-LAW: It was canceled, I said!

GERDA: Well, are you going to look to the household now?

SON-IN-LAW: You're amusing tonight, but then Fredrik is a gay companion!

GERDA: We've been playing freemasons!

SON-IN-LAW: Watch out for that!

SON: Then we'll play secret gang instead! or vendetta!

SON-IN-LAW (*uncomfortable*): You're talking very strangely. What are you up to? Secrets?

GERDA: You don't tell your secrets, do you? Maybe you don't have any secrets?

SON-IN-LAW: What has happened? Has anyone been here?

SON: Gerda and I have become spiritualists. We've had a visit from a dead spirit.

SON-IN-LAW: Let's stop this nonsense now; otherwise it may turn out badly. Though it's becoming to Gerda to be a little happy—generally you're moody . . . (*He wants to pat her on the cheek, but she draws back.*) Are you afraid of me?

GERDA (*attacking*): Not at all! There are feelings that resemble fear but are something else; there are gestures that say more than facial expressions, and words that conceal what neither gesture nor expression can reveal . . .

   (SON-IN-LAW *amazed, tapping a bookshelf*)

SON (*gets up from the rocking chair, which keeps on rocking until the* MOTHER *comes in*): Now Mother's coming with the porridge!

SON-IN-LAW: Is that . . .

MOTHER (*enters, catches sight of the rocking of the chair; shudders, but controls herself*): Won't you come and have some porridge?

SON-IN-LAW: No, thanks! If it's oatmeal, give it to the hunting dogs, if you have any; if it's rye flour, put it on your boil . . .

MOTHER: We're poor and have to save . . .

SON-IN-LAW: One isn't poor when one has twenty thousand!

SON: Yes, if one lends money to those who don't repay!

SON-IN-LAW: What's that? Are you crazy, boy?

SON: I probably have been!

MOTHER: Are you coming?

GERDA: Come on! Courage, gentlemen! You'll get a sandwich and a steak from me . . .

MOTHER: From you?

GERDA: Yes, from me in my house . . .

MOTHER: That's something, that!

GERDA (*with a gesture toward the door*): Come on, gentlemen!

SON-IN-LAW (*to the* MOTHER): What is all this?

MOTHER: They're up to something!

SON-IN-LAW: I suspect they are!

GERDA: Go ahead, gentlemen! (*All go toward the door.*)

MOTHER (*to the* SON-IN-LAW): Did you see the rocking chair move? *His* rocking chair?

SON-IN-LAW: No, I didn't! But I saw something else!

[CURTAIN]

The same set. The waltz, "Il me disait" by Ferrari is being played. GERDA *is sitting reading a book.*

MOTHER (*enters*): Do you recognize it?

GERDA: The waltz? Yes.

MOTHER: Your wedding waltz, which I danced way into the morning hours!

GERDA: I?—Where's Axel?

MOTHER: What does that have to do with me?

GERDA: There! Have you already quarreled? (*Pause. Play of facial expressions*)

MOTHER: What are you reading, my child?

GERDA: The cookbook. But why doesn't it say how long anything should be cooked?

MOTHER (*embarrassed*): It varies so, you see; people have such differing tastes—one does this, the other that . . .

GERDA: I don't understand that; food should certainly be served when just prepared; otherwise it's warmed up, consequently ruined. For example: you roasted a grouse for three hours yesterday; the first hour there was a fragrance of glorious wild game in the kitchen; and when it was served, it lacked that fragrance and tasted only of air! Explain that!

MOTHER (*embarrassed*): I don't understand!

GERDA: Explain why there wasn't any gravy, then! Where did that go? Who ate it up?

MOTHER: I don't understand anything!

GERDA: But I've been asking around, and I know about some things . . .

MOTHER (*interrupts sharply*): I know all that, and you're not going to teach me anything, but I am going to teach you the art of housekeeping . . .

GERDA: With soya sauce and cayenne pepper, you mean? I know that already, and how to select dishes for parties that no one eats so you have it left over for next day . . . or invite company when the pantry is filled with leftovers . . . I know all that; that's why I'm taking over the housekeeping from today on!

MOTHER (*furious*): Am I to be your maid?

GERDA: I yours and you mine; we'll help each other!—Axel's coming!

SON-IN-LAW (*enters; a heavy cane in his hand*): Well-l? How do you like the chaise longue?

MOTHER: Well, all right . . .

SON-IN-LAW (*threateningly*): Isn't it fine? Is there anything wrong with it?

MOTHER: Now I'm beginning to understand!

SON-IN-LAW: Oh!—But, and since we don't get enough to eat in this house, Gerda and I intend to eat by ourselves.

MOTHER: What about me?

SON-IN-LAW: You're as fat as a fat lady at the circus, so you don't need very much; you should reduce a little for the sake of your health, as the rest of us have had to do . . . How—ev—er, Gerda, step out for a minute; however you [*to the* MOTHER] are going to start a real fire in the stove! (GERDA *goes.*)

MOTHER (*trembles with fury*): There's wood there . . .

SON-IN-LAW: No, there are only a few sticks, but you're going to go after wood, enough to fill the stove!

MOTHER (*hesitates*): Is a person going to burn up her money?

SON-IN-LAW: No, but wood has to be burned if it's to give any warmth! Quick!

  (MOTHER *hesitates.*)

SON-IN-LAW: One, two—three! (*Strikes the table with the stick*)

MOTHER: There isn't any more wood, I think . . .

SON-IN-LAW: Either you're lying or you've stolen the money . . . we bought a cord the day before yesterday!

MOTHER: Now I see who you are . . .

SON-IN-LAW (*sits down in the rocking chair*): You would have seen that a long time ago, if your age and experience hadn't fooled me in my youth and inexperience . . . Quickly! Get out there after wood, or . . . (*Lifts the cane*)

  (MOTHER *goes out, returns immediately with wood.*)

SON-IN-LAW: Now make a real fire, and don't pretend!—One, two, three!

MOTHER: How you resemble the old man when you sit there in his rocking chair!

SON-IN-LAW: Light it!

MOTHER (*crushed, but furious*): I will, I will!

SON-IN-LAW: And keep it going while we go out into the dining room to eat . . .

MOTHER: What will I get?

SON-IN-LAW: Gerda set out the porridge for you in the kitchen.

MOTHER: With blue skim milk . . .

SON-IN-LAW: Since you've consumed the cream, that's proper, and just!

MOTHER (*dully*): Then I'll go my way.

SON-IN-LAW: You can't—I'll lock you in!

MOTHER (*whispers*): Then I'll jump out the window!

SON-IN-LAW: Do that! You should have done that a long time ago—then the lives of four people would have been spared! Light it!—Blow on it!—Like that! Sit here until we come back. (*Goes*)

  (*The* MOTHER *stops the rocking chair first; listens at the door; then she takes some of the wood out of the stove and hides it under the chaise longue. The* SON *comes in; he has been drnking.*)

MOTHER (*startled*): Is that you?

SON (*sits down in the rocking chair*): Yes!

MOTHER: How are you?

SON: Not at all well—I'm done for soon, I think.

MOTHER: That's just your imagination!—Don't rock like that!—Look at me. I've reached a certain age . . . though I've worked, slaved, and done my duty to my children and my house. Haven't I?

SON: Ha!—Like the pelican who never gave its heart's blood—the zoology books say it's a lie.

MOTHER: Have you had anything to complain about?

SON: Listen, Mother; if I were sober, I wouldn't answer frankly—then I wouldn't have the strength, but now I'm going to tell you that I've read Father's letter, which you stole and threw in the stove . . .

MOTHER: What's that? What letter?

SON: Always lying! I remember when you taught me to lie the first time; I could barely talk. Do you remember that?

MOTHER: No, I don't remember that at all! Don't rock!

SON: And when you lied about me for the first time?—I remember as a child—I had hidden under the piano, and a woman came to visit you; you sat lying to her for three hours, and I had to listen!

MOTHER: That's a lie!

SON: But do you know why I'm weak like this? You never nursed me, but had a wet nurse and a bottle; and when I got older, I was allowed to go with her to visit her sister, who was a prostitute; and there I got to see secret scenes, which otherwise only dog owners offer the children in spring and fall on the open street! When I told you—I was four—what I had seen in that den of iniquity, you said it was a lie, and you spanked me for telling a lie though I spoke the truth. That maid, encouraged by your approval, initiated me at the age of five into all the secrets . . . I was only five . . . (*He sobs.*) And then I had to starve and freeze, like Father and the rest. Now I learn for the first time that you stole from the household money and the money for wood . . . Look at me, Pelican; look at Gerda who hasn't any real bosom!— How you murdered my father, you know, when you drove him to despair that can't be punished by the law; how you murdered my sister, you know best, but now she knows, too!

MOTHER: Don't rock!—What does she know?

SON: What you know, but I can't say! (*Sobs*) It's terrible I've said all this, but I had to; I feel when I get sober, I'll shoot myself; so I'll keep on drinking; I don't dare to get sober . . .

MOTHER: Lie some more!

SON: Father said in anger once that you were one single great distortion of nature . . . that you didn't learn to talk as a child but learned to lie right away . . . that you always shook off your duties so you could live it up! And I remember when Gerda was deathly sick you went to see an operetta in the evening—I remember your words: "Life is heavy enough without one's needing to make it heavier!" And that summer you were in Paris for three months with Father, having a good time so he got into debt.

Gerda and I lived here in town, shut up with two maids in this apartment; in our parents' bedroom a fireman lived with the housemaid, and your bed was used by that intimate pair—

MOTHER: Why didn't you tell me that before?

SON: You've forgotten I told you, and that I was spanked because I told on them or lied, as you called it alternately, for, as soon as you heard a true word, you said it was a lie!

MOTHER (*walks about the room like a newly captured wild animal*): I've never heard the like from a son to his mother!

SON: It's a little unusual, of course, and it's quite against nature—I know that, but it had to be said once. You went about like a sleepwalker and couldn't be awakened; that's why you couldn't change either. Father said that if they put you on the rack and tortured you, you couldn't be made to admit a fault or admit that you had lied . . .

MOTHER: Father! Do you think he lacked faults?

SON: He had great faults; but not in relationship to his wife and children!—But there are other secrets in your marriage, which I have sensed, suspected, but have never wanted to admit to myself . . . Father took those secrets with him into the grave, partly!

MOTHER: Have you talked enough now?

SON: Now I'll go out to drink again . . . I can never take a degree; I don't believe in the legal system; the laws seem to be written by thieves and murderers in order to set the criminal free; *one* honest man isn't an acceptable witness, but two false witnesses are full proof! At eleven-thirty my case is just, but after twelve I've lost; an error in writing, an inadequate margin, can put me, innocent as I am, into prison. If I'm merciful to a scoundrel, he punishes me for libel. My contempt for life, humanity, the community, and myself is so boundless I don't have the energy to try to live . . . (*Goes toward the door*)

MOTHER: Don't go!

SON: Are you afraid of the dark?

MOTHER: I'm nervous!

SON: They go together!

MOTHER: And that chair's driving me crazy! It was always like two chopping knives when he was sitting there . . . chopping my heart.

SON: Surely you don't have anything like that!

MOTHER: Don't go! I can't stay here—Axel's a scoundrel!

SON: I thought so, too, until a little while ago! Now I think he's the sacrifice for your criminal passion . . . Yes, he was the young man who was seduced.

MOTHER: You must keep bad company!

SON: Bad company! Well, I've never been in good!

MOTHER: Don't go!

SON: What can I do here? I'd only torture you to death with my talk . . .

MOTHER: Don't go!

SON: Are you waking up?

MOTHER: Yes, I'm waking up as if from a long, long sleep! It's terrible! Why couldn't anyone wake me up before?

SON: What no one could do was impossible, I suppose. And when it was impossible, I suppose you weren't responsible for it.

MOTHER: Repeat those words!

SON: I suppose you couldn't be different.

MOTHER (kisses his hand "slavishly"): Say more.

SON: I can't!—Yes, I beg you: don't stay here to make what's bad worse!

MOTHER: You're right! I will go—away!

SON: Poor Mother!

MOTHER: Do you have any pity for me?

SON (sobs): Yes, of course I have! How often I've said about you: She's so wicked, she's to be pitied!

MOTHER: Thank you for that.—Go now, Fredrik!

SON: Can't something be done about this?

MOTHER: No, it's hopeless!

SON: Yes, it is!—It's hopeless! (*Goes. Pause*)

(*The* MOTHER *alone; her arms over her bosom for a long while. Then she goes to the window, which she opens, and looks out— downward; draws back into the room and gets ready to take the leap to jump out; but then she changes her mind when someone knocks sharply three times on the door at the back.*)

MOTHER: Who is it? What is it? (*She closes the window.*) Come in! (*The doors at the back are opened.*) Is someone there? (*The* SON *can be heard crying out inside.*) It's he—in the garden! Isn't he dead? What shall I do? Where shall I go? (*She hides behind the chiffonier. The wind begins to blow as before so that papers fly about.*) Shut the window, Fredrik! (*A flowerpot crashes to the floor.*) Shut the window! I'm freezing to death, and the fire in the stove's going out!

(*She turns on all the electric lights; closes the door, which opens again; the wind sets the rocking chair going; she walks around and around in the room until she throws herself head first on the chaise longue and hides her face in the pillows.*)

("*Il me disait*" *is played outside.*)

(*The* MOTHER *lies as before on the chaise longue with her face hidden.* GERDA *comes in with the porridge on a tray, which she puts down. Then she turns off all the electric lights but one.*)

MOTHER (*awakens, raises her head*): Don't put out the lights!

GERDA: Yes, we have to economise!

MOTHER: Are you back already?

GERDA: Yes, he didn't think it was fun when you weren't there.

MOTHER: There you are!

GERDA: Here's your supper.

MOTHER: I'm not hungry.

GERDA: Yes, you are, but you don't eat porridge.

MOTHER: Yes, sometimes.

GERDA: No, never! But not because of that but because of your malicious smile every time you tortured us with oatmeal—you enjoyed

our suffering . . . and you cooked the same thing for the hunting
dog!

MOTHER: I can't eat blue milk—it makes me freeze!

GERDA: After you've skimmed off the cream for your eleven o'clock
coffee! Go on! (*Serves the porridge on a small round table with
one leg*) Go ahead, eat so I can look on!

MOTHER: I can't!

GERDA (*bends down and takes the wood from under the chaise
longue*): If you don't eat it, I'll show Axel you stole wood.

MOTHER: Axel, who missed me . . . he won't do me any harm! Do
you remember the wedding when he danced with me . . . to "Il
me disait"! There we have it. (*She hums the second refrain,
which is now played.*)

GERDA: You'd be wise not to remind me of that atrocious behavior . . .

MOTHER: And I got verses, and the most beautiful flowers!

GERDA: Hush!

MOTHER: Shall I recite the verses for you? I know them by heart . . .
                             "In Ginnistan . . ."
Ginnistan is a Persian word for the Garden of Paradise, where
gracious spirits live on fragrance . . . They're genii or fairies,
who are so put together that the longer they live, the younger they
become . . .

GERDA: Good God! Do you think you're a genie?

MOTHER: Yes, that's what it says here, and Viktor has proposed to
me. What would you say if I remarried?

GERDA: Poor Mother! You're still walking in your sleep as we all
have been doing. Won't you ever wake up? Don't you see how
they're laughing at you? Don't you understand Axel insults you?

MOTHER: Does he? I always think he's politer to me than to you . . .

GERDA: Even when he raised his cane against you?

MOTHER: Against me? That was against you, dear!

GERDA: Mother, have you lost your mind?

MOTHER: Why, he missed me tonight, we always have so much to talk about, he's the only one who understands me, and you're only a child . . .

GERDA (*takes her* MOTHER *by the shoulders and shakes her*): Wake up, for heaven's sake!

MOTHER: You're not fully developed yet, of course, but I'm your mother and have nourished you with my blood . . .

GERDA: You gave me a bottle and a pacifier for my mouth, and then I had to go to the cupboard and steal, but there was only hard rye bread that I ate with mustard, and when it burned my throat, I drank vinegar to cool it; the spice cabinet and the bread basket—that was the pantry!

MOTHER: So you stole even as a child! That was nice, and you're not ashamed to admit it? What children I've sacrificed myself for!

GERDA (*weeps*): I could forgive everything, but that you took my life away from me—yes, he was my life, because with him I began to live . . .

MOTHER: It's not my fault he preferred me! He probably found me —how shall I put it?—more attractive . . . yes, he had better taste than your father, who didn't appreciate me until he got rivals—(*Someone knocks loudly three times on the door*.) Who's knocking?

GERDA: Don't say anything bad about Father! I don't think my life will be long enough to regret what harm I did to him, but you're going to pay for that, you who set me on him! Do you remember when I was a little, little child, you taught me to say mean hurtful words that I didn't understand? He was wise enough not to punish me for the arrows, for he knew who had stretched the bow! Do you remember when you taught me to lie to him, to say I needed new schoolbooks, and when we had got money out of him, we shared it!—How am I going to forget all of that past? Is there any drink that extinguishes one's memory without ending one's life? If I only had the strength to walk out on all of it! But I'm like Fredrik—we're feeble sacrifices, your sacrifices, without strength or will . . . you hardened soul, who can't suffer for your own crimes!

MOTHER: Do you know about *my* childhood? Do you have any idea of what a bad home I had, what wickedness I learned there? It's inherited, I think, from above, from whom? From our first parents, it said in the children's books, and that seems to be right . . . So don't blame me; then I won't blame my parents, who could blame theirs, and so on! Besides, it's like this in all families, but the rest of them don't show it to outsiders . . .

GERDA: If that's how it is, I don't want to live, but if I'm forced to, I'll go through this miserable life deaf and blind in the hope there'll be a better hereafter . . .

MOTHER: You exaggerate so, dear; if you have a child, you'll have other things to think about . . .

GERDA: I won't have any children . . .

MOTHER: How do you know?

GERDA: The doctor said so.

MOTHER: He's mistaken . . .

GERDA: Now you lied again . . . I'm sterile, incomplete, like Fredrik, so I don't want to live . . .

MOTHER: Nonsense . . .

GERDA: If I could do evil as I'd like to, you'd not exist any longer! Why should it be so hard to do evil? And when I raise my hand against you, I hit myself!—

(*The music ends hastily; the* SON *can be heard screaming.*)

MOTHER: Now he's been drinking again!

GERDA: Poor Fredrik, yes . . . what's he to do?

SON (*enters, half-drunk*): It's . . . smoking . . . I think . . . in— the kitchen!

MOTHER: What's that?

SON: I think . . . I . . . I think it's . . . on fire!

MOTHER: On fire? What are you saying?

SON: Yes, I . . . think . . . it's on fire!

MOTHER (*runs to the back, opens the doors, but is met by a red glow of fire*): Fire!—How are we going to get out?—I don't want to burn!—I don't want to! (*Walks about*)

GERDA (*takes her* BROTHER *in her arms*): Fredrik! Run, the fire's over us! Run!

SON: I haven't the strength!

GERDA: Run! You must!

SON: Where? . . . No, I don't want to . . .

MOTHER: I'd rather jump out the window . . . (*Opens the balcony doors and plunges out*)

GERDA: Lord God, help us!

SON: It was the only way!

GERDA: You did this!

SON: Yes, what was I to do?—There wasn't any other way!—Was there?

GERDA: No! Everything has to burn up; otherwise we'll never get out of here! Hold me in your arms, Fredrik; hold me tight, little Brother; I am happier than I have ever been; it's becoming lighter! Poor Mother, who was so wicked, so wicked . . .

SON: Little Sister, poor Mother, do you feel how warm it is, how nice, now I'm not freezing any longer. Listen how it's crackling out there! Now everything old is burning, all the old wicked and bad and evil things . . .

GERDA: Hold me tight, little Brother; we won't burn; the smoke will choke us. Don't you feel how good it smells—that's from the palms that are burning, and from Father's laurel wreath. Now the linen closet is burning—it smells of lavender—and now the roses. Little Brother, don't be afraid; it will soon be over; dear, don't fall. Poor Mother who was so wicked! Hold me, tighter, hug me, as Father used to say! It's like Christmas eve when we could eat in the kitchen, dip in the kettle, the only day we got enough to eat, as Father said. Smell the fragrance—it's the cupboard that's burning with the tea and the coffee, and the spices, the cinnamon and the cloves . . .

SON (*in ecstasy*): Is it summer? Why, the clover's blooming, summer vacation's beginning. Do you remember how we walked down to the white steamboats and patted them when they were newly painted and waiting for us? Then Father was happy, then he was alive, he said, and the examination books finished! The way life should always be, he said. I think he was the pelican who stripped himself for us; he always had wrinkled trousers and a worn velvet collar while we walked about like little aristocrats . . . Gerda, hurry up; the steamboat's ringing; Mother's in the forecabin—no, she isn't along. Poor Mother! She's gone—is she still on shore? Where is she? I don't see her—it isn't fun without Mother—there she comes!—Now summer vacation begins! (*Pause*)

(*The doors at the back open; the red glow has become stronger. The* SON *and* GERDA *sink to the floor.*)

[CURTAIN]

Bibliographic

and Biographic Notes

THE STANDARD SWEDISH EDITION of Strindberg's works is John Land-quist's *Strindbergs samlade skrifter* (55 vols. Stockholm: Bonnier, 1912–20). *A Dream Play* (*Ett drömspel*) appears in volume 35, and the four chamber plays—*Stormy Weather* (*Oväder*), *The House That Burned* (*Brända tomten*), *The Ghost Sonata* (*Spöksonaten*), and *The Pelican* (*Pelikanen*) appear in volume 45.

For those who know Swedish the best bibliographies are in E. N. Tigerstedt's *Svensk litteraturhistoria* (Stockholm: Bonnier, 1948–) and in the Swedish journal *Samlaren,* which prints an annual bibliography.

For those who must rely on English sources, the basic bibliographies are: Esther H. Rapp's bibliography of Strindberg in England and America in *Scandinavian Studies* 23 (1950): 1–22, 49–59, 109–137; Alrik Gustafson's bibliography in his *A History of Swedish Literature* (Minneapolis: University of Minnesota Press, 1961), 601–10, which lists both Scandinavian and non-Scandinavian items; the annual American Scandinavian Bibliography in the May or August number of *Scandinavian Studies,* 1948 on; and the annual bibliography in *Publications of the Modern Language Association.* Since articles, books, and reviews of books about and productions of Strindberg plays appear frequently, it is rewarding to check these bibliographies, the annual ones regularly, and the others probably once.

It cannot be denied that Strindberg used his experiences, thoughts, and observations in his works to a remarkable degree, and that many of his works are autobiographical and even confessional. Nevertheless, there is a very real danger in concentrating so much on the autobiographical basis of any of the plays that one loses sight of it as an independent work of art. For those who are particularly interested in the autobiographical background of any of the plays in this volume, any biography in English will do. Elizabeth Sprigge's *The Strange Life of August Strindberg* (New York: Macmillan, 1949) is as readable as any. An English translation of Gunnar Brandell's *Strindbergs Infernokris* (Stockholm: Bonnier, 1950) is about to appear. Martin Lamm's *August Strindberg* (Stockholm: Bonnier, 1948), in Harry Carlson's translation, is now available (New York: Blom, 1971). The Brandell volume is the standard study of Strindberg's experiences in the 1890's, which affected all his literary works after 1897; the Lamm biography is useful not only as the authoritative treatment of Strindberg's life but also as a brilliant presentation of all of his works from the biographical point of view.

Some of the Strindberg items basic to an understanding of the plays in this volume are available in English: *Inferno, Alone and Other Writings* (Anchor Books A492C; Garden City, N.Y.: Doubleday & Company, 1968); *From an Occult Diary* (New York: Hill and Wang, 1965); *Letters of Strindberg to Harriet Bosse* (New York: Thomas Nelson & Sons, 1959); and *Open Letters to the Intimate Theater* (Seattle: University of Washington Press, 1966).